The Martha's Vineyard Cookbook

Over 250 Recipes and Lore from a Bountiful Island

Praise for previous editions:

"This culinary tribute will enchant Islanders, visitors, and food lovers everywhere."

   —*Cape Cod Life*

"No ordinary cookbook. It could qualify as a book on New England foods. And it could stand alone as a cookbook on seafood."

   —*The Christian Science Monitor*

"Many thanks to these island cooks for presenting the true foods of coastal New England, from the esoteric to the simple but sublime. As I read through these pages I could almost smell the briny-sweet summer breeze on the Vineyard."

   —Jasper White, Chef/Proprietor of Jasper's, Boston

THE

Martha's Vineyard

COOKBOOK

THIRD EDITION

Over 250 Recipes and Lore from a Bountiful Island

BY LOUISE TATE KING & JEAN STEWART WEXLER

The Globe Pequot Press

GUILFORD, CONNECTICUT

For Hilary

and

For Carolina

Cover design by Laura Augustine
Cover photograph by Alison Shaw
Text design by Nancy Freeborn
Illustrations by Gil Fahey

Library of Congress Cataloging-in-Publication Data
King, Louise Tate.
    The Martha's Vineyard cookbook : over 250 recipes and lore from a bountiful island /
  by Louise Tate King & Jean Stewart Wexler.—3rd ed.
      p. cm.
  Includes index.
  ISBN 0-7627-0569-8
    1. Cookery—Massachussetts—Martha's Vineyard. 2. Martha's Vineyard (Mass.)—Social life and customs. I. Wexler, Jean Stewart. II. Title.

TX715 .K53 1999
641.59744'94—dc21

                                                      99-049132

Manufactured in the United States of America
Third Edition/Second Printing

Contents

Foreword

Island settlements must of necessity be self-sustaining. A sturdy population draws its nourishment not only from the soil but from the surrounding sea that separates it from the mainland. It is from such thrifty, salty independence that the cooking of Martha's Vineyard has evolved—cooking that, as this newest edition of *The Martha's Vineyard Cookbook* proves, remains perennially relevant.

Nostalgia aside, there is much to be learned from the examples of a simpler, less industrialized era and the contributions of this island's original Wampanoag Indian inhabitants, especially now that high priority has been given to protecting the environment and managing the resources of land and sea. Reflecting these concerns, the recipes herein make good use of less common ingredients—fish like tautog, shellfish like Jonah crabs, and wild plants that yield rose hips and day-lily buds.

At the same time, who could not be tempted by a bowl of thick chowder? Rum tea or Max Eastman's daiquiris? Or the wealth of homey fruit crumbles and pies? This book's thoughtful text has always honored these as well as the wholesome delicacies that vacationing urbanites have only recently started to appreciate: fish right off the boat, corn freshly picked from a farm, and blackberries gathered with care.

Attitudes toward proper diet have certainly shifted in the ten years since this satisfying volume was last published. But anyone on speaking terms with a few burners and a fridge is probably capable of adjusting a recipe like the one for eels with herbs, for example, by replacing half a stick of butter with a little olive oil.

What makes this cookbook so compelling is that it has always offered recipes for the likes of eel. And beach plums. And mussels. And herbal teas. The lashing of butter and cream or generous dicings of salt pork are matters of style, not substance. So, too, is the inevitable pesto that is now suggested for anointing a thick fillet of striped bass.

More recipes for salads and vegetables have been included to cater to contemporary tastes. Equally welcome is the seductive glimpse of the West Tisbury Farmers' Market, which was actually started nearly sixty years ago, faltered, and was subsequently revived in 1974 to become a thriving weekly enterprise that offers a microcosm of island food and society.

Gently revising *The Martha's Vineyard Cookbook* every decade appears to have become yet another durable tradition of the island. Which leads to speculation about what the cookbook might be like ten years hence, after the turn of the century. Surely it will continue to evolve as food habits shift. But the basic ingredients that sustain island appetites are likely to remain, continuing to reflect a heritage that reaches back some 400 years.

FLORENCE FABRICANT
Food Columnist
The New York Times
1993

Foreword

A dd ten years to a volume of recipes already as well aged in wisdom and practicality as these, and the extra decade is nothing much— except as it may represent absence from kitchens where it ought to be but isn't because the first edition was sold out. It is ten years since the hardcover *Martha's Vineyard Cookbook* came out, and here is the subtler and a bit more pliable edition in paper covers, certain of the welcome it will have.

Along with most of maritime New England, Martha's Vineyard has been a victim of the misguided impression that its cooks were chiefly inclined to the overcooking of vegetables, monotonous preparation of the stoutest foods, and a Puritanical avoidance of delicacy and imagination. In spite of evidence to the contrary, these assumptions have persisted. They have persisted to such an extent that the present cookbook brought not only revelation but some of revelation's best delights—in this case the mouth-watering delights that lie beyond expectation.

It is true that Vineyard housewives could make sea voyage ginger-bread that would last well around Cape Horn and into the Pacific or even into the Arctic; and it is true that a biting northeaster and a hard day's work on the water would assist the ingestion of a hearty eel stifle. But times have changed, old exigencies have been completely relaxed, and today's eel stifle may be put down as a gourmet dish. Yes—read what it says here. Or, for variety, here is an invitation to eels with herbs, including sage, rosemary, thyme, and so on. Who, ten years ago, would have expected so much?

Half a century ago swordfish was hardly known in the important markets with the exception of Boston. Vineyard recipes helped in the missionary spread of swordfish fame, now far flung; and there are imaginative ways to cooking swordfish. Nobody wants to be in a rut when there are inviting possibilities to explore.

If, besides the resourcefulness exhibited in these pages, resulting in so wide a range of choice, there is a characteristic emphasis, it lies not in any stuffiness of tradition, but in basic excellence with chowders, shellfish, and seafood generally, and in the rewarding use of the Island's bounty—windfall apples, elderberries and elder flowers, cranberries, wild grapes, beach plums, blackberries, beach peas, Irish moss, and so on. Not to be overlooked is the contribution in such diverse forms as Easter bread and linguica, which came by sea in the whaling era of the past century. So it is that a hint runs from first to last of the savor provided by blown spray, insular kinship, and the lean paradox of the Vineyard's own soil.

HENRY BEETLE HOUGH
Editor
Vineyard Gazette
1983

Acknowledgments

Since my coauthor, Louise Tate King, was unable because of illness to participate in assembling this new edition, my friend and neighbor Linda McGuire offered to help. And help she did. Without her hours of typing and retyping, consistent good humor, endless patience, infectious enthusiasm, and above all, expertise as both professional-level cook and meticulous assistant, there would be no third edition of *The Martha's Vineyard Cookbook*. To her, my boundless gratitude.

Jean Stewart Wexler

Introduction

A cookbook about Martha's Vineyard, the picturesque island lying 5 miles south of the heel of Cape Cod, could well be a New England cookbook. Or it could be a seafood cookbook, describing ways to prepare the fish and shellfish that live in the Island's ponds and in the salt waters that encircle it. Vineyarders do use these foods from the sea—and have for the 300-odd years since the Island acquired its present name: "Martha's" after the daughter of one of the first settlers, Bartholomew Gosnold; "Vineyard" because of the profusion of wild grapevines that still blanket large sections of the Island's interior.

But today's Vineyarders draw on an expanded heritage in preparing their meals. Some of their recipes, like a simple but satisfying cornmeal mush (called Hasty Pudding), were used by the Wampanoag Indians who hunted and trapped amongst the riches of the Island long before the white man moved in. Some were brought in by the Portuguese fishermen who signed on with the Edgartown whalers when they stopped off at the Azores and the Cape Verde Islands and who returned with the ships to settle and prosper in the quiet Island towns. Other dishes have English or Scottish origins and were prepared by the wives of the whaling captains and other early settlers, whose descendants still live in the proud white houses with their widow's walks. And much of their food came, as some still does, from the Island's own riches—the meadows and woodlands, the Great Ponds, and the smaller freshwater ponds.

New England ways of cooking are traditional on the Vineyard, but individual adaptations have crept into the lore, and an Island chowder—or stifle, or blueberry pudding—will taste a little different from one made in Boston, or even one made on Cape Cod. Of course, we may be prejudiced. Swordfish straight off the boats at Menemsha, the farmers' first sweet corn, summer's first blueberry pie, a delectable chowder made from the unappetizing creatures your children dug out of the primeval black muck of a Great Pond—this is Vineyard fare that somehow would never taste the same "off-Island."

Ecology—the relation of organisms to the environment—has become a primary concern in populated areas throughout the world. Preserving a delicate balance between man and nature is vital on the Vineyard, whose boundaries are defined forever by the sea. The Great Ponds must remain saline and unpolluted to maintain the fish and shellfish that inhabit them, valuable sources of food and income. There must be farmers to plant and land for them to plant on, space for cows and sheep to graze and poultry to range, if the Island is to survive in the way its residents want it to survive. Vulnerable to two vastly different but almost equally threatening forces—the sea that ravages its coastline and developers who have begun to ravage its beauty—Martha's Vineyard is constantly struggling to sustain its environmental heritage.

Evidence of this struggle becomes more pronounced and more disturbing every year, even though everything that could negatively affect the Vineyard's welfare is constantly monitored by one committee or another. Now the Island's animal and plant life have begun to experience continuous pressure because of the ongoing fragmentation of their habitats by unending development.

Of course, an ever-expanding population means ever-increasing quantities of refuse that must be disposed of. No longer do residents drive to what used to be called dumps to toss their own trash on the heap or to scrounge for treasures. Nor is someone arriving at one of the strictly regulated landfills likely to discover, as someone did one summer evening years ago in Chilmark, a lady down in the pit perched on a crate in front of a decrepit upright piano energetically pounding out a hymn. But despite the various thorny issues, for many, life on the Vineyard goes on pretty much as it always has.

It was gratifying to be asked to put together a revised version of this cookbook in 1993, and we were even more challenged by the preparation of this third edition. There are a good many new recipes as well as a new "Vineyard Inns and Restaurants" chapter containing signature dishes from some of the Island's favorite eating spots. We are very grateful to the chefs and managers who cooperated with us on this project.

The bulk of the book, however, remains unchanged, since we feel it reflects the essence of this very special place.

One final comment: Residents of the historic Up-Island town of Gay Head recently voted to have their town's name officially changed to Aquinnah. Though this name is now correct, longtime residents find it difficult to drop "Gay Head" from their vocabulary. To many, for instance, the Gay Head Cliffs will always be so named. We have chosen to leave our Gay Head references intact, not in defiance of the law, but for nostalgic reasons.

CHAPTER 1

Chowders

Chowder, if built with due respect for both clock and calendar, improves with age. In many chowder recipes one encounters the phrase "remove to back of stove," and there is a good deal of eloquence there. On the back of the stove is where much of the perfection comes in.

—*Vineyard Gazette*

The word *chowder* probably derives from the French word *chaudière,* meaning an iron pot. On their native islands of Guernsey and Jersey, the Channel Islanders who settled along the north shore of Massachusetts more than 300 years ago had long combined food from the sea with the rich milk from their cows in the iron pots they used for cooking. Other settlers in the new land, after sampling this delightful combination, soon were concocting chowders from whatever base they had at hand, applying the resourcefulness and ingenuity long identified with the New England housewife. Besides all types of seafood—fish, clams, lobsters, scallops, shrimp, oysters, and eels—chicken, beefsteak, corn, potatoes, parsnips, even eggs went into the pot with the bread, onions, and milk. Tomatoes, however, used instead of milk in the chowders made farther south, have always remained anathema in the chowders of New England.

In early days corn was the staple of the Vineyard diet through the winterbound months, and early chowders were a thin corn gruel to which was added fish, eels, shellfish, or some sort of meat. Potatoes in place of bread, now traditional in the chowders of Martha's Vineyard, are said to have been introduced by one John Pease, who came from Salem, Massachusetts, to settle in Edgartown around 1656. He had eaten potatoes in the Virginia colony, and one lean fall, when Vineyard grain crops had been devastated by flocks of wild fowl (probably wild pigeons), he begged a few potatoes from the trading vessels that moved along the eastern coast and tried them in his chowder—with historic results. Later, salt pork was added to fill out and enrich the chowders when clams were poor in flavor; it too became traditional. On the Vineyard, the browned bits of salt pork are often left in the finished chowder as they were 300 years ago, not removed as they usually are in mainland chowders.

Chowders, like stews and other dishes developed when cooking was a pleasurable and time-consuming art, do need to be "built" with care and allowed time to mellow. Vineyard housekeepers, working in the same houses or home sites as their whaling-wife or Wampanoag (the Indian tribe native to the Vineyard, a branch of the Algonquians) ancestors, today use blenders, electric stoves, and freezers to prepare and preserve their chowders. But, to quote a letter written by the grandmother of a present-day West Tisbury cook, chowder is still "better the second day than the first, and the third day than the second, if it lasts that long."

There are many chowders, all structured the same way. We have included only the ones that we consider most indigenous to the Island. Following the procedures detailed in the Basic Recipe on page 4, you can concoct your own. Or see what you can produce from this list for a salt-pork chowder, taken from the recipe book of a "Boston Housekeeper" of 1854: salt pork, onions, sweet herbs, fresh sliced cod, biscuits, Madeira wine, Jamaican pepper, stewed mushrooms, oysters, and truffles. With this, we leave you on your own!

Vineyard Clam Chowder

The clams in this heartwarming, satisfying brew are known off-Island as steamers; quaintly enough, they are also named Nanny-Noses. This is *the* clam of New England; it is a soft clam, thin-shelled, with a projecting neck. Unlike its sturdier-flavored relative, the hard-shelled clam (known on the Vineyard as the "quahog," from the longer, less pronounceable Algonquian Indian *"p'quaughaug"*), the steamer imparts a delicate, subtle sea flavor to chowder; the quahog produces a robustly aromatic dish. Vineyarders, like all New Englanders, without question imply the use of the soft clam when they set out to build a clam chowder.

The quahog, pronounced *ko*-hog and also spelled *quahaug,* finds its way into chowders, too. But the dish is then specifically labeled "quahog chowder." Here on the Island a clam and a quahog are thought of as two very different bivalves. And so they are. The quahog in its youthful stages is recognized off-Island as the familiar little-neck or cherrystone clam. Then it is at its tender best, eaten raw on the half shell. Or the clams are broiled, with appropriate seasonings, as Clams Casino, for example (see page 51). Grown up and measuring 3 inches or more in diameter, the quahog is chopped or ground and forms the basic ingredient of quahog chowder.

BASIC RECIPE
1 quart shucked steamer clams, including their liquor
¼ pound salt pork, cut into ½-inch dice
2 medium onions, chopped medium fine
4 medium potatoes, peeled, cut in ½- to ¾-inch dice (about 3 cups)
4 cups whole milk (or half milk, half evaporated milk)
2 tablespoons butter
Salt to taste
¼ teaspoon freshly ground black pepper

Lift clams out of their liquor; this helps somewhat to drain off the sand. (Some cooks rinse the clams briefly in running water.) Strain the clam liquor through a strainer lined with cheesecloth or a clean dish towel; set aside. Separate the firm parts of the clams from the bellies, or soft parts. Cut away the black portion of the necks, if desired. Coarsely chop only the firm part, or put through the coarse blade of a food chopper. Set aside the clams, keeping the firm and soft parts separate.

In a heavy kettle or Dutch oven, cook diced salt pork over moderate heat until crisp and golden. Remove the dice, drain on a paper towel, and set aside. Add the chopped onions to the fat in the kettle; cook slowly until tender and transparent. Add the diced potatoes, the strained clam liquor, and sufficient water to rise about 1 inch above the potatoes. Simmer, covered, until potatoes are tender, but don't overcook them. Add the chopped firm parts of the clams; simmer a little longer—about 5 minutes. Add the soft parts of the clams and the reserved salt-pork bits; cook 5 minutes longer.

In a saucepan heat the milk with the butter over moderate heat; it must not boil. Add to the chowder kettle. Add salt to taste and the black pepper. (Salt may not be needed; if the clams are very fresh, they contribute considerable saltiness; so, too, the salt pork.) Remove the kettle from the heat immediately and allow the chowder to "ripen" at least an hour or two.

Reheat, uncovered, on low heat until the mixture begins to steam. It must not boil, or it will curdle. The use of a double boiler is recommended; set the top of the double boiler over, not in, boiling water. Remove from heat and serve immediately in heated bowls.

Optional: Vineyard cooks rarely thicken their chowders, thinking, with culinary justification, that the potatoes will bind the mixture sufficiently. If, however, you wish a thickened chowder, blend 3 tablespoons softened butter with 3 tablespoons flour; stir this mixture gradually into the chowder kettle several minutes before the heated milk is added. Stir over very low heat until chowder thickens slightly. Do not allow it to boil, or the mixture will curdle. If this happens, drain off the liquids and blend them in an electric blender 5 to 10 seconds. The result is a fully reconstituted mixture.

Note: Common crackers are traditionally served with chowders, usually split and soaked in milk, then added to each bowl of chowder. Toasted (see note about them under Fish Chowder on page 9), they make a good accompaniment, too. Legend has it that these crackers were first made in Massachusetts one hundred or more years ago by Artemus Kennedy, who baked them on the floor of a brick oven, then peddled them on horseback, using his saddlebags as containers. Today's efficient methods of preparation and transportation make them available in any good grocery store.

Makes 8 to 10 portions.

Quahog Chowder

In New England we simply ask at the fish market for quahogs for chowder, and all is well. Elsewhere, however, it is prudent to request *clams* for this chowder, whereupon one receives the familiar hard-shelled bivalve, a grade or two larger than the cherrystone clam. This, the quahog, differs considerably in structure from the steamer clam. It ingests less sand than the steamer; there is less likelihood, therefore, of encountering those annoying particles.

Buy 1 quart of these clams, shucked. Lift them out of their liquor, chop them coarsely by hand or, using the coarse blade, put them through a food chopper. Put the liquid through a fine strainer lined with cheesecloth or a clean dish towel.

Proceed with the Basic Recipe (see page 4).

Makes 8 to 10 portions.

Will Holtham's Quahog Chowder

Thousands of cups of this rich, creamy chowder are served every summer at its creator's busy Menemsha restaurant.

20 large quahogs, steamed open in 1 quart water (save broth)
¼ pound butter
¾ cup chopped onions
1 stalk celery
2 cloves of garlic, chopped
1 tablespoon chopped fresh dill
½ teaspoon dried thyme
3 pinches of black pepper

1 dash Tabasco sauce
2 dashes Worcestershire sauce
3 tablespoons flour
2 pints chopped sea clams from fish market (defrost if frozen)
4 or 5 large potatoes, peeled and diced
1 quart light cream

Chop quahogs after removing them from shells. Melt butter in heavy soup kettle or Dutch oven. Add onions, celery, garlic, dill, thyme, pepper, Tabasco sauce, and Worcestershire sauce. Sauté ingredients 5 to 6 minutes. Add flour and continue cooking for another 5 or 6 minutes over low heat, stirring occasionally. Add sea clams, chopped quahogs, and saved broth, and bring to a boil. Add potatoes and boil on medium heat until they are tender. Warm light cream and add it to chowder.

Makes 10 portions.

Fish Chowder

Among the chowders, fish chowder in particular invites experiment. If you already know the dish as made with the traditional cod or haddock, try making it with some other fish. John Pachico, longtime fish vendor on the Vineyard, recommended an elegant blending of swordfish and striped bass. Blackfish or black bass (known on the Vineyard as "tautog" and catchable from nearly any rocky shore) and filleted flounder, which Vineyarders call "sole," are both good in any combination. This melding of various fish textures and tastes adds character to an already delicious dish. If a family fishing expedition leaves you with an assortment of fish you don't quite know what to do with, have the fishermen clean and bone them, and toss them all in the chowder pot.

Off-Island, or if no one in your household wants to bother with catching or cleaning fish during your stay on the Vineyard, have your fish dealer fillet whatever fish you choose. Be sure to have him give you the bones, skin, heads, and tails for making your fish stock, the most important ingredient in this chowder. One Island fishmonger stews these trimmings in seawater, a masterful touch. If seawater for you means a trip to the East River or to some polluted bay, use bottled clam juice to make your stock, or settle for the water from your kitchen faucet.

FISH STOCK

Trimmings from a 4-pound cod or haddock or from 4 pounds of fish of choice (heads, bones, skin, tails)
Cold water to cover fish (or half bottled clam juice, half water)
3 or 4 stems fresh parsley
1 small onion, peeled, thinly sliced

½ carrot, cut into ¼ -inch-thick circles (don't bother to peel it)
1 small stalk celery
6–8 whole black peppercorns
1 tablespoon lemon juice
1 bay leaf
Salt to taste (less if using clam juice; as the clam juice cooks down, it gets saltier)

Place these ingredients in a 4- to 6-quart kettle, preferably enamel or stainless steel, using enough cold water (or half clam juice, half water) to rise an inch or two above the surface of the fish trimmings. Bring to a boil; then, reducing heat to low, cook at a gentle simmer for ½ hour. Strain the stock through a fine strainer; reserve it.

THE CHOWDER

¼ pound salt pork, cut in ½-inch dice
2 medium onions, chopped medium fine
4 medium potatoes, pared and cut in ½-inch dice (about 3 cups)
2 cups reserved fish stock
Raw fish, trimmed, boned, skinned, and cut in 2-inch chunks (at least 2½–3 pounds)

4 cups whole milk (or half milk, half evaporated milk)
2 tablespoons butter
Salt to taste
¼ teaspoon freshly ground black pepper
Chopped parsley (optional)

Over moderate heat cook the salt-pork dice in a heavy 4- to 6-quart kettle or Dutch oven until crisp and golden. Remove the "cracklings," drain on a paper towel, and reserve. Add the onions to the fat in the kettle; cook slowly until transparent. Add the diced potatoes and the reserved fish stock. There should be enough of this liquid to cover the potatoes by an inch or two. Add water, if necessary. Simmer the potatoes over low heat until tender. Do not overcook them. Add the cut-up fish and the reserved salt-pork cracklings, and cook very slowly 8 to 10 minutes. It is important not to overcook the fish; it is done when it flakes easily when pierced with a fork.

In a saucepan heat the milk with the butter; be careful not to let it boil. Add it to the chowder with salt to taste and the black pepper, and remove immediately from heat. Allow the chowder to "ripen" for at least an hour or two.

At serving time heat slowly and carefully so that the chowder does not boil, and serve immediately. The use of a double boiler is recommended; set the chowder over, not in, boiling water.

A garniture of chopped parsley may be sprinkled over the chowder in each serving bowl.

Note: The chowder may be thickened slightly with a paste of 3 tablespoons softened butter and 3 tablespoons flour, added to the chowder gradually a few minutes before the heated milk goes into the chowder kettle.

Traditional Island accompaniments: A dish of sour pickles and some common crackers or pilot crackers. Or try the common crackers split, soaked in hot water until soft, drained, spread with softened butter, and toasted under the broiler.

Makes 8 to 10 portions.

Henry Beetle Hough's
Chicken Chowder

When asked for his favorite recipe, Henry Beetle Hough, editor of the *Vineyard Gazette,* replied that he thought it was his mother's recipe for chicken chowder. Quoted intact from a clipping he sent us from *Gazette* files for the year 1923, here is the recipe:

Following recent editorial discussion of chowder, several readers have requested a recipe for chicken chowder. The formula, an invaluable one, seems to deserve a place in this department. Accordingly, the recipe of a Vineyard housewife and cook of considerable reputation is given as follows:

Put three slices of salt pork into an iron kettle. One tablespoon of butter can be used instead. Remove the pork after it has cooked out. Slice in four or five onions and cook, but not long enough for them to brown. When onions are cooked, put in three pints of boiling water. Add one chicken, cut in pieces. Cook about two and a half hours, then slice in three or four potatoes. Cook about a half hour. Heat a quart of milk. Mix two tablespoons of flour together with enough cold water to make a thin paste. Stir together well, then add salt and pepper to taste, smooth out and add to milk. Bring milk to boil and add to ingredients in the kettle. Bring whole to a boil and then set on back of stove.

. . . and the concoction is as good or better the second day as it is the first.

The use of a good plump fowl is suggested.
Makes 6 to 8 portions.

Corn Chowder

Follow Basic Recipe (page 4), using 4 cups of corn (half cream-style, half whole-kernel) instead of clams. Use only 2 cups diced raw potatoes. Combine corn and potatoes and cook in 2 cups chicken stock instead of clam liquor and water. Reduce amount of milk from 4 cups to 3 cups.

Makes 6 to 8 portions.

Parsnip Chowder

Peel and cut into small chunks enough parsnips to make 3 cups. Follow Basic Recipe (page 4), using parsnips instead of clams. Reduce amount of potatoes to 2 cups. Cook vegetables in 2 cups chicken stock instead of clam liquor and water. Add only 3 cups heated milk. Garnish each portion with a sprinkle of chopped parsley.

Makes 6 portions.

Potato Chowder

Follow Basic Recipe (page 4) but eliminate clams. Cook potatoes in 2 cups of chicken stock instead of clam liquor and water.

Makes 4 to 6 portions.

CHAPTER 2

Fish

Whales, Tortoises, both on land and sea, Seales, Cods, Mackerel, Breames, Herrings, Thornbacke, Hakes, Rockefish, Dogfish, Lobsters, Crabbes, Muscles, Wilks, Cockles, Scallops, Oisters.

—Brereton (1602), quoted in Banks, *History of Martha's Vineyard*

Alewife, Bass, Bluefish, Butterfish, Cod, Dogfish, Eel, Flounder, Goosefish, Haddock, Hake, Halibut, Mackerel, Marlin, Perch, Pollock, Puffer, Sculpin, Sea Robin, Scup, Shark, Shockfish, Skate, Skipjack, Smelt, Squeteague, Sting Ray, Sturgeon, Swordfish, Tautog, Tomcod, Toadfish, Trout, Tuna, Whiting.

—Compiled from Elvin, *The Fishes of Martha's Vineyard*

Martha's Vineyard has a long and honorable history of fishing and fishermen. The journal of the Gosnold expedition to the Island in March 1602 reports that the crew "had pestered our ship so with Cod fish that we threw numbers of them over-bord again." The abundance of these fish gave the area its name—Cape Cod. Early records are full of references to fish and fishing. The Island Indians, hospitable from the beginning to the English adventurers, taught the new settlers ingenious methods for capturing this elusive but essential food; and many of the Island's waters bear names deriving from the Indians' use of them—Katamuck (Katama), a crab-fishing place, for instance, or Quanaimes (Quenames), the long-fish place.

Despite pollution, overcommercialization, and all the other hazards of our technological age, the magic and mystery of the primitive rituals involved in taking food from the sea still persist on the Island. Traps and nets are still spread out to dry behind the weatherworn houses of the fishermen; and be it fair weather or foul, the *Unicorn* and the *Quitsa Strider* chug through Menemsha Bight into the uncertain waters of the Sound and return with their holds heavy with glistening cod or monstrous green lobsters. Little boys dangle their lines from every bridge and dock on the Island, and in the fall the fires of the bass fishermen glimmer here and there on the misty beaches as the men cast their lines out into the dark water all through the night.

Proportionately, saltwater fish are of course more important and more abundant on and around the Vineyard than are freshwater fish. Many of the pretty land-locked ponds can yield up a good mess of shiny sunfish in a short time, however; and trout fishermen often net beautiful specimens of these sleek, spotted fighters in certain ponds or along the fresh, sparkling streams that traverse some parts of the Island.

SWORDFISH

A summer on the Vineyard without swordfish is almost as unthinkable to some people as a summer on the Vineyard without sun is to others. Those picturesque fishing trawlers with the elongated fish-spotting structures on their bows are not tied up at the Menemsha docks just so tourists can snap pictures of them. They are working boats that may depart anytime, day or night, if the tide is right.

The aptly named long-line method of catching swordfish is still often used. This involves letting out as much as 40 miles of line, baited every 60 to 300 feet with mackerel, behind the boat once it is in open water. For understandable reasons, gill nets and harpooning (harpooned fish has better flavor and brings premium prices) are preferable methods of catching these huge sea dwellers. The captain of a trawler made this very clear some years ago when he and five other men spent forty-eight hours straight, working in shifts untangling their long line, which was not only tangled but also loaded with more than 300 swordfish as well as sharks, tuna, and other smaller fish.

Years ago, trawlers used to come in from a two-week trip with one hundred or so swordfish weighing 100 to 150 pounds apiece, though one boat caught 550 in ten days. Nowadays, their main catch is likely to be tuna, which is fortunately now a steady seller in American fish markets.

Swordfish and other fish such as codfish have become increasingly scarce because they have been grossly overfished, particularly in the waters off the eastern seaboard. In the past our fishing boats plied their trade back and forth along the Atlantic and Pacific coasts, venturing out as far as they needed to in pursuit of their prey. Now the U.S. Government has established imaginary boundaries called Hague Lines 200 miles off both coasts and in the Gulf of Mexico, and American fishermen are forbidden to cross them. Since few other countries have such restrictions, swordfish for sale in this country is increasingly imported from elsewhere.

Vineyarders, however, can still buy and relish swordfish caught by the Menemsha trawlers—often the sought-after harpooned kind—from mid-June until the end of September in a good season, and if you happen to be around Menemhsa the day the first swords are brought in, you'll probably hear about it, as word spreads throughout the community the way word of the arrival of spring warblers is passed from one birdwatcher to another. And, once you've become addicted to freshly caught swordfish, you're not likely to settle for any other kind. Choose some other item on the menu if you are out for a seafood dinner at a restaurant during the winter.

Charcoal-Broiled Swordfish

Two factors are important here. First, the swordfish steaks should be marinated in an aromatic mixture of herbs, oil, lemon juice, and seasonings after being cut into serving-size portions. But, more important: Never, never purchase anything but the freshest swordfish. During the summer, this is usually not difficult if one lives in the North Atlantic states (though we, of course, feel Vineyard-bought swordfish is matchless). At the risk of antagonizing the frozen-food processors, we do not recommend frozen swordfish at any time.

Swordfish, ⅓–½ pound per serving, cut at least 1½ inches thick
Marinade (see below)
Lemon wedges
Melted butter

Marinate fish pieces at least 4 hours, turning several times. Drain pieces well; broil over charcoal (or about 4 inches from broiler heat in your kitchen range) about 6 to 7 minutes on each side for ½-inch slices, or until fish begins to flake when tested with a fork. Serve with lemon wedges and pour a little melted butter over the top.

Note: The fish may be broiled on one side only—approximately 12 to 14 minutes.

SWORDFISH MARINADE

1 cup vegetable oil
Juice of 2 lemons
2 tablespoons white-wine vinegar (optional)
1 teaspoon salt
⅛ teaspoon freshly ground black pepper

½ teaspoon dried basil (or 1 teaspoon chopped fresh basil or rosemary)
Very small pinch cayenne pepper
1 medium clove garlic, minced (optional)

Stir together all ingredients.
Makes about 1½ cups.

Skewered Swordfish

Swordfish Marinade (see page 17)
1 tablespoon soy sauce
1½–2 pounds fresh swordfish, sliced 1 inch thick, cut into 24 cubes
24 medium-size mushrooms
16 small white onions, peeled and parboiled 5 minutes
2 large green peppers, cut into 24 1½-inch squares
16 cherry tomatoes
About ½ cup melted butter
Salt
Freshly ground black pepper
Fennel sprays (optional)

Prepare marinade, adding the soy sauce to the other ingredients. Marinate swordfish cubes at least 2 to 3 hours. Remove from marinade and drain well, then dry with paper towels. Preheat broiler to maximum. (A charcoal grill is preferable, and should be started about 20 minutes before swordfish is removed from marinade.)

Thread eight 10- to 12-inch skewers with fish and vegetables. Brush with melted butter and sprinkle with salt and pepper to taste. If you like, tie one or two fennel sprays lengthwise on each skewer.

Broil 5 to 6 minutes, turn skewers, broil another 5 to 6 minutes. Skewers may be brushed again with melted butter while cooking.

Makes 8 portions.

STRIPED BASS

Two types of bass are found in Vineyard waters—the black bass (also called blackfish or tautog), which according to one Island fisherman is "by all odds the finest chowder fish," and the more familiar "striper," or striped bass. Concern that the venerable striper might be disappearing from the waters of the East Coast prompted the sponsors of the annual fall Martha's Vineyard Striped Bass and Bluefish Derby in 1985 to disallow striped bass entries until its future is assured. Seven years later, huge bass were again being caught in quantity, to the delight of both fishermen and conservationists, and in the fall of 1992 the Derby committee voted to reinstate striped bass in the 1993 Derby. Anyone keeping an undersized bass is liable to a heavy fine.

The weighing-in station on the Edgartown docks remains a night-long social center during Derby month, a place where pipes and cigars are chewed on as tales are swapped involving jigs, tides, favored beaches, bottoms crawling with skate, and of course the big one that got away. And when a seventy-five-year-old Chilmark woman hauled in a 54-pound striper back in the 1960s, another tale was added to the annals.

The fortunate fishermen who land the 40- and 50-pounders can feast on this noble, firm-fleshed fish, give chunks away to friends, and still have plenty to pile in the freezer for winter dinners. Most of us, though, have to buy our bass, all ready to be stuffed and baked or grilled in the backyard.

Fish   *19*

Baked Striped Bass with Herb Stuffing

3–4 pounds striped bass, cut into two fillets
Salt and freshly ground black pepper
3 or more tablespoons butter
½ cup chopped shallots or green onions (use some of green stems)
1 clove garlic, minced fine
½ cup finely chopped celery
½ cup coarsely chopped fresh mushrooms
1 tablespoon chopped fresh chervil (or 1 teaspoon dried)
½ teaspoon chopped fresh sage (or ¼ teaspoon dried)
½ teaspoon minced fresh summer savory (or ¼ teaspoon dried)
½ teaspoon minced fresh basil (or ¼ teaspoon dried)
¼ cup chopped fresh parsley (the Italian type is best)
1 cup dry white wine
5 slices whole-wheat bread, toasted and coarsely crumbled
¼ cup grated Parmesan cheese
¼ cup olive oil
4 slices salt pork, thinly sliced (optional)
1 teaspoon lemon juice
Lemon wedges
Parsley sprigs

Preheat oven to 400°F.

Rinse fish well under cold water, dry with paper towels, and rub with salt and pepper inside and out.

Over moderate heat melt butter in a heavy skillet; when butter foam subsides, add shallots or onions, garlic, and celery. Reduce heat and sauté about 5 minutes, or until vegetables are wilted. Stir occasionally. Add a little more butter if indicated. Turn heat to high, add mushrooms and cook 3 to 4 minutes more. Add chervil, sage, savory, basil, parsley, and ½ cup of the wine; stir well, reduce heat, and let simmer for several minutes.

Remove skillet from heat, stir in bread crumbs and grated cheese, lifting lightly with a fork to combine all ingredients. Additional salt and pepper may be added, if required. Allow mixture to cool slightly.

Place one fillet on a shallow baking pan lined with greased foil. If fish slabs are thick and it looks as though the dish would be unwieldy when assembled, lay two pieces of twine on pan first and use to tie stuffed fillets together. Use larger piece of fish for bottom, if they differ. Arrange stuffing neatly on top of fish, then lay second fillet on that. Press stuffing inward if needed to help hold it in place. Rub top of fish with olive oil and dust lightly with salt and pepper if desired. Optional salt-pork slices should be added at this point. Tie with twine if needed.

In a small saucepan heat remaining wine, olive oil, and the lemon juice. Pour over fish and bake, uncovered, about 30 to 45 minutes, or until fish flakes easily when pierced with a fork. While the fish is baking, baste it three or four times with the liquids in the baking pan. Transfer fish to a heated platter and discard twine.

Serve the fish very hot, garnished with lemon wedges and sprigs of parsley.

Note: For fewer diners, the stuffing can be carefully piled on a single bass fillet, the salt-pork slices (if used) placed on the stuffing, a dusting of salt and pepper added if desired, and the mixture of wine, olive oil, and lemon juice poured over the top. Adjust proportions and baking time accordingly. If salt pork is not used, a piece of foil placed over the fish during final 10 minutes or so of baking will help keep stuffing from drying out too much.

Makes 6 to 8 portions.

Grilled Striped Bass with Pesto

3–4-pound striped bass fillet, skin on
Light cooking oil
Approximately 1 cup pesto (see page 295)

Prepare grill for cooking. When hot, lightly oil bass fillet on both sides and place meat side down on grill. Cook about 5 minutes. Turn carefully over and cover top with pesto. Continue to grill until fillet flakes when pierced in middle with fork, or to desired doneness.

Note: Mayonnaise may be used if pesto is out of season.
Makes 6 to 8 portions.

BLUEFISH

Fishing for "blues," according to former Island chronicler Joseph Chase Allen, was probably the first Vineyard sport. Years and years ago, when the bluefish schooled along the shores, young and old lined the beaches and fished for the fun of fishing, throwing most of their catch down to flop their lives away on the sand. To get in form for these outings, the fishermen held casting practice sessions with their heavily leaded lines in Island meadows, and Joe Allen commented that the "distances to which these Vineyarders could cast a bluefish jig were unbelievable, fifty fathoms being considered only moderately fair."

No one parts with a just-caught bluefish these days without good cause, such as being able to present a cleaned 10-pounder to the lady the fisherman is courting. Many consider them the finest-flavored fish of all, rating them even higher than striped bass or swordfish. This is a moot point that we will not debate here; but from the tiny "snappers" that weigh only a few ounces to the huge "choppers" often caught off shore on trolling jigs thrown out from boats, bluefish, when carefully prepared, are a sea delicacy worthy of the highest praise.

Baked Bluefish and Bass

½ pound chunk of bluefish
½ pound chunk of striped bass
½ cup finely diced mixed red and green peppers
1 teaspoon tarragon
½ teaspoon salt
Freshly ground black pepper to taste
2 tablespoons melted butter

Preheat oven to 400°F.

Lay fish in a flat, oiled baking dish about 6 by 9 inches. Do not overlap. Combine peppers, tarragon, and salt, and sprinkle evenly over fish. Add black pepper to taste. Dribble melted butter over the top. Bake about 20 minutes or until fish flakes easily when prodded with a fork.

Makes 2 generous portions.

Bluefish or Tuna Provençale

[Baked with Aromatic Herbs and Seasonings]

An entree from Louise Tate King's former restaurant, this is a considerably simplified version of a traditional French dish from Provence, where tomatoes, garlic, and olive oil are part of the culinary heritage. There tuna is likely to be used in preparing this dish, as it easily can be in this country, now that this elegant fish has become more widely available. An asset is that you may prepare it ahead by browning the bluefish slices quickly, preparing the sauce ahead, and combining all a half hour or so before serving time.

4–5 pound bluefish, cleaned and cut into 2-inch-thick slices (bone in)
or
2 pounds of thick tuna steaks, cut in to 2-inch-thick slices

MARINADE

1 cup olive or vegetable oil
½ cup red-wine vinegar
1 tablespoon lemon juice
1 teaspoon salt

¼ teaspoon freshly ground black
* pepper*
2 cloves garlic, minced fine

Place the fish slices in a shallow container; combine the oil, vinegar, lemon juice, salt, pepper, and garlic, and pour over the fish. Marinate the fish in this mixture 2 to 3 hours, turning occasionally. Refrigeration is not required.

Preheat oven to 450°F.

Remove fish from marinade; dry it thoroughly with paper towels. Discard marinade.

SAUCE

2 tablespoons butter

2 tablespoons olive or
    vegetable oil

1 cup onions, thinly sliced

3 cups fresh tomatoes, cut in
    chunks (canned may be
    substituted)

2 cloves garlic, minced fine

1 teaspoon salt

¼ teaspoon freshly ground black
    pepper

1 cup dry white wine

4 tablespoons tomato paste

2 beef bouillon cubes

½ cup chopped parsley

½ teaspoon dried thyme

Scant teaspoon dried oregano

Over high heat melt the butter with the oil in a heavy skillet until the butter foam subsides. Quickly brown the fish on both sides, allowing 2 to 3 minutes per side. Remove from skillet and arrange in a shallow, flameproof baking dish.

In the same skillet, over moderate heat, cook the onions until transparent. Add a little more butter or oil if the onions demand it. Add the tomatoes, garlic, salt, pepper, wine, tomato paste, bouillon cubes, ¼ cup of the chopped parsley, thyme, and oregano. Cook over high heat, stirring frequently, about 10 minutes, allowing the liquids to evaporate sufficiently so that sauce is thickened slightly.

Pour the sauce over the bluefish or tuna slices, sprinkle with the remaining ¼ cup chopped parsley, cover the dish tightly with foil, and bake 15 to 20 minutes, or until the fish flakes easily when pierced with a fork.

Transfer the fish to a heated platter; keep warm. Place the baking dish with its remaining sauce over high heat and boil rapidly, stirring constantly, until about 2 cups of sauce remain. Pour sauce over fish slices and serve immediately.

Note: The sauce may be thickened slightly with a paste of 1 tablespoon flour mixed with 1 tablespoon softened butter.

Makes 4 to 6 portions.

Betty Ann's Bonito

2 bonito steaks, ¾-inch thick

3 tablespoons dry vermouth

1 medium garlic clove, minced

2 tablespoons finely chopped scallions, or 1 tablespoon each
  finely chopped onion and chives

1 tablespoon chopped parsley

Salt and freshly ground black pepper

2 tablespoons mayonnaise

1 teaspoon Dijon mustard

Dash each of Worcestershire and Tabasco sauces

½ teaspoon sugar

2 tablespoons grated Parmesan cheese

Preheat oven to 400°F.

Place the fish steaks in a small flameproof casserole just big enough to hold them. Pour vermouth over top, adding a bit more if needed to cover bottom of pan. In a small dish, mix garlic, scallions or onion and chives, and parsley. Sprinkle over top of steaks. Salt and pepper if desired. Place dish in oven and bake 12 minutes to partially cook.

While fish bakes, mix the mayonnaise, mustard, two sauces, and sugar in a small dish. Remove fish from oven at end of cooking period and spread mixture over top of each steak. Sprinkle half the grated cheese on each steak and place fish about 4 inches below heated broiler for 3 to 5 minutes. Check several times to make sure top is not burning. If it is, lower broiling tray. Remove and serve.

Note: This is an elegant but rich and filling way to prepare this sleek beauty whose capricious behavior taunts countless Vineyard fishermen each summer. If you prefer to prepare the fish a simpler way, marinate it in fresh lemon juice for 3 to 5 hours, then broil in the usual manner. Minced garlic, salt, and pepper may be added to the marinade, but do not add oil, as this fish is quite oily like its relative the tuna.

Makes 2 portions.

Shirley's Grilled False Albacore

If when fishing for bonito you manage to land one of these less tasty relatives (false albacore stripes go around, bonito's run lengthwise) you can make your catch very palatable with the following recipe. It was devised by the wife of Vineyard mystery writer Philip Craig, who has been concocting ways to cook whatever fish they catch for many years now.

1 false albacore
½ cup lemon juice
¼ cup olive oil
1 teaspoon salt
1 teaspoon oregano
¾ teaspoon garlic powder
½ teaspoon freshly ground black pepper

Fillet and skin fish, then cut into good-size chunks. Put chunks into a resealable plastic bag. In a small bowl whisk together remaining ingredients. Pour in with fish, seal bag, and refrigerate overnight. Turn bag once or twice to redistribute marinade.

Drain fish chunks and grill until flesh is opaque and flakes easily when pierced with a fork. Turn chunks once or twice during cooking period. Serve with lemon slices or tartar sauce.

Makes 4 to 8 portions, depending on size of fish.

Poached Mako Shark

These cousins of the great sharks can weigh up to 1,000 pounds, swim more than 50 miles an hour, and swallow whole swordfish. Most of those caught and sold locally, however, are in the 50- to 175-pound range. Virtually unknown here until the last decade or so, this firm-fleshed fish is increasingly popular as a less expensive alternative to swordfish. Usually broiled, mako is also delicious poached according to this recipe, which is adapted from one designed for salmon.

1 tablespoon butter
2 tablespoons each chopped carrots, celery (include some leaves),
    and onions
¼ cup white wine
2 tablespoons fresh lemon juice
2 or more cups water
2-pound slab of mako shark, cut 1 inch thick
Salt
Freshly ground black pepper
Mayonnaise

In a skillet at least 2 inches wider than fish slab, melt butter over low heat. Add carrots, celery, and onions. Stir to coat with butter, then raise heat slightly and sauté vegetables 5 minutes, stirring to avoid sticking. Add wine, lemon juice, and water. Bring to boil, lower heat, and simmer 5 minutes. Add fish, salt, and pepper as desired. If liquid does not come at least halfway up side of fish, add more water. Alternatively, a smaller skillet may be used so liquid will cover fish, in which case it does not need turning. Bring mixture to low boil, lower heat, and simmer fish about 15 minutes, or 8 minutes per side if fish is to be turned over. Slab can be cut in half to make turning easier. Fish is done when center flakes easily when pierced with a fork. Carefully lift fish from the skillet, and cover the top with a layer of mayonnaise. Allow fish to cool somewhat before serving.

Note: Fish slab may be wrapped in cheesecloth before lowering it into liquid. This facilitates removal when it is cooked.

Makes 4 portions.

HERRING

Next to the whale—which, however colorful, does not figure in a Vineyard cookbook—the lowly herring seems to have the most interesting Island history. During the 1920s and 1930s, hundreds of thousands of barrels (some fishermen brought in a thousand a night during the six-week spawning season) of these silvery fish were trapped in the herring creek off Edgartown Great Pond and were used to make, of all things, artificial pearls. According to a fascinating account in the *Vineyard Gazette* of May 24, 1923, two Cape Cod men evolved a process for converting the scales from the herrings' bellies (no other part of the fish was used) into a liquid into which glass beads were dipped to produce so-called Priscilla pearls. Since the days of salting and pickling these fish had already passed, the remains were not eaten but were "plowed into the ground for fertilizer." The *Gazette* doesn't say where, but perhaps this accounts for the lushness of some of our Vineyard gardens.

Salted and smoked, the herring used to be known on the Vineyard as Oldtown Turkey. "Alewives" is a more familiar name for these fish. Webster's gives two possible derivations for this euphonious term; we prefer the second: "possibly . . . American Indian (a form *aloofe* is recorded in 1678)."

Little used today by American housewives, herring have long been an important food fish and are still an important part of European cuisine, particularly

Scandinavian. Today's Vineyarders still trap the herring when they come wriggling up the creeks off the Great Ponds every spring as they have for untold centuries, but nowadays this is mainly to extract the females' roe. As herring is both plentiful (though seasonal) and good, it deserves to be eaten more often, particularly in one of its many pickled forms.

Sautéed Fresh Herring Roe

16–20 fresh herring roes, whole
1 teaspoon salt
¼ teaspoon freshly ground black pepper
Flour or cracker meal
1 beaten egg (optional)
About 2 tablespoons butter
About 2 tablespoons vegetable oil
Cooked bacon
Few sprigs parsley

Place a heavy 10- to 12-inch skillet (preferably black iron) over low heat. Season roes with salt and pepper, and coat them with flour or cracker meal. Handle them gently; they are fragile. Roes may be dipped into beaten egg before coating with flour or meal. Add half butter, half oil to skillet in sufficient quantity to cover the bottom well. Increase heat to moderate. When butter foam subsides, add the roes and sauté each side until golden brown. Do not overcrowd skillet. If necessary, sauté one batch and remove to a heated platter, then repeat the process. Serve with crisp, golden bacon, and garnish with a few sprigs of parsley.

Makes 4 portions.

John Pachico's Herring Roe Bake

Mr. Pachico, skilled fisherman and former proprietor of a Vineyard Haven fish market, suggested this simple method of preparation. The finished dish is unexpectedly good, and it is not only quickly prepared but, unlike sautéed roe, requires no attention while it is cooking.

12 slices raw bacon
16–20 whole fresh herring roes
Flour or cracker meal
Salt and freshly ground pepper
2 eggs, lightly beaten (optional)

Preheat oven to 475°F.

Place half the bacon slices on the bottom of a shallow casserole or baking dish. Dip the roes into flour or cracker meal. Handle them gently; they are fragile. Season well with salt and pepper. If desired, dip first into beaten eggs and then into flour or cracker meal. Carefully distribute the roes over the bacon. Cover with remaining bacon slices. Bake approximately 25 minutes. If bacon topping is not crisp enough, place dish under the broiler for a few moments.

Makes 4 portions.

Fillet of Sole Louise

6 small fillets of very fresh sole (or flounder or halibut)
Dry white wine
Bottled clam juice
2 tablespoons chopped shallots (or white part of scallions)
¼ teaspoon salt
¼ teaspoon white pepper
1 tablespoon fresh lemon juice
5 tablespoons butter
2 tablespoons flour
1 cup cream or whole milk
18 large fresh shrimp, shelled and deveined

Preheat oven to 400°F.

Carefully place fish in an enamel or glass baking dish, about 9 by 14 inches, so that all are equally spaced. If the tails seem especially thin, turn them under an inch or so. Pour enough wine and clam juice (in equal quantities) over fillets barely to cover them. Spread chopped shallots or scallions over top, season with salt and pepper, sprinkle with the lemon juice, and dot with 2 tablespoons of the butter. Cover baking dish tightly with a piece of aluminum foil. Bake approximately 10 to 12 minutes, then lift a corner of the foil and check fish. It should appear opaque and should be just starting to flake.

Remove baking dish from oven and allow fish to cool for an hour. If the fish is very fresh, this will make it easier to remove from the pan. With a spatula or pancake turner (or both), carefully transfer fish to a heatproof platter. Strain the fish stock. Reduce it to 1 cup by boiling rapidly in an uncovered pan. Make a roux by melting the remaining 3 tablespoons butter in a saucepan over moderate heat, then adding the flour and blending it in thoroughly. Allow roux to simmer several minutes, then add the fish stock and cream or milk. Bring the mixture to a simmer, stirring constantly. Taste for seasoning. Pour any accumulated liquids from fish platter into sauce. Stir well, then pour sauce over fish.

Simmer shrimp slowly in boiling salted water for 3 to 5 minutes. Cut in half lengthwise and garnish each fillet with 6 pieces. Heat in 450°F oven only long enough to bring fish to serving temperature.

Note: Prepare this dish in the morning if you like, saucing and garnishing the fish just before reheating.

Makes 6 portions.

Poached Haddock or Codfish with Egg Sauce

Off-Island, this is sometimes referred to as "Cape Cod Turkey." Incidentally, Vineyarders who schedule a trip to the mainland often say that they are going to the United States of America. A small smile invariably accompanies this statement, and in it can be read a quiet contentment, a strong feeling of "place"—engendered, perhaps, by the Island's physical and psychological insularity. Also revealed is the inimitable flash of Yankee humor, never far below the surface.

4-pound haddock or codfish (pollock, which runs in the fall,
*   is also good), cleaned and left whole*
Salt
Egg Sauce (see page 34)

If time permits, sprinkle fish with ½ cup salt inside and out and let it stand overnight. Then rinse thoroughly. Otherwise, salt fish and let stand at least half an hour, then rinse. Fill a 6- to 8-quart pot or fish steamer with enough water to cover fish; add about 2 tablespoons salt. Bring water to simmering point. Carefully tie the fish in cheesecloth and place it in the pot of simmering water. Allow it to simmer for about 30 minutes. Fish will be done when it just barely begins to flake when tested with a fork. Transfer fish to a heated platter, remove cheesecloth, and serve with Egg Sauce.

Note: Canadian salt cod (use 1½ pounds fillets) may also be used in this recipe, but the fish must be "freshened" to remove its salt. To do this, soak it in water to cover for at least 12 hours, draining water and replacing it with fresh water at least twice during this period. Or the salt cod can be covered with cold water, brought to a simmer, and drained at once; repeat this process three times, until the fish loses enough salt to be edible when tasted. The fish must *not* be boiled during this desalting process.

Makes 3 to 4 portions.

EGG SAUCE

2 tablespoons butter
2 tablespoons flour
¼ teaspoon dry mustard
¼ teaspoon salt

1½ cups milk (or half milk, half chicken stock or canned chicken broth)
2 hard-boiled eggs, sliced

Melt butter in small saucepan over moderate heat, add flour, mustard, and salt and stir thoroughly until well blended. Reduce heat. Cook a minute or so longer. Slowly stir in the milk or milk and stock. A wire whisk is good for this purpose. Still stirring, cook slowly until mixture comes to a simmer. Add the hard-boiled eggs and serve immediately.

Makes 4 portions.

Scup (Porgy) au Gratin

Scup is suggested in this recipe from the files of the *Vineyard Gazette*. Filleted flounder makes an admirable substitute, as do other filleted fish—young mackerel, haddock, or pollock. Nor is it essential to adhere conscientiously to the amounts of other suggested ingredients. For instance, a little more zucchini or tomato, particularly if both are freshly plucked from one's garden, heightens enjoyment of the finished dish.

4 servings filleted scup (or other filleted fish)
1½ teaspoons salt
¼ teaspoon freshly ground black pepper
2 small zucchini, sliced ½ inch thick
2 medium tomatoes, coarsely chopped (or 1 cup drained
*   canned tomatoes)*
2–3 tablespoons finely chopped shallots or green onions
½ cup fresh bread crumbs, preferably from day-old home-style bread
½ cup melted butter (or half butter, half oil)
2 tablespoons lemon juice
¼ cup grated Parmesan cheese (freshly grated is preferable)

Preheat oven to 425°F.

Place fish fillets in shallow baking dish, season lightly with about half the salt, and dust with pepper. Cover with zucchini slices, tomatoes, and shallots or green onions. Sprinkle remaining salt over vegetables, and dust with pepper. Combine bread crumbs, butter, and lemon juice in a small bowl, mix, then spread over vegetables. Top with grated cheese. Bake until fish flakes easily when tested with a fork, about 20 to 30 minutes.

Makes 4 portions.

Sautéed Fish

A popular Vineyard version of fried fish, good for small freshwater fish as well as for the little mackerel, snapper blues, scup, flounder, and other saltwater dwellers that are too small for broiling or baking.

5 tablespoons butter (or half butter, half vegetable oil)
8–12 small fish, cleaned (or 2–3 pounds filleted fish)
2 eggs, beaten
Salt
Freshly ground black pepper

In a heavy skillet (preferably black iron), heat the butter until foam subsides. Dry each fish or fillet slightly with a paper towel, dip in beaten eggs, place in skillet, and brown over moderate heat. (The egg will run a little; scrape it back toward the fish pieces.) When one side of fish is browned, dribble a little additional beaten egg on top of each piece, salt and pepper lightly, and turn over to brown on other side. Salt and pepper to taste; serve very hot.

Makes 4 portions.

Captain Poole's Fish

Menemsha stalwart Everett Poole is said to be almost as uncompromising about how fish is to be prepared as his father Captain Donald was, though he will sometimes settle for fish that has been broiled or baked. Donald Poole used to insist there was no way to cook fish except rolled in cornmeal and fried in salt-pork fat. Even a slab of his son's magnificent swordfish received this treatment. That was the way he ate fish as a child and the way his wife prepared it for him up to his death in 1984.

If you have always used some other kind of fat for frying fish, try using salt pork. You may become as reluctant as the Captain was to give it up.

4 frying-size fish (mackerel or ocean perch should be good) or
  4 good-sized fish steaks or fillets
2 teaspoons salt (slightly less if preferred)
½ teaspoon black pepper
½ cup yellow cornmeal
Piece of salt pork (about ¼ pound), cut in ½-inch dice
Lemon wedges or tartar sauce

Clean fish and remove heads, if using whole fish. Rinse in cold water, pat dry with paper towels. Rub all surfaces (including inside cavities if using whole fish) with combined salt and pepper, then roll in cornmeal. Cook salt-pork dice over moderate heat until skillet has a good coating of fat—at least ¼ inch deep. Remove dice; fry fish in hot fat over moderate heat until crisp and brown on both sides. This should take 6 to 8 minutes. Fish should flake easily when tested with fork. Do not overcook. Drain slightly on paper toweling and serve very hot. Browned salt-pork dice may be served with fish for those who like it, as may the traditional lemon wedges or tartar sauce.

Makes 4 portions.

Mixed Seafood in Clam Shells

Sometimes, instead of arriving home with a catch of handsome bluefish or a mess of steamers, children, husband, or house guests show up in the kitchen and proudly present the cook with a conglomeration of sea treasures that, if used separately, wouldn't even make enough appetizers to go around. The next time this happens, try this recipe, adapted to utilize whatever you find dumped in the kitchen sink. Mussels instead of clams could be used, or several of each; more fish and less crab could be used, or vice versa. Almost any way, it's good.

6–8 medium quahogs
2 or 3 small fish (flounder, scup [porgy], tautog, or perch),
 cleaned but left whole
Canned clam juice
Meat from 8 rock crabs or 2 or 3 blue crabs (or ¾ cup cooked crabmeat)
1 cup fresh bread crumbs (use day-old French or Italian type if possible)
⅓ cup each chopped onion, green pepper, and celery
2 tablespoons melted butter
1 teaspoon chopped fresh parsley
2 slices bacon, cooked crisp
Salt
Freshly ground black pepper
Paprika

Preheat oven to 400°F.

Open the quahogs and remove from shells. Reserve liquid and at least twelve shells. Wash the shells.

Place the fish in a saucepan of sufficient size, add the reserved quahog liquor and sufficient canned clam juice barely to cover the fish. Cover tightly and cook over gentle heat about 5 to 10 minutes, or until fish flakes easily when prodded with a fork.

While fish is poaching, chop clams fine; place in mixing bowl with crabmeat, bread crumbs, onion, green pepper, and celery.

Remove fish from its poaching liquid, reserving several tablespoons liquid; place on cutting board and discard skin, remove flesh from bones, using two forks. Add fish, melted butter, and chopped parsley to bowl. Crumble the bacon over the mixture. Mix lightly with a fork, adding several tablespoons of the reserved fish liquor. Salt and some freshly ground pepper may be added to taste.

Place the seafood mixture in the quahog shells, dividing it evenly. Bake the filled shells in a shallow pan, covered tightly with foil, about 20 minutes. Remove foil, sprinkle the shells lightly with paprika, and place under a moderately heated broiler long enough to brown.

You may cook these also over a charcoal grill by wrapping each filled shell in heavy foil and placing them on the grill about 25 minutes.

Serve in the shells.

Makes 4 portions.

EEL

Dreaded by timid bathers, despised by most fishermen, and scorned by contemporary cooks, at least in America, these snakelike water creatures with a unique and fascinating life history can be transformed into epicurean delicacies. In pioneer days eels were used in coastal settlements as an important food and were trapped largely in eel pots. Nowadays, eels are usually caught—off the Menemsha docks, for instance—by someone who is fishing for something else and discarded as quickly as they can be freed from the fishhook.

If you land an eel and can survive the dehooking, skinning, and hacking-to-pieces process, try cooking the eel meat. It has a rich, slightly oily flavor and tastes more like chicken than fish, according to devotees. There are several ways to disgorge the hook from the eel's mouth, but they are too involved to be described here. If there is an Islander nearby, ask him. To skin an eel, cut through the skin all the way around just below the head. Hold the eel's head in one hand, and yank the skin off with a pair of pliers (don't forget to kill your prey first by striking him hard on the head with some heavy object). Pull hard, and remember the eel is proverbially slippery. Slit the belly and remove the innards. Hack off the head; then cut the meat into chunks of 2 or 3 inches. Wrap these in foil and refrigerate until used. Like any fish, eel should be eaten (or pickled) soon after it is caught.

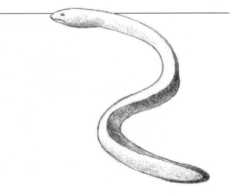

Eels with Herbs

1½ pounds cleaned, skinned fresh eels

4 tablespoons butter

½ cup chopped spinach or sorrel

½ cup chopped fresh parsley

2 tablespoons fresh chervil (or 1 tablespoon dried)

1 teaspoon chopped fresh tarragon (or ½ teaspoon dried)

Pinch each of dried sage, thyme, and rosemary

½ teaspoon salt

¼ teaspoon freshly ground black pepper

1 cup white wine

1 cup or more chicken stock (or canned chicken broth)

2 egg yolks, lightly beaten

1 tablespoon lemon juice

Rinse eels in cold water; dry thoroughly with paper towels, or they will not brown when sautéed. Cut them into 2- to 3-inch pieces.

Heat butter in a heavy skillet over moderate heat until foam subsides; add eels and brown evenly on all sides. Add the spinach or sorrel and the herbs; add the salt and pepper. Pour the wine and chicken stock over the eels and herbs, using enough broth barely to cover fish. Cover pan tightly and reduce heat; simmer the eels about 20 minutes, or until a fork pierces the flesh easily.

Remove eel pieces; place in shallow casserole or bowl.

Pour pan liquids into top of a double boiler; place over, not in, boiling water in bottom of double boiler. Stir egg yolks into liquids and cook, stirring constantly, until sauce thickens slightly. Stir in lemon juice; pour sauce over eels. Sauce will thicken as it cools. Chill well in refrigerator before serving.

Makes 4 to 6 portions.

Martha's Vineyard Eel Stifle

2 pounds eels, skinned and cut in 1-inch slices
¼ pound salt pork, cut in ½-inch dice
4 medium onions, cut ½ inch thick
4 cups sliced potatoes, ½ inch thick
¾ teaspoon salt
¼ teaspoon freshly ground black pepper
Flour

Prepare eels according to directions on page 40. In a heavy iron or cast-aluminum kettle, cook the salt-pork dice over moderate heat until crisp and golden. Drain on paper towels and reserve. Place a layer each of onions, potatoes, and eels in the kettle. Sprinkle with some of the salt and pepper and about ½ teaspoon flour. Repeat layers until all the ingredients are used. Sprinkle the salt-pork dice over the top and add enough cold water barely to cover layers. Simmer over low heat, tightly covered, until tender—about ½ hour.

If preferred, this dish may be baked in a 300°F oven, in which case it must be cooked a little longer.

Makes 6 to 8 portions.

Sautéed Squid

Squid, familiar fare in Mediterranean countries, can also be caught and cooked on Martha's Vineyard. Menemsha children introduce their summer playmates to squid jigging in the murky, swirling waters below the docks. Intrepid adults can usually haul in a fair catch with the right combination of patience and luck. Buy a cane pole and some line, wrap a bit of fluorescent orange tape around a treble hook, attach hook to line and line to pole (a half-ounce sinker might be advisable in a swift tide), and lower your line into the water where the children fish. Yank your prey up sharply when he attacks, or he may drop off. If you don't catch anything, don't settle for a package of frozen squid. That is for fish, not for humans.

4 small fresh squid (do not use frozen)
½ cup flour
½ teaspoon salt
¼ teaspoon black pepper
½ cup olive oil (more if needed)
2 small eggs, beaten
Lemon juice
Lemon slices

Prepare squid for cooking by removing the head and cutting off the tentacles. Slit open the body and clean it well in cold water. Cut body and tentacles into ½-inch rings. Pat pieces with paper towels to absorb most of the moisture on them. Combine flour, salt, and pepper in a paper bag, add squid pieces a few at a time, and shake until well coated with flour mixture. Remove and keep on a plate while heating oil to sizzling hot (use a good-sized heavy skillet). Using a slotted spoon, dip squid pieces into beaten eggs, let drain slightly, then place in hot fat. Cook pieces quickly over moderate heat, turning to brown all sides. Do not overcook, or squid will be tough—5 minutes should be the maximum cooking time allowed. Drain cooked pieces briefly on paper towels, sprinkle with a few drops of lemon juice, and serve very hot with lemon slices.

Note: The flouring process may be omitted. Simply pat washed squid dry, salt and pepper pieces well, dip into beaten egg, and fry as outlined above.

Makes 4 portions.

CHAPTER 3

Shellfish

The fish and shellfish of the great ponds formed the basis of the very sound economy of the Island Indians before the coming of the English. The great ponds, depending on the salinity of the water, will produce variously great quantities of oysters, quahaugs, soft shell clams, scallops and blue mussels. . . . The Indians ate all those shellfish as is indicated by the shell heaps and kitchen middens that mark the sites of their villages. They also ate other shellfish that are no longer generally used for food, such as the little quarterdecks or boatshells which used to be called sweetmeats, and the big whelks which Vineyarders called winkles.

—E. Gale Huntington, *An Introduction to Martha's Vineyard* [†]

As anyone knows who has ever investigated the insides of a clam or oyster, shellfish are not like other "fish"; they are defined as "aquatic invertebrate animals." The category includes mollusks, such as clams, oysters, mussels, slugs, and snails; and crustaceans, such as lobsters, crabs, shrimp, and—oddly enough—wood lice. Like the rest of us on this increasingly polluted planet, shellfish are at the mercy of their environs. A change in the saline content of the vast, beautiful Great Ponds has often killed off the resident shellfish; and though a mussel can live to a shell-encrusted

[†] Dukes County Historical Society, Edgartown, Massachusetts, 1969.

old age on a jetty at Menemsha Bight, the waters from which he constantly syphons his food may turn him into a live health hazard as a carrier of infectious hepatitis.

Now the Vineyard, like other communities, is concerning itself with the condition of its precious waters, since much of its livelihood is derived in one way or another from the sea. Surely this jewel of an island, to which thousands of people come to escape the filth and frustrations of city life, won't be allowed to succumb to the same ills as more metropolitan areas.

Clamming, scalloping, oystering, crabbing, and musseling have been nearly as important as fishing on Martha's Vineyard since the days when the Indians feasted on shellfish cooked in salt steam over seaweed and hot stones—a custom that evolved into the more elaborate clambake of the white man. In almost every saltwater pond on the Vineyard, summer wanderers still encounter one or another of these intriguing creatures. A scallop may bubble past a young skindiver in Sengekontacket Pond; a crab glide off into the seaweed at the approach of a Sailfish skimming toward him; a steamer clam squirt a watery warning out of his sandhole and withdraw deeper into the black muck as picnickers pass. And once an immense oyster turned up high on the pebbles at Lambert's Cove beach. Though barnacled and worm-burrowed, he was still tight and alive. Carried from his moorings and deposited miles away by some freakish tide, he came nonetheless to a glorious end—chilled, sprinkled with lemon juice, and savored at sunset on a North Tisbury porch.

CLAMS

Though certainly the most popular and familiar bivalve on the Island, clams, for some curious reason, are not included in the 1602 list of "fishes" recorded by the Gosnold expedition. The Indians were using them for food long before that, and their popularity has developed until today clams and clamming are an integral part of the summer scene all up and down the East Coast.

The hard-shelled quahog or little neck (the slightly larger ones are the well-known cherrystones) and the soft-shelled or steamer are routed out of their sand beds and used every way from raw to exotic recipes in which they are minced, ground, stuffed, sauced, spiced, or otherwise tampered with. There are other edible clams to be gathered on the Island, if you can find enough of them to make it worth your while. Surf clams, the inhabitants of those huge rounded shells that make such handy ashtrays, have tough bodies, but the muscles that keep the creatures closed against the perils of life in the sea can be cut out and treated like the equivalent muscle in the scallop (the only part of that bivalve that is eaten). Small surf clams can be ground for chowder. And the razor clam, though difficult to capture and extremely perishable, is thought by some to be even more delectable than its more accessible relatives.

Hard-shelled clams and oysters both freeze very satisfactorily, mussels do not. Since oysters are so misshapen and sharp edged, it is preferable to shuck them and freeze them with their liquid in small plastic containers. But clams can be frozen as they come from the pond. Scrub off the worst of the muck and sand, dry them slightly, then store them in bags in the freezer to be used as needed. At least one Vineyard household enjoys defrosted clams both raw and cooked right into April.

When frozen or thoroughly chilled, clams relax their muscles slightly, making them very easy to open. We prefer this method to heating them in the oven to facilitate opening.

Steamer Clams with Herbs

I f you have friends who are rather blasé about steamed clams, having had them at every New England resort town every summer since early childhood, take them on a clamming expedition along the tidal sands of one of the Great Ponds (or to your own favorite, secret place) and invite them over that night for supper. Or you may want to wait until the next day, and soak your clams overnight in sea water with a handful or so of cornmeal thrown in it. Set the container in a cool place during the soaking period. This rids them of most of their ingested sand. Confronted with a steaming bowl of this savory blending of seafood and herbs, even the most indifferent diner is likely to forget himself and demand more.

1 gallon steamer clams
1 cup dry vermouth
1 cup butter
1 small clove garlic, crushed
1 teaspoon dried basil (or 2 teaspoons chopped fresh basil)
1 small bay leaf (or 2 dried Vineyard bayberry leaves)
Freshly ground black pepper, a lot or a little
¼ cup lemon juice
2 tablespoons chopped fresh parsley (optional)

Even if you have bought your clams, try to get them as sandless as possible—sand tends to cling in the "necks." (We recommend soaking them overnight as detailed above.) Rinse them gently under cold running water. Use only fresh, live clams. If you have any doubt as to their state of health, smell them. Live clams smell like the sea. Dead ones smell foul, like the black muck they live in.

Place the washed clams in a large, deep, 6- to 8-quart kettle with a tight-fitting cover. Combine vermouth, 4 tablespoons of the butter, garlic, basil, bay leaf, and black pepper in a small saucepan and heat until the butter melts. Pour this mixture over the clams and mix in gently with a slotted spoon. Try not to break the clam shells. Cover the kettle and place over high heat until the pot is full of steam. Lower heat and steam about 10 minutes, or until shells fall slightly open. Do not overcook.

While clams cook, combine the remaining ¾ cup butter and the lemon juice in a small saucepan and heat until butter melts. Mix well; keep warm. Ladle clams into a large, warmed bowl. Pour the liquid in the pan through a strainer lined with cheese-cloth into a pitcher and serve it in cups or small bowls as a broth with the clams. Serve the warm lemon butter in several small dishes for diners to dip their clams into. The soup may be garnished with chopped parsley, if desired.

Note: If the clams have been freshly dug, they will not require the addition of salt; if not, you may wish to add salt to taste.

Makes 3 to 4 generous portions.

Clams Casino

Though not exclusively a Martha's Vineyard recipe, here is a wonderfully savory way of using the outcome of a clamming expedition. Proportions given produce a satisfactory prelude to a meal; more, of course, would be needed if clams are to be used as a main course.

Rock salt
24 quahogs, little-neck size, opened and left in the half shell
¾ cup soft bread crumbs (use day-old French or Italian type,
   if possible)
¼ teaspoon freshly ground black pepper
5 tablespoons chopped parsley, preferably flat Italian kind
Pinch of cayenne pepper (optional)
4–6 tablespoons olive oil (or other vegetable oil)
1 clove garlic, minced

Preheat oven to 500°F.

Partially fill a shallow baking dish (a rimmed cookie sheet is suggested) with rock salt. This provides a bed for the quahogs; it prevents them from tipping and losing their juices. Set the half-shell quahogs on the rock salt.

Mix the bread crumbs, black pepper, 3 tablespoons of the parsley, and the cayenne pepper if desired. Spoon this mixture equally over the clams. Mix the oil and garlic thoroughly; pour carefully over each clam. Bake for about 10 minutes. If the crumbs have not sufficiently browned, place the dish under the broiler just long enough to achieve the desired browning. Sprinkle clams with remainder of chopped parsley and serve immediately.

Note: Salt has been deliberately omitted from this recipe. If the quahogs have been out of the water only a matter of hours, they will be delightfully seasoned with the brine from their natural environment.

It is suggested that the quahogs be refrigerated until icy cold; opening them is then a simple matter. The muscle that acts as a hinge, almost locking the two shells in place, will relax considerably when chilled.

Quahogs can also be "dressed up" by following a recipe for Oysters Rockefeller, substituting clams for oysters.

Makes 4 portions as an appetizer.

Clambake

No two clambake enthusiasts agree about the ingredients essential in preparing a true clambake. In Rhode Island, white and sweet potatoes, as well as onions, are important. Sometimes chicken or fish is added to the pile. In other lands, both food and procedure vary—the Polynesians, for instance, steam their foods over hot stones in earthen ovens.

New England clambakes—and those on Martha's Vineyard—are conducted more or less as follows: First, a huge pit is dug in the beach and lined with large beach stones. Then a large fire is laid and lighted, and enough cordwood is thrown on to keep the fire going for about an hour and a half. The embers are then raked away, and a 4-inch layer of wet seaweed is placed on the stones. Rockweed, a seaweed that is full of "blisters" that break open and contribute additional liquid and flavor, is especially good for this purpose. Then comes the food. Potatoes, if used, go first; then chicken wrapped in cloth. A layer of rockweed follows. Next comes corn, left in the husk, then live lobsters, and last, steamer clams—bushels of them—poured into burlap bags and arranged over the top. Another layer of rockweed is thrown on, then a wet canvas is thrown over the entire pit to confine the steam. The edges of the canvas should be weighted down with stones to form a tight cover; additional seaweed may also be used to hold it down. Sand raked onto the perimeter of the canvas will provide an even tighter seal. The clambake should then be left to steam for about an hour.

When the clambake is opened, the steamed clams are served first, poured out into some huge receptacle and dipped into by each participant, who should be supplied with a paper cup partly filled with melted butter to dunk his clams in. After everyone cleans up a little in the sea (often getting his feet wet in the process), the rest of the food is hauled out and served. Tomatoes and cucumbers, salt, pepper, more butter can be set out on a big rock or portable table, and a few cases of cold beer are usually welcome. Big chunks of watermelon provide a suitably messy conclusion to the feast, if anyone has room for them; and a few blankets should be spread around on the perimeter for people to rest on between trips to the pit for seconds or thirds or fourths.

When properly organized and begun early enough in the day, an old-style clambake can be an experience long remembered with nostalgia. Get to the beach early enough for a swim while the fire burns down, and another while the food cooks. And remember to program everything so that all cleaning up can be done while there's still light. If people want to linger, start a bonfire and sit around it for a while.

MUSSELS

The blue mussel is one of this country's least utilized, most abundant, and—when properly prepared—most delicious seafoods. Mussels are simple to gather and simple to fix, using only the simplest of seasonings—a little onion and parsley, some pepper, a splash of white wine. And in Massachusetts, at least, one doesn't need a permit to collect them, another indication of their lowly state. ("If you can find a mussel, you can have it," said the Chilmark town clerk when this fact was checked for the new edition of this book.) Skindivers in the Menemsha area report massive black beds of these beautiful mollusks spreading nearly across the inlet in some places. There are vast beds among the Tashmoo rocks, and at several places on the south side of the Island thousands of mussels sometimes wash up on the beach, displaced by an angry ocean during a mighty storm. Don't bother to collect a pailful of nice fat ones, though, even if they are still fresh. They will be full of sand that won't wash out. And one more caution: Mussels, like other shellfish, can carry infectious hepatitis, so take a good look at the water they're sieving their food from. If you mussel in Menemsha, you might be wiser not to do so during the weeks those elegant cruisers are tied up at the new marina.

Steamed Mussels

[With White Wine and Aromatic Seasonings]

Irma Rombauer, the personality responsible for the continuing success of the best-selling *Joy of Cooking,* wrote that ". . . in France the mussel is called the oyster of the poor [but] there are many definitions of poverty."

3 quarts mussels
1 small carrot, scraped and cut into ½-inch dice
1 medium clove garlic, minced
¼ cup green onions, minced (or finely minced shallots or onions)
1 cup dry white wine or ⅔ cup dry vermouth
½ cup water
¼ teaspoon freshly ground black pepper
2 tablespoons parsley, coarsely chopped (preferably the flat-leaved
*   Italian type)*

Scrub the mussels thoroughly under running water. Snip beards off with scissors.

Don't worry about removing barnacles and other shells—most of them will drop off during the cooking process and add flavor to the broth. Put the carrot, garlic, onions, wine, water, pepper, and 1 tablespoon of the parsley into the pot. Cover and simmer until carrot dice are tender, about 10 minutes. Add the mussels, raise heat to high, and cover pot. Lift and stir mussels occasionally as they cook. Do not have the pot too full to manage this. The mussels are ready for the table the moment the shells open. This will take 5 to 10 minutes. Serve the mussels in good-sized soup plates. Spoon the delicious liquid generously over the shells, sprinkle each dish with parsley, and serve at once. Do not eat any mussels that are unopened. Try cooking them a little more—they may just be underdone.

Note: While the vegetables are simmering, there may seem to be too little liquid in the pot, but the mussels will add their own good juices as they open.

Makes 4 portions.

Mussels with Tomato, Bacon, and Linguine

2 quarts mussels, scrubbed and debearded
4 slices lean bacon, cut in bits
1 tablespoon butter
2 garlic cloves, minced
½ cup chopped onions
½ cup dry white wine
8 plum tomatoes, chopped fine,

or 1½ cups drained or canned plum tomatoes
Juice and zest of 1 orange
1 pound linguine
Salt
Freshly ground black pepper
3 tablespoons chopped flat-leaved parsley

Place well-scrubbed mussels in a large saucepan (be sure to remove grit and tiny stones; barnacles can be left on). Cover saucepan and cook mussels over high heat until they open. Shake or stir mussels frequently to distribute heat. Do not overcook—5 minutes should be sufficient unless mussels are huge. Pour mussels into a large, fine sieve placed over a bowl and allow to cool slightly. Put large kettle of salted water on to heat for linguine. Remove mussels from shells. If any have not opened, put them back over heat for a minute or two. They may not have gotten hot enough. Discard any that fail to open. Save mussel liquid.

In a large, flat saucepan, cook bacon bits until brown. Remove with slotted spoon and drain on paper towel. Pour off bacon grease. Melt the butter in pan and cook garlic about 15 seconds, stirring. Do not brown. Add chopped onions and cook, stirring, over medium heat about 3 minutes or until soft. Pour in 2 cups of the strained mussel liquid (leave any debris on bottom of measuring cup—it might be sand) and the wine and cook over high heat until reduced about one half, 8 to 10 minutes. Add tomatoes and juice and zest of orange, reduce heat, and simmer until mixture thickens somewhat. Stir as needed. When linguine water is boiling, add pasta and cook al dente, around 10 minutes. Drain.

Combine mussels and bacon bits with tomato mixture. Heat thoroughly, then mix with cooked linguine. Salt and pepper as desired, sprinkle with chopped parsley, and serve.

Makes 4 generous portions.

Mussel Soup

A near relative of Billi Bi, another delicious mussel soup, the following is less rich and not quite so complicated to prepare.

3 quarts fresh mussels

1 medium onion, chopped

2 tablespoons chopped fresh
  parsley

1 stalk celery, chopped

1½ cups dry white wine

1 quart fish stock (see page 8) or

bottled clam juice

1 cup medium cream

Salt (optional)

¼ teaspoon freshly ground black
  pepper

3 tablespoons chopped chives
  (optional)

Clean mussels (see page 54).

In a deep kettle cook onion, parsley, and celery in the wine and 1 cup of the fish stock or clam juice over moderate heat until vegetables are tender.

Add mussels to the kettle, cover tightly, and cook over high heat only until mussels open. Lift and stir mussels several times to distribute heat more evenly. Do not overcook. (Mussels are sufficiently cooked when their shells open.) When cool enough to handle, remove mussels from shells. Discard any that seem reluctant to open (or replace in kettle and cook a few minutes more—sometimes they are just not quite done).

Add remainder of fish stock or clam juice to the liquids in the kettle. Cook over high heat until liquid is reduced by about one-third. Strain through a fine sieve lined with cheesecloth or a clean dish towel, pressing down on vegetables with back of spoon.

Return liquid to pan, add cream and mussels, and reheat but do not boil, stirring constantly. Add salt if needed, dust with black pepper, and serve. This may also be served cold with chopped chives sprinkled on each serving.

Note: Thicken with a paste of 3 tablespoons softened butter and 3 tablespoons flour before adding the mussels, if desired.

Makes 6 generous portions.

Mussels Vinaigrette

This is a fine way to use leftover steamed mussels. Strain them, discard the shells, and pour any good French (vinaigrette) dressing over the mussels in sufficient quantity to cover them. Allow the mussels to marinate 4 or 5 hours or overnight. Serve them (drained) as an hors d'oeuvre preceding lunch or dinner or with cocktails. Refrigerated in the dressing, they will keep for days. Just before serving, sprinkle the mussels lavishly with chopped fresh parsley.

OYSTERS

Despite the fact that the mature oyster can produce up to sixty million eggs during a single season, the beachcomber who comes across an oyster shell nearly always finds it empty. Oysters, obviously, have a rough time of it. Since the 1950s, when a disease hit the North American oyster beds, this mollusk has lost much of its vigor and now has to be coddled into maturity by well-researched oystermen who set out the oyster seed in the backwaters of the Vineyard's salt ponds, then carefully transplant the spat to mature in the sands off Cape Cod. Pollution has hit the oyster as it has every other living thing; but the oyster has other enemies as well. Fish and crabs feed on the defenseless oyster spat as they roam the pond bottoms. Starfish clasp the rough shells with their tentacles and pry them open to eat the soft insides; and the tiny oyster drill manages to burrow through the oyster's protective housing and siphon out the nourishing innards.

Small wonder, then, that the oyster is carefully guarded from ravaging humans. Oysters should not be taken anywhere during the months that lack an "r"; this is not because they are not edible during warmer weather (though their flavor is poorer then), but to allow them to revitalize their colonies. A shellfish permit is required for anyone planning to gather oysters on the Vineyard, and even then the ponds are often closed to oystering to give the beds a chance to build up.

If you do go oystering and pick the shells up as they're usually found, in jagged clumps, we offer two precautions. Wear gloves—almost every surface of an oyster seems to have a razor-sharp protrusion that is hard to avoid. And check each shell before you carry it home. A good many of them, you will find, are full not of plump oyster but of smelly black muck, which makes the unenviable chore of cleaning and scrubbing even less attractive.

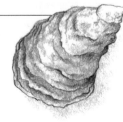

Oyster or Clam Fritters

2 cups oysters or steamer clams
2 cups sifted flour
2 teaspoons baking powder
½ teaspoon salt
¼ teaspoon freshly ground
    black pepper
Restrained pinch cayenne pepper
½ cup milk, more or less

2 egg yolks, lightly beaten
2 egg whites, beaten until stiff
Vegetable oil for deep-fat frying
    (or ½ cup vegetable oil for skil-
    let frying)
Lemon wedges
Parsley sprigs

Strain the oysters or clams, reserving liquor; chop coarsely.

Prepare the batter by sifting the presifted flour with the baking powder, salt, pepper, and cayenne. Measure reserved shellfish liquor, add enough milk to make 1 cup, and add gradually with beaten egg yolks to flour mixture, stirring until batter is smooth. Add chopped oysters or clams and blend well. Stir in 1 or 2 tablespoons of the beaten egg whites, then carefully fold in remainder until no white streaks remain.

In a deep-fat fryer drop batter a tablespoon at a time into oil heated to 375°F. (There should be at least 3 inches of oil in fryer.) Don't overcrowd the fry kettle. When the fritters are puffed and golden, turn once, cook briefly on other side, remove, drain on paper towels, and keep warm in a preheated 200°F oven until all the fritters are cooked.

If using the skillet method, heat ½ cup oil in a 10- or 12-inch heavy skillet over moderate heat until a light haze forms over oil. Immediately drop in fritter batter, a heaping tablespoon at a time. Cook until golden, turn, and cook on other side.

Garnish with lemon wedges and parsley sprigs and serve at once.

Note: Frozen oysters or canned minced clams may be substituted; the flavor, however, will not be as robust.

Makes 30 to 36 fritters.

Oysters with Mushrooms

½ pound fresh mushrooms, sliced
5–6 tablespoons butter
1 pint oysters, undrained
2 tablespoons flour
1 cup milk
½ cup cream
½ teaspoon Worcestershire sauce
½ teaspoon salt

¼ teaspoon freshly ground pepper (white, if possible)
Pinch of dry mustard (optional)
6 slices buttered toast, cut in triangular halves
1–2 tablespoons chopped fresh chives

Cook the mushrooms in 2 to 3 tablespoons of the butter in a skillet (preferably enamel, cast iron, or stainless steel) over moderate heat. Allow the butter foam to subside before tossing in the mushrooms. Stir occasionally; cook 5 to 6 minutes, or until delicately browned. Remove from skillet and reserve.

Add the oysters in their liquor to the skillet and simmer only until edges curl. Remove from pan immediately, drain, and set aside. Reserve oyster liquor.

Add 2 more tablespoons butter to skillet. Melt over moderate heat. Add the flour and blend well. Reduce heat and cook the roux a few minutes longer. Add milk, cream, and reserved oyster liquor and cook over reduced heat, stirring constantly, until mixture thickens and bubbles a little. Add Worcestershire sauce, salt, pepper, and the mustard, if used. (Mix the mustard with the Worcestershire sauce to avoid lumps.) Add oysters and mushrooms; cook only long enough to reheat the mixture. Add the last tablespoon of butter, swirling it in thoroughly.

Serve immediately on hot buttered toast with chives sprinkled on top.
Makes 4 portions.

Oyster Pie

1 pint oysters, shucked
3 tablespoons butter
¼ pound fresh mushrooms, sliced
3 tablespoons flour
Approximately 1 cup whole milk
(or half milk, half cream)
½ teaspoon salt

¼ teaspoon white pepper
Dash of Worcestershire sauce
1 teaspoon lemon juice
Cayenne pepper
Pastry crust, ½ recipe (see crust
used for Beefsteak-and-
Kidney Pie, page 112)

Preheat oven to 425°F.

Drain oysters through a fine strainer; reserve the liquor.

In a heavy skillet melt 2 tablespoons butter over moderate heat; when foam subsides, cook the sliced mushrooms only until lightly browned, about 5 minutes. Remove mushrooms and set aside. Add remaining tablespoon butter to skillet; when it has melted, add the flour and stir it until well blended. Cook another minute, then add the strained oyster liquor combined with enough milk to make 1½ cups. Reduce heat and cook, stirring constantly, until mixture thickens. Remove from heat. Add the oysters, salt, pepper, cooked mushroom slices, Worcestershire sauce, lemon juice, and a restrained dash of cayenne pepper.

Pour the creamed mixture into a round, shallow, 8-inch casserole. Cover with the pastry crust, rolled about ¼ inch thick. Seal and crimp the edges, cut slits in the crust (which may be brushed with a little cream), and bake 10 to 15 minutes, or until crust begins to brown. Reduce heat to 375°F and bake an additional 15 to 20 minutes.

Makes 4 portions.

Oyster Casserole

A small, family-operated restaurant in Edgartown, unfortunately no longer there, used to serve this oyster preparation. One of the sons, who shared the cooking honors with his mother, was a true deep-water sailor, having spent considerable time at sea both working sail and in yacht galleys. He therefore was familiar with the shellfish of many islands, far and near, and knew multiple ways of preparing these delicate foods from the sea. The oysters in their casserole, however, were fresh from one of the Island's Great Ponds in proper season, a factor that contributes to the superiority of the dish. Though the use of the oysters is not dissimilar to that involved in scalloped oysters, this young man wisely restrained the use of bread crumbs and seasoning, allowing the flavor and succulence of the plump, fresh oysters to dominate the finished casserole.

25–30 small oysters, freshly shucked but undrained (if oysters
*   are large, adjust number proportionately)*
4 saltines or common crackers, coarsely crushed
¼ teaspoon freshly ground black pepper
3 tablespoons melted butter
1 tablespoon fresh lemon juice
Dash of cayenne pepper (optional)

Preheat oven to 475°F.

Place a layer of half the oysters and half their liquor in a 1-quart ovenproof casserole. Sprinkle half the crushed crackers over them and dust with half of the black pepper.

Repeat the layering process. Combine the melted butter with the lemon juice and pour over the ingredients in casserole. Top with a sprinkle of cayenne pepper, if desired.

Bake, uncovered, on top shelf of oven approximately 20 minutes, but only until the edges of the oysters curl. The size of the oyster will determine the baking time.

Note: Salt is deliberately omitted from this recipe. If you are blessed with oysters fresh from one of the Vineyard's Great Ponds, salinity will be at its maximum. If not, add salt with discretion.

Makes 2 portions.

SCALLOPS

Most of us living on the Vineyard never encounter the larger varieties of scallops except on a seafood platter in an off-Island restaurant, but we all have admired, sought, and, when wading or clamming, even been pinched by bay scallops, the Vineyard's most precious commodity. Flitting through the waters of the salt ponds in their colorful housings, these decorative creatures are usually literally and figuratively out of reach of most of the Island's summer visitors. Anyone caught out of season with even a handful of scallops will be fined a flat and substantial fee, and the season begins long after the vacationers have gone home. In November the licensed Islanders—lone workmen, husbands and wives, sturdy young men—don their hip boots and scalloping gloves and move out onto the cold, still ponds to net their limit of these delicious mollusks. Control laws, the time spent freezing in your boat, the tedium of extracting the edible muscles, the relatively low yield of these per bushel of scallops, and the high demand for these inimitable delicacies all contrive to make scalloping and scallops an expensive taste to indulge. But every Vineyarder should allow himself a few feasts every winter, if only to remind him how vastly varied are the fruits of land and sea that this Island can provide.

It is possible, in these days of quick and careful transportation of perishable foods, to buy bay scallops from good markets in other parts of the country. If you happen to see them during the winter, and they look firm and fresh and show no watery leakage, buy them and enjoy the inimitable sweetness of these fragile sea creatures.

Broiled Bay Scallops

1 pound bay scallops, drained
¼ teaspoon salt
Pinch of freshly ground black
*   pepper*
¼ cup (or a little more) melted
*   butter*
1 teaspoon lemon juice

1 small clove garlic, chopped fine
¾ cup fresh bread crumbs (use
*   day-old French or Italian*
*   type, if possible)*
Sprinkle of paprika
Parsley sprigs (optional)

Preheat oven broiler, using maximum setting.

Place the bay scallops in a shallow heatproof baking dish; sprinkle them with salt and pepper. Combine melted butter, lemon juice, and garlic; mix in the bread crumbs thoroughly. The crumbs should be quite buttery; add additional melted butter, if desired. Pat the crumbs lightly over the scallops; sprinkle lightly with paprika.

Broil about 3 inches under the broiler heat for about 10 minutes. Do not overcook; shellfish toughens and shrinks when exposed to too much heat. Serve immediately, garnished with sprigs of parsley, if desired.

Note: It is essential to choose an appropriate-size baking dish for this recipe. There should be only one layer of scallops, and they should be completely contained by the baking dish. A heavy enamel or stainless-steel shallow casserole about 6 by 9 inches is suggested for the quantities given.

Makes 2 generous portions.

Scallops in Mushroom Caps

2 dozen good-sized mushrooms
Salt and pepper
4 dozen bay scallops (or 2 dozen sea scallops)
6 slices bacon
Chopped parsley for garnish (optional)

Preheat broiler, using maximum setting.

Wash mushrooms; pat dry with paper towels. Cut stems off (save them to use some other way). Place mushroom caps upside down on a cookie sheet large enough to hold them all without touching. Dust each cap with salt and pepper, and place two bay scallops or one sea scallop on each mushroom. Lay ¼ slice bacon over each mushroom. Broil about 2 inches from heat for 8 to 10 minutes, depending on size of mushrooms. Garnish with chopped parsley before serving, if desired.

Makes 4 portions.

LOBSTERS

A person sitting down to a sumptuous lobster dinner probably doesn't notice that his *pièce de résistance* is "right-handed"—that is, its right pincer is usually much heavier than its left one. Nor does he care that his lobster took at least six years to grow to an edible 1-pound size, is rigidly protected by state and local laws, and has a name derived from an Anglo-Saxon word for spider. He is much more likely to be conscious that, bite for bite, his meal will cost him four times as much as a good steak dinner (as this page was being written, fresh lobster meat was selling for $29.50 a pound in a Menemsha market), and that if he finishes all that extra butter, he'll wish he hadn't a few hours later.

People on the Vineyard have various reasons for being interested in lobsters. Not only are lobsters trapped in the offshore waters in pots set out by licensed lobstermen (and often illegally raided by unlicensed ones), but they are hatched by the thousands at the Martha's Vineyard Lobster Hatchery and Research Station, which the Commonwealth of Massachusetts established in 1951 to improve lobster production. Since then, several million *Homarus americanus* (American lobsters) have been hatched, reared, and released by former director John T. Hughes and his successors. But lobster fry, like many other shellfish, have a host of predators (including their own kind, since they eat each other), and relatively few eggs—only an estimated 60 out of the 60,000 eggs that can be released each season by an adult female lobster—survive the first three stages of growth and are mature enough to drop into the dark, murky depths and begin the defensive, nocturnal existence they are destined for. Small wonder, then, that lobsters are scarce and expensive.

Strangely enough, not only are lobsters scarce, but lobster recipes are few as well. Upon reflection, we concluded that people prefer their lobsters in simple style—broiled or boiled. They are so good in these ways that they really don't need to be improved on.

Baked Stuffed Lobster
[A Martha's Vineyard Version]

*4 live lobsters, weighing about
    1½ pounds each*
24 Ritz crackers
½ cup melted butter
1 tablespoon lemon juice
½ cup pale dry sherry
¼ teaspoon salt

*¼ teaspoon freshly ground black
    pepper*
*½ pound uncooked bay scallops,
    shrimp, or crabmeat, chopped*
Lemon wedges
Parsley sprigs

Preheat oven to 450°F.

Kill lobster by severing the vein on the back of its neck with a sharp knife or cleaver. Prepare each lobster for stuffing by placing it on its back and splitting it lengthwise. Reserve the tomalley (green liver) and roe, if any.

Crush the crackers coarsely with a rolling pin. In a mixing bowl combine the melted butter, lemon juice, and sherry; add the crushed crackers, salt, pepper, and the chopped shellfish. Add the reserved lobster liver and roe. Mix these ingredients lightly with a fork, then spoon stuffing into the prepared cavity of each lobster. Bake the lobsters in a shallow pan 20 to 25 minutes, depending on their size. Transfer to a large, heated platter; garnish with lemon wedges and sprigs of parsley.

Makes 4 portions.

Lobster Sauté

Lobster meat—delectable and elegant at any time—is especially so in this form. A further virtue is that the lobster may be prepared in practically no time, after your guests have arrived, as the procedure is unbelievably simple.

5 tablespoons butter

2 small cloves garlic, minced fine (optional but delicious)

1–1½ pounds cooked fresh lobster meat, cut in chunks

½ teaspoon salt

¼ teaspoon freshly ground black pepper

1 tablespoon chopped fresh herbs (a mixture of parsley, chives,
  basil, and tarragon is very good)

In a heavy skillet, melt butter over moderate heat. When butter foam subsides, add the minced garlic, if used. Immediately add the lobster meat and stir and turn it frequently; sprinkle with the salt and pepper. The lobster is ready to serve as soon as it is heated through. Sprinkle half the herbs over the lobster and mix them well into the lobster meat. Remove skillet from heat, transfer contents to a heated serving platter, sprinkle remainder of herbs on top, and serve immediately.

Makes 3 portions.

Lobster Salad Rolls

A stop in Gay Head at Mrs. Grieder's geranium-decked luncheonette or Manning's Snack Bar for a lobster roll and chowder was for years one of the delights of a summertime tour around the Island. Now, alas, Mrs. Grieder has died and the snack bar is gone, so it might behoove you to make your own lobster rolls and carry them along for a beachside picnic, if you are fortunate enough to know of an unposted spot.

The secret of her delicious filling, Mrs. Grieder once told us, was to chop the lobster meat very fine—"People don't like chunks in sandwiches." She also emphasized the importance of buttering every bit of the frankfurter roll and of grilling the roll a long time very slowly. Proper preparation was so important to her that she never let anyone else make the lobster rolls but tended to each order herself.

2 cups finely chopped lobster meat	Grated onion (optional)
½ cup finely chopped celery	Salt
Sprinkle of lemon juice	Freshly ground black pepper
½ cup mayonnaise (approximate)	5 frankfurter rolls
Pinch of curry powder (optional)	Softened butter
	Shredded lettuce

Combine lobster meat and celery and sprinkle lightly with lemon juice. Mix slightly, then add enough mayonnaise to bind mixture, and stir well. Add a pinch of curry powder and grated onion to taste, if desired. (Vineyarders omit these two ingredients, but you may like them.) Add salt and pepper to taste and mix well.

Partially slice frankfurter rolls, if necessary, and butter the outside surfaces well. Heat griddle or heavy skillet, and toast rolls slowly on both sides until golden. Put about 2 tablespoons shredded lettuce inside each toasted roll (this makes a bed for the salad) and spoon about ½ cup of the salad on the lettuce, spreading evenly. Keep cool until eaten.

Note: Do not carry unrefrigerated lobster rolls around with you on a hot day. The combination of seafood and mayonnaise is a frequent source of food poisoning. *Makes 5 filled rolls (about ½ cup salad per roll).*

CRABS

*C**rab* is of Anglo-Saxon derivation, "akin to crawl," says Webster, and anyone who has seen a member of the order Decapoda scuttling for cover, out-maneuvering even the subtlest thrusts of the stalker's net, will appreciate this association. Vineyard winds and waters are too frigid for many of these quaint crustaceans to be attracted to the Island; and blue crabs in particular have behaved erratically over the past twenty years or so, appearing, disappearing, and reappearing in Vineyard waters in some mysterious, unpredictable cycle. For several years during the midsixties, for instance, there just didn't seem to be any blue crabs. Then they came back. When you're exploring the margins of any brackish ponds or creeks during a beach outing, look in the murky, weedy areas for a dark, roundish patch that scoots into hiding when you approach. Remember the spot, and come back with a net, a bushel basket floated on an inflated inner tube, a pair of old tennis shoes, and a will to do battle. If you're a poor sport, you can tie chunks of old meat, rotten fish, or almost anything no longer edible on short lengths of string, toss them into the murk or weeds, and lure the creatures into the shallow water where you can block their escape and net them. But a good forthright hunt, human after crab, is fairer and much more exciting. It's also an excellent sport for the ten-to-fourteen age group who become bored with clamming, are too impatient to fish if it involves waiting, and think beachcombing is sort of a drag. An eye-to-eye confrontation with an 8-inch blue crab, pincers held high and open, ready to battle to the death with the outsize monster that has all the advantages, becomes an experience for child or adult to store away with the other treasured souvenirs of a Vineyard summer.

Basic Steamed Crabs

Cooked crabmeat can be used in many delectable ways. Some dishes require a good deal of preparation and a great many ingredients, but the crab recipes in this book are relatively simple, as all summer-resort cooking should be. To obtain the crabmeat needed for them, the crabs may be cooked in the following way.

It will take four to six large blue crabs to provide a cup of cooked meat, and at least twice that many of the other varieties. Allow at least ½ cup meat for each portion. Cook only live crabs. They can be kept alive for some hours in a cool, shaded place and protected by wet seaweed.

Heat about 6 inches of water to boiling in the largest covered kettle you have. Clean seawater is excellent for cooking crabs or any other seafood. Grab each crab with kitchen tongs, rinse it under cold running water, and plunge it into the kettle of live steam. This is not a chore for the soft-hearted. There is a fair amount of rattling about in the kettle, but the authorities assure us that this level of creature does not feel pain. Keep the flame high, and the steam will quickly kill them. Cook the crabs a few at a time, steaming each batch about 10 minutes. Stir them around once or twice during this time. Remove cooked crabs from kettle. They can be cooled fairly quickly under running water, or left in the sink until they can be easily handled. If blue crabs are used, lift the little "tail" on the bottom and rip off the top shell. These are male crabs; the females have large "aprons." Discard these tops, along with the feathery "devil's fingers" along each side and the soft pouch under the eyes. Using a nutcracker and nutpick, remove the meat that remains. Crack claws and remove all meat. This meat may be cooled and eaten just as it is, sprinkled with lemon juice, and dipped in melted butter. Or it may be reserved for other recipes.

If other varieties of crabs are used, such as rock crabs, use only the meat from the leg sections. There is not enough in the body to bother with.

Note: Good sports keep only the male crabs, returning the females to ensure future generations. This is not easy, since the biggest captives almost always have the distinctive aprons.

Blue Crabs in Beer

3–4 quarts beer
1 tablespoon cayenne pepper (less if desired, or omit)
20–24 good-sized live blue crabs
1 cup melted butter
2 lemons, cut in slices

A large canning kettle is useful for cooking crabs. If you have nothing big enough to hold them all, cook them in batches, using about 2 cups beer and about ¼ teaspoon cayenne for every six crabs. Put beer and pepper in kettle, cover, and heat. When kettle is full of steam, grasp each crab with kitchen tongs, rinse under cold running water, and pop into kettle, replacing lid each time. Cook crabs over high heat for 10 to 12 minutes, until they turn red. Remove lid and stir crabs around two or three times during cooking process, so all will be cooked. Remove cooked crabs from liquid and cool until they can be handled easily. Serve with melted butter, lobster forks or nutpicks, nutcrackers or lobster crackers, and large bowls of cool water. Float lemon slices on the water for diners to use to clean up their hands and arms from time to time. (Demolishing and ingesting a mess of crabs is not for the fastidious.) Mugs of cold beer help cool the palate if you've been properly lavish with the cayenne.

Makes 4 or more portions.

Rock-Crab Cakes

Though too small to be eaten like blue crabs, the Jonah and rock crabs found mainly along the Island's north shore among the rocks and breakwaters are equally as tasty as their larger relatives and make delicious crab cakes. It takes a good many crabs to feed several people, so save this dish for a special small luncheon.

3–4 cups cooked crabmeat
1 egg
½ teaspoon salt
About 1 cup dried bread crumbs
4–6 tablespoons fat (butter or bacon grease is especially good)
Black pepper
Small lemon wedges
Parsley or watercress

Prepare crabmeat according to recipe for Basic Steamed Crabs (see page 72). Beat egg lightly, add crabmeat and salt, mix and mash well. Dampen hands and shape mixture into small balls. Roll in crumbs, then refrigerate several hours. Heat fat in a large, heavy skillet. Fry crab cakes, slightly flattened, until golden brown, turning to brown all over. Dust with black pepper and serve at once with lemon wedges and parsley or watercress garnish.

Note: If you can't be bothered with catching enough rock crabs for this recipe, make them with the same amount of cooked blue-crab meat (see page 73).

Makes 4 portions.

CHAPTER 4

Moors and Meadows

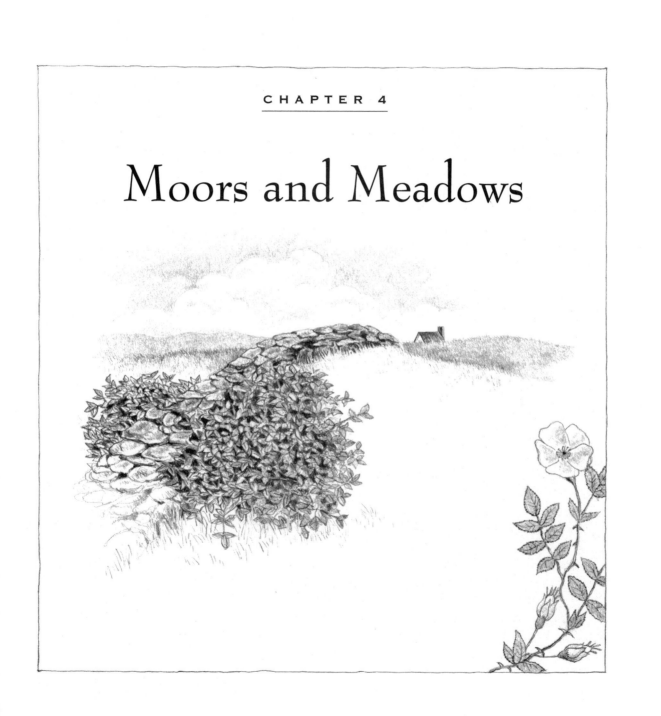

In its interiors were valleys with winding streams . . . secret swamps well-hidden from the sea, great thickets. . . . One could find . . . the aromatic bayberry, and the beach plum with its gnarled and windbeaten attitudes. . . . In season the air was perfumed to ecstasy by the wild grape, and Islanders went into the swamps and glades to return with [high-heaped] baskets. . . . On the Great Plain the sweetfern grew, wildflowers in profusion, and, especially after a spring fire, blueberries and huckleberries of large size and succulence.

—Henry Beetle Hough, *Martha's Vineyard, Summer Resort*

The Vineyard, befitting its name, abounds in foodstuffs that any resourceful cook can collect from its roadsides, meadows, woods, and waters. Some of the "edible" things usually listed in books on the subject might be used for survival but really aren't very good, especially when one considers the bother of finding and preparing them. Delicate new fern fronds, for example, treated according to several recipes, invariably turn out fuzzy and acrid, disturbingly suggestive of steamed, buttered caterpillars. Wild greens, unless chosen with care and picked while young, cook up into a stringy, harsh-flavored mess. Milkweed shoots toughen when only a few inches high and can cause nausea when overindulged in or undercooked; and most wild fruits are better left to the wasps, worms, and birds who seem to get at them first in any case.

But a fortuitous encounter with a patch of bright green watercress thriving in a hidden stream or the discovery of a mass of tangy, red-brown fox grapes in a thicket off

Indian Hill Road should tempt any culinary-minded Vineyarder to transport his find back to the kitchen for the unique enjoyment that can come from eating food from the wild. Leaves, berries, nuts, seeds, flowers, roots, and stalks can be brought to the table—some left just as they're picked, others transformed almost beyond recognition, but all retaining to the last taste an ineffable hint of their wild origin.

BEACH PLUMS

The beach plum (*Prunus maritima*) grows rampantly on dunes and coastal plains from Virginia to Nova Scotia, but beach-plum–jelly makers tend to regard their favorite picking places as regional treasure spots, revealed only to close friends or relatives. One young Vineyard housewife who covets her special thicket was quite unhappy when visiting New Yorkers brought her a jar of jelly made out of plums from *their* favorite bushes near their Long Island summer place. All beach-plum jelly should come from the Vineyard, she felt (though she'd heard it was also produced on that unmentionable mainland place, Cape Cod).

Prunus is a large and important genus of the rose family, which includes all the plums, cherries, and apricots, though oddly enough the peach is usually put in another category. The beach plum is a native American shrub that grows anywhere from nearly prostrate to a height of 6 feet or so. When picking the fruit, one should investigate the tiny, sprawling varieties, as fruit production is often disproportionate to plant growth, and the biggest, plumpest plums often hide under the scrawniest bushes. In winter, beach-plum bushes are distinctively black-barked and twiggy; in spring, clusters of dainty white flowers appear in such profusion that some Vineyard thickets in low-lying sections of the Island look almost as though a small cloud were resting on them. Around Labor Day, the picking begins, so late-staying summer people can usually carry some jelly home with them.

If you plan to start your own beach-plum patch on your Vineyard property, you would be wiser to purchase stock from a nursery than to laboriously transplant wild bushes. There are reasons for this. Beach plums, like many wild-food sources, often thrive in the midst of equally thrifty poison ivy. Wild beach plums love poor, sandy soil and usually die when moved to more cultivated land. Their roots are deep-growing and brittle, making them hard to dig up. And, furthermore, if you do manage to stagger through the poison ivy and soft sand the several hundred yards back to your car with your by-now bare-rooted and probably broken-rooted prize, get it comfortably established in your own meadow, inspect it anxiously the next spring for signs of life, see it finally put forth a few green leaves and perhaps a feeble cluster or two of blossoms—if your transplanted beach plum survives that long—chances are it will turn out to have bacterial leaf spot on its leaves and brown rot on its fruit and be utterly unsatisfactory for either culinary or decorative purposes. Leave beach plums where you can admire them on your way to the beach or the airport (there are masses in that vicinity, but not many are fruit-producing) and purchase a half dozen young plants. Take heart that one cultivated variety is called Squibnocket. Surely it must have Vineyard sap in it.

Beach-Plum Juice

A tart, tangy breakfast or hot-afternoon drink—a far cry from the bland concoctions arrayed on city supermarket shelves—can be made very simply out of beach plums, sugar, and water. Don't drink it too strong or too abundantly, as it seems to affect some people's digestive systems adversely.

Pick over a gallon or so of ripe beach plums, discarding any that are bronze-colored, pulpy, or blistered by blight. Don't be too particular—it is almost impossible not to miss a few bad ones. Wash fruit in cold water; remove and throw out any plums that float. Place fruit in large kettle, mash well with potato masher, add enough water barely to show through fruit, bring to a boil, and cook over moderate heat for 10 minutes. Let fruit cool in pan until it can be worked with. Place in cheesecloth bag over a large pan or bowl and squeeze juice through bag until pulp begins to show through cheesecloth. Discard pulp and wash bag thoroughly for future use. Taste juice and add sugar to taste (about ¾ cup per quart of fruit). Let juice cool, and store in refrigerator. Dilute half and half with cold water or apple juice before drinking.

This concentrated juice can be canned by the regular steam-bath processing method (see government bulletin, or any canning guide, under fruit juices).

Beach-Plum Jelly

Prepare fruit as in preceding recipe, with two exceptions. If jelly is to be made at once, simply follow the directions enclosed with whatever pectin product you choose for making the jelly. And do not squeeze the juice out of the bag by hand if you want your jelly crystal clear, but let it drip through (you will get more juice, by far, however, if you do squeeze the bag). If you are too busy to make the jelly at beach-plum time, can the juice in the approved manner, adding 1 cup sugar per quart and noting this fact on the jar label. When you want to convert juice into jelly, simply open the jar, add the additional sugar, and proceed according to the pectin maker's instructions.

Note: Vineyard housewives who market their jelly usually bottle the plum juice during beach-plum season and convert it into jelly in the spring to sell to summer visitors, claiming it tastes fresher than jelly made during the winter months.

ROSE HIPS

Vineyard roses are not felt by Nantucketers to be nearly as spectacular as those that swarm in colorful profusion over that island's cottages. This is only a minor reflection of the long-standing rivalry between the two neighboring but not particularly neighborly islands. Actually, Vineyard roses can also be awe inspiring, especially in Edgartown, where carefully tended tea roses and climbers grace borders and white fences and the sides of the neat houses. Along the roads, the old-fashioned single-petaled ramblers sprawl over the stone fences and scent the June air. Up-Island, especially across the Gay Head dunes, the *Rosa rugosa,* of Japanese heritage, thrives on what seems to be pure sand, huge, deep green clumps that in early summer are dotted with pink or white blooms and later will bear hundreds of succulent Chinese-red rose hips, or rose apples.

Actually, only the plumpest and ripest of these fruits could be termed succulent when picked from the bush, but the hips are surprisingly tasty if picked—and eaten—with discrimination. Bite off the pulpy outside, avoiding the seeds; as you chew, remember this is one of the richest known sources of vitamin C.

If you can avoid the insidious poison-ivy stalks that always seem to infiltrate whatever anybody wants to pick, and don't mind pricks and scratches, take home a few quarts of the biggest, ripest rose hips you can find (they should be at least the size of large cherries) and turn them into marmalade for breakfast on a cold winter morning in the city—a sweet reminder of the Vineyard summer.

Grambs' Rose-Hip Marmalade

There are various ways of making rose-hip jam. The standard one involves putting the stewed, deseeded pulp through a food mill or sieve, adding 1 cup sugar to 1 cup pulp, and boiling the mixture until it is thick enough to spread. Sometimes pineapple is used. This recipe requires both orange and lemon rind and suggests adding ginger, which we recommend. If you have never tasted rose hips, stew a few in sweetened water and taste them before going to the trouble of preparing the rest of the fruit. Most people like the flavor, vaguely reminiscent of quince.

2 cups prepared rose hips (about 1 quart unprepared)

1 cup water

Rind of 1 orange, cut into julienne strips

Rind of 1 lemon, cut into julienne strips

1½ cups sugar

2 tablespoons minced preserved or crystallized ginger; or same
amount of cut-up fresh ginger root, if available (optional)

Pick only large, bright red or dark red fruits. Grate off their flesh on a medium grater, saving seed residue. Place residue in a small saucepan and add the water. Cover the saucepan and simmer seeds over low heat about 10 minutes. Turn off heat. Combine the prepared rose hips, the orange and lemon strips, and the sugar in a heavy saucepan. Strain the liquid off the seeds and add it to the fruit mixture. Stir to combine. Cook mixture over moderate heat until it boils. Stir in minced ginger. Reduce heat immediately and cook marmalade until fruit is somewhat translucent and mixture is thick enough to spread. It will thicken a little as it cools. Add a small amount of water during cooking, if necessary. Pour marmalade into hot, sterilized jars, seal, and process 5 minutes in a hot-water bath.

Makes about 3 cups.

Rose-Hip Soup

People of other countries—especially the Scandinavians—make delectable fruit soups from cherries, peaches, plums, apricots, and all kinds of berries, using the fruits separately or in combination. This is a similar soup, using a wild fruit that is available in season to anyone on Martha's Vineyard who seeks it out. Dressed up with sour cream and a bit of nutmeg, this rose-hip soup is elegant enough to grace any formal dinner menu.

3 cups rose hips
6 cups water
½ cup sugar
1 tablespoon cornstarch
1 tablespoon water

2 teaspoons lemon juice
½ teaspoon grated lemon rind
½ teaspoon powdered ginger
4 tablespoons sour cream
More ginger

Pick over rose hips, using only fully ripe but not overripe fruit for measuring. Rinse well, remove stem and bud ends. In a 2-quart saucepan, combine rose hips and water, bring to a boil, and cook over moderate heat for 25 minutes (do not boil too fast or too much water will evaporate). Let fruit cool slightly, then put through a food mill. Measure pulp; if necessary, add enough water to make 3 cups pureed fruit. Put pulp in a smaller saucepan, add sugar, stir well, and bring to a low boil. Mix the cornstarch and 1 tablespoon water thoroughly and stir slowly into fruit mixture. Continue to stir slowly until mixture comes to a low boil again. Cook, still at reduced heat, about 2 minutes, until soup thickens evenly. Turn off heat; stir in lemon juice and rind. Stir in ginger. Let soup cool, then refrigerate until well chilled. To serve, top each portion with a tablespoon of sour cream and add a dash of ginger.

Makes 4 portions.

THE ELDER

Tree, Berry, and Flower

The elder, a small tree conspicuous on the Vineyard only when its umbels of off-white flowers appear in June—and to a lesser degree in August when the red-purple berries ripen—has a long, impressive history of service. "Cooked berries, preserves, pies, beverage, soup, breadstuff, pickles, asparagus-substitute, tea" is the list given in one book; another, in quite a different vein, recommends elder canes for "peashooters, blowguns, water pistols, popguns, whistles and flutes." Elder grows almost everywhere, perhaps because it was long thought to be a protection against witches and thus was never cut down. A tisane (medicinal tea) from the dried flowers is said to be delightfully reminiscent of muscatel and is suggested in an English herbal as a "pleasant alternative to aspirin, particularly when mixed with equal parts of lime flowers and chamomile." Dried mint is also good in elder tea. Elderberry juice, rich in vitamin C, is recommended in the same book for chills, neuralgia, and sciatica; and elderberry wine, of course, is an old-time favorite.

Some find the flavor of the elder disagreeable—the berries in particular are bland and slightly rank, but they become very tasty when dried. Since elder is so useful, nutritious, and abundant, it should be tasted in some form or other during your summer stay. There is a lovely display of elder near the West Tisbury millpond, but you'd better leave those for the tourists to enjoy (especially since the police station is only fifty yards or so down the road) and check some of the swampy areas along Middle Road. A hazard here, however, is one of the few exposed stands of poison sumac on the Island, so be careful.

Dried Elderberries

These berries adapt well to drying, taste much better in this form than when fresh, and can be used dried throughout the winter in a variety of ways. Collect the berries when they are fully ripe and remove them from their stems, taking care not to bruise them too much. If feasible, dry your berries in the sun; otherwise, the oven may be used. Outdoors, spread them on an elevated screen in full sun. Be sure to move them indoors before evening moisture begins to collect on them. Repeat this sunning until berries no longer produce a watery juice when squeezed. For oven drying, place berries on shallow pans and place them in the oven. If small pieces of screening are available, they are better, as they allow heat to circulate evenly around the berries. Turn oven to lowest setting, prop oven door slightly open, and let berries dry until the same stage is reached as in sunning. This will take some twelve hours or so. They can be stored in clean fruit jars until used (give them a little air now and then to prevent spoilage).

To stew the dried berries, cook them in water until tender with a little lemon juice and peel, and sugar to taste. For pie, stew them in a little water until tender, and use the cooked berries in any blueberry-pie recipe.

Elder-Flower Fritters

A recipe published in London in 1776 says the flowers should be "marinated as the Apples on Pedestals" but gives no hint as to what marinade was used or what Apples on Pedestals were. This more contemporary version makes an unusual, if somewhat esoteric, Sunday breakfast.

16–20 elder-flower heads
1 cup sifted all-purpose flour
2 tablespoons sugar
½ teaspoon salt
1½ teaspoons baking powder
1 egg, well beaten
¾ cup milk
1 teaspoon salad oil

1 teaspoon chopped marigold
   petals (if available)
Nutmeg (optional)
Cinnamon (optional)
Fat or oil for frying
½ cup orange juice
Sugar

Pick the flower heads at the height of their bloom, and use them as soon as possible.

Do not wash flower heads. Trim stems to about 1 inch. To make the batter, resift the flour with the sugar, salt, and baking powder. Combine the well-beaten egg in a bowl with the milk; gradually add the sifted dry ingredients. Add the teaspoonful of salad oil; mix well. Stir in the marigold petals, if used. A few shakes of nutmeg or cinnamon may be added.

Heat fat to frying temperature; fritters may be deep-fried in about 3 cups oil or fat, or fried in a skillet with just enough oil or fat to cover flowers.

Dip flower heads in batter, shake gently to remove excess, and cook about 4 minutes, until light brown. Drain on paper towels; sprinkle with orange juice and a little sugar. Serve at once.

Note: An eighteenth-century Boston housewife made dessert fritters by soaking the flower heads for an hour in brandy before cooking and adding ½ teaspoon grated lemon peel to her batter.

Makes 4 portions.

Elderberry Rob

*R*ob, according to Webster, derives from the Arabic word *rubb*, by way of France, and is the "thickened juice of ripe fruits." The mild flavor of the elderberry benefits especially from this melding with pungent spices. When made from undiluted fruit, as our source recipes specify, the rob is more a syrup than a beverage. We give a diluted recipe here because without water the sugar and juice mixture tends to stick and requires careful simmering and frequent stirring. If you want to try it both ways, omit the water specified and use the thick sauce as a topping for cottage pudding or vanilla ice cream. Then add equal parts apple juice or water to the rob if you want to drink some iced on a hot afternoon or warmed and served on a rug by the fire on a snowy night.

> *1 quart well-ripened elderberries, removed from stems*
> *About 1 pint water*
> *1 scant cup sugar*
> *1-inch piece stick cinnamon*
> *12 cloves*
> *1 scant teaspoon nutmeg (freshly grated is best)*

Pour about half the elderberries into a good-sized saucepan and crush them with a potato masher. Add more berries and repeat process until all berries are crushed. Bring berries to a low boil, lower heat, and simmer 10 minutes, stirring once or twice to make sure berries cook evenly. Set colander or strainer over a large bowl. Lay a double-folded piece of cheesecloth in the colander and pour berries into it. Let cool until you can work with them, then tighten cheesecloth around berries and strain and press to extract juice until pulp begins to show through cloth. If clearer rob is desired, allow sediment to settle several hours before pouring off juice. Measure juice back into original saucepan and add enough water to give you about 1 quart liquid. Add sugar and spices, place over medium heat, and stir until sugar dissolves. Reduce to a simmer and cook slowly ½ hour. Let juice cool, then strain off into clean jar or pitcher. Store in refrigerator until needed. Serve hot or cold.

Note: Other robs are equally good—try making one with blackberries or grapes.
Makes about 1 quart (diluted form).

Fried Wild Apples[†]

S ince one author of this book is by heritage a Southerner, some of the recipes, like this one, depart from traditional New England styles and tastes, principally in the use of bacon and bacon fat for frying and seasoning. This dish does need the southern touch and is delicious for an early-fall lunch or for your teenagers' breakfast, especially if served with hot, freshly baked cornbread.

3 quarts wild apples or 1½ quarts regular apples (these never taste
*   as good)*
3 slices bacon
½ teaspoon salt
¼ to ½ cup brown sugar (or to taste)
Cinnamon, cloves, or nutmeg (optional)

Wash apples, cut into halves or quarters, remove cores and the worst of the wormholes and bruises, but do not peel. Some may have to be thrown away entirely—thus 3 quarts are specified to start with. In a large frying pan, fry bacon until crisp,

[†] By "wild" apples we mean fruit from an abandoned orchard or from one of the many roadside seedling trees on the Vineyard (also referred to as "windfall" apples).

remove from pan, and add apples to the hot fat. Lower heat, sprinkle apples with salt and brown sugar, and fry until tender—about 15 minutes. Spices may be added if you like them. Turn the fruit frequently so it will cook evenly. Add a small amount of water or apple juice if the pan seems too dry. When apples are done, crumble bacon over the top of them and mix well. Serve while hot.

Makes 4 portions.

Old-Orchard Pear Butter

If you are lucky enough to know the location of one of the Vineyard's old homesites, way back off the main roads, you probably know where there's an old pear tree—winter, Seckel, or even Bartlett—whose branches droop heavy with pears every September, years and years after the householders have died or moved away. Pears don't store as well as apples, but they can easily be converted into a wonderful sort of butter that can double as a dessert sauce. Plan to can some of this butter—it really takes very little time, and the jars will be waiting for summer breakfasts when you come back to the Island the next summer.

Gather as many pears as you think you will use, take them home, wash them, and cut them up, removing the cores. Don't bother to peel them; and don't worry about the size or shape of the pieces, as they will be reduced to pulp in no time. Add enough water to the cut pears to enable them to boil (cider or apple juice may be used instead of water), and cook them, stirring and lifting the fruit to facilitate the cooking process, until they are soft and mash easily. Remove from heat and allow to cool in pan until you can work with them. Put pulp through a food mill, removing the cores and seeds from the mill if it becomes clogged. Replace pulp in kettle (use a large one, as the mixture will splatter as it thickens) and cook slowly until desired thickness is reached. Stir well now and then to prevent sticking. You don't really need sugar if the pears are sweet enough to eat raw; otherwise, add sugar to taste. Stir in about ½ teaspoon each nutmeg and ginger per quart of butter; or season with whatever spices you like. The butter does need something to spruce up the bland pear flavor, but don't overspice.

If mixture is to be canned, follow processing instructions for applesauce as given in any canning guide.

Spiced Wild-Grape Jelly

Plain wild-grape jelly may be prepared by following any recipe for regular grape jelly, but here are the directions for a tart, spicy garniture for roast meat or poultry, from a 1963 collection of Vineyard recipes published by the local hospital auxiliary.

4 quarts wild grapes, removed from stems	*¼ cup whole cloves*
1 pint vinegar	*¼ stick cinnamon, broken up*
	3 pounds sugar (approximately)

Do not wash grapes. Place in a large kettle, crush with a potato masher, add vinegar and spices, mix, and crush again. Cook mixture 15 minutes. Pour off juice, pressing out as much as you can from the grapes. Then, either (a) let juice drip through a regular jelly bag, or (b) let juice settle in bowl overnight, then dip out or pour off carefully, leaving sediment in bottom. Measure juice and add sugar cup for cup. Heat to boiling, stirring sugar to help dissolve it. Cook fairly rapidly until jelly thermometer registers 220°F. Cool slightly, skim, pour into hot, sterilized containers, and seal. Process 5 minutes in a hot-water bath.

Makes about 12 jelly glasses.

Blackberries with or without Cream

If you disdain blackberries as being "too sour," "too full of seeds," or for any other reason, sensory or otherwise, you are missing out on one of the finest fruit flavors there is. It is a humble berry and is best served in a humble way. Seek out the brambles that grow in damp places and remember that the best berries ripen in the shade of the leaves and canes. Those along dry sunny roadsides are apt to be tiny and tasteless. Beware the ubiquitous poison ivy—it masquerades as a bramble. Long sleeves and long pants and a pair of tongs for pulling the out-of-reach canes closer are all recommended. A good way to find all wild fruits is to watch for the blossoms when you're traveling around the Island in June, then check for fruit late in the summer. Blackberries abound on Chappaquiddick, if you can find them; and there are fairly good patches along Moshup's Trail that are easily accessible.

Pick your blackberries either early or late in the day. Use two containers—one for the plumpest and ripest, the other for all the rest. Use these less perfect specimens for pie, pudding, juice, jam, or jelly. Treat the prize berries carefully. Don't bruise them, wash them, refrigerate them, or drop them in the sand. Keep them fairly cool and out of the sun until you are ready to eat them, then roll them into a bowl and serve them just as they are. Some people insist a sprinkle of sugar improves their flavor; and most enjoy them more with cream than without. The cream melds with the tart berry juice to produce a different taste—undeniably delicious, but the purist will still prefer his blackberries unadorned.

Barberry Jelly

These fiery-red berries, dangling in prickly splendor along so many Vineyard driveways and house fronts from fall into winter, seem an uninteresting food source, but we found so many references to barberry jelly in old cookery books that we donned gloves, managed to collect a quart of berries, and were rewarded with some of the tastiest and most colorful jelly we've ever had. Tart, suggestive of both plum and currant, barberry jelly fulfills the usual breakfast requirements, but is also wonderful spooned onto vanilla ice cream, pancakes, or cornbread, or served as a side dish, like cranberry sauce, with a roast meat or fowl. In gathering the berries, wear cotton gloves and strip the heaviest-laden sprigs toward you, holding a pan underneath to catch the berries. You can't avoid a few imbedded barbs, but the hazards are minimal compared to the treats in store once the filled jelly jars are safely on the shelf.

Gather the barberries before they freeze; otherwise, they lose their flavor. Pick out the most obvious twigs and any berries that are obviously spoiled. Rinse under cold water. Place in a saucepan and add 1 cup cold water to each quart of berries. Bring to a boil and cook slowly about 5 minutes, stirring to mix berries well. Line a colander with a double thickness of cheesecloth, place over a large kettle, and pour cooked berries into cheesecloth. Allow to drain thoroughly. If more jelly is desired, fold cheesecloth around berries and squeeze out remaining juice. The finished product will not be so clear, but the flavor will be improved. Boil this plain juice 5 minutes, then measure, and add 1 cup sugar for each cup of juice. Bring to a boil again and cook until jelly is 8°F above the boiling point of water (on jelly thermometer) or until mixture sheets from a metal spoon. Turn into hot, sterilized jars, seal, and process 5 minutes in a hot-water bath.

Autumn Olive Jelly

Autumn olive (*Elaeagnus umbellata*), often incorrectly referred to as Russian olive (*Elaeagnus angustifolia*), grows in profusion on Martha's Vineyard. Almost everyone admires the silvery foliage of these tall shrubs, but usually only birds make use of the heavy clusters of amber-red berries that dangle from their branches every fall. A lovely jelly, a bit like currant in taste, can be made from these berries if they are gathered when fully ripe, usually around the middle of October. Though the jelly can be made with pectin, following the product's directions for currant jelly, this recipe relies on the natural jelling quality of the berries.

4 quarts ripe autumn olive berries
3½ cups water
5 cups sugar
1 tablespoon fresh lemon juice
1 teaspoon margarine
2 teaspoons grated orange peel (optional)

Pick over berries and remove all stems, leaves, and anything that moves—various insects dote on these berries. Place berries in a large stainless-steel kettle, mash well, add the water, stir, and bring to a boil. Boil for 2 minutes, then turn off heat and let sit 5 minutes. Reheat to a low boil and cook 5 more minutes. Let sit until cool enough to work with.

Line a large colander with a jelly cloth or a double layer of cheesecloth, place over a big bowl, and pour in about half the cooked berries. Squeeze gently to extract the juice. If you prefer clearer jelly, you can allow the berries to drip overnight, but you will end up with far less jelly of an odd shade of pinkish green. Discard the squeezed pulp (don't squeeze too much) and repeat with rest of berries.

Measure the berry liquid into a large, broad, stainless-steel kettle. You should have around 4 cups. If more or less, adjust quantity of sugar accordingly. Add the sugar, lemon juice, and margarine, which helps keep the jelly from boiling over and makes it easier to skim. Stir well, bring to a boil, and sustain at a rolling boil until the jelly sheets from a large spoon or a jelly thermometer reaches 221°F. Set kettle off stove and skim off froth. Stir in orange peel, if used. Ladle jelly into hot, sterilized jelly jars, seal, and process 5 minutes in a hot-water bath.

Makes four 8-ounce jars.

Day-Lily Buds

In mid-July, great, grasslike clumps of green along the Vineyard's roads burst almost overnight into spectacular bloom. These are the blossoms of the orange day lily (*Hemerocallis fulva*), one of our loveliest wildflowers, escaped long ago from cultivated gardens and now naturalized throughout our countryside. Though day lilies are almost as familiar to summer vacationers as daisies or goldenrod, few know that the buds of these slender plants are good to eat. Euell Gibbons, in his fascinating book on using wild plants for food, *Stalking the Wild Asparagus* (New York: David McKay Company, Inc., 1978) details the importance of day-lily buds—both fresh and dried—in Far Eastern cuisine. We tried steaming the fresh buds and agree that they are delicious—in flavor and texture somewhere between green beans and okra. Pick with discrimination, if you want to try them, leaving a succession of new buds for you or other summer people to enjoy in flower.

24 day-lily buds
2 tablespoons butter
½ teaspoon salt
Freshly ground black pepper

Pick buds that are somewhat swollen and tinged with orange. Place them in a vegetable steamer over 1 inch of boiling water, cover, and steam 5 minutes. Remove carefully with tongs into a small, warmed bowl; add butter, salt, and pepper; mix gently, and serve at once.

Makes 2 portions.

Sautéed Giant Puffball

Calvatia gigantea, the giant puffball, is one of the easiest edible fungi to identify because of its size, which can range from several inches to a foot or more in diameter. The largest ones can weigh more than 50 pounds. Huge ones, however, are likely to be old and tough, and some people find them indigestible. The primary rule concerning puffballs is: *Never consume one with dark or discolored flesh.* Only those with firm, white flesh are safe. Consult a mushroom guide if you have any doubts at all about your find.

Giant puffballs often appear, sometimes year after year, in colonies, springing up as if by magic on a hillside or lawn. A bumper crop popped up one summer on the lawn of the West Tisbury church but was soon demolished by the kicks of passing children. These monstrous fungi also often grow in thickets.

If you find one of these oddities, gently detach it from the soil and take it home. Cut off the dirty base, remove the tough, brownish skin, and slice the creamy insides into ¾-inch slices. Melt enough butter in a large frying pan to cover the bottom and gently sauté the slices about 5 minutes, adding a bit more butter if the pan dries out. Turn them carefully once or twice so they brown lightly on each side. They crumble easily, so use caution. With a sprinkling of salt, some freshly ground pepper, a little chopped chives or parsley, and a squeeze or two of fresh lemon juice, they are delicious.

Note: The slices are not only delicate, they shrink considerably as they cook. A grapefruit-size puffball may feed only three dedicated mushroom eaters.

Sorrel Soup

This common weed is infuriatingly familiar to gardeners, as its roots creep underground like vine roots, and when one plant is pulled up, five others seem to crop up overnight. Furthermore, it presumably thrives in poor, overly acid soil and thus reflects adversely upon the condition of one's garden! The sorrel family, genus *Rumex,* has, however, long enjoyed culinary status in Europe, particularly in France, where *crème d'oseille* is a cherished soup in the cuisine of many households and restaurants. We write at this length because our weedy sorrel (*Rumex acetosa*) is quite different from the more highly cultivated, broad-leaved French variety that is described in an English cookbook as "a slender perennial plant about 2 feet high with spikes of reddish green flowers." This need not dismay you in your search, however, as in a particularly delinquent garden area American sorrel (which also produces spikes of reddish green flowers) produces succulent leaves 3 to 4 inches long, and enough for a quart of soup can be yanked up in a few minutes.[†] (We suggest using scissors or a knife instead, or cutting the roots off the plant at the source, to avoid having to wash them.) Consult a wildflower guide or other authority if you aren't familiar with the leaves. The plant likes moist, loose soil (it grows in almost everything, including sandy gravel paths and undernourished lawns, but in such locations the leaves are useless as food) and can be gathered from early spring to the first hard freeze of winter. The greens can be cooked up like a rather stringy spinach (it is sometimes described as a "sour spinach"), or a few leaves can be chopped into salad, but we think the soup pot is by far the best place to transform this ubiquitous pest into a *potage extraordinaire.*

Sorrel was used by Greek and Roman doctors as a diuretic, is considered good for the blood and an appetite stimulant, and has been recommended in times past as a cure for kidney stones. We don't vouch for any of this, but we do know there is noth-

---

[†]Seeds for the French sorrel (*oseille*) can be purchased from several seed specialists or obtained from France, if you want to try growing the more civilized variety.

ing better for lunch on a hot summer day than a bowl or two of chilled sorrel soup, served out in the shade, perhaps with a good Camembert, some crackers, a fruit salad, and a cold bottle of Chablis.

2 cups sorrel leaves, firmly packed
3 tablespoons butter
1 medium onion, chopped fine (or ¾ cup finely chopped green onions)
1 tablespoon flour
3 cups chicken stock (canned stock may be used)
½ teaspoon salt
Freshly ground black pepper
2 egg yolks
1 cup medium cream
2 tablespoons chopped parsley or chopped chives

Prepare the leaves by trimming off the stringy parts. Rinse them and drain thoroughly on paper towels. Chop fine, or use scissors to cut the leaves. Melt the butter in a heavy 2-quart saucepan, add the onions and cook over low heat until golden and transparent. Stir in the flour thoroughly. Stir in the chopped sorrel and cook until the leaves are wilted. Add the chicken stock, salt, and pepper, and cook until mixture comes to a simmer. Cook an additional 5 minutes. Beat the egg yolks; gradually beat in the cream. Then slowly beat in 2 cups of the hot soup. Return this mixture to the soup pot and cook carefully over very low heat, stirring constantly, for another moment or two. Do not boil. Additional salt and pepper may be added. Serve hot or very cold. Garnish with chopped parsley or chives, or both.

Makes 4 to 6 portions.

Beach Peas

This decorative relative of the garden-grown green pea forms pods after its magenta-pink blooms have faded. Beach peas are rampant across the road from the Menemsha docks and equally common though less accessible along most of the South Shore sand dunes and banks. If you can find enough pods to fill a basket while the peas in them are still bright green and before they have hardened—and if you have the time and patience to shell them—they make a very tasty vegetable. Since they are smaller than the cultivated pea, they take an inordinate amount of time to prepare, but both picking and shelling would provide a worthy afternoon project for the children on a poor beach day.

2½ cups shelled beach peas
½ teaspoon salt
1 teaspoon sugar
4 tablespoons butter

½ cup medium cream
Freshly ground black pepper
1 tablespoon chopped fresh
chives (optional)

Place a vegetable steamer and about 1 inch of water in a saucepan, cover, and bring water to a boil. Put peas in steamer, cover pot, and steam about 10 minutes. Remove strainer and peas from pan, pour out water, replace peas and add all other ingredients except chives, if to be used. Simmer over low heat for 5 minutes, stirring once or twice. Do not boil. Serve hot with chives sprinkled on top if desired and an additional dusting of black pepper.

Note: You might like to try cooking beach peas like snow peas—leaving them in the pod for steaming. In this case, the tedium of shelling would be eliminated, but peas would have to be gathered when very young.

Makes 3 to 4 portions.

WILD GREENS

Spring is the time to collect greens, though some make fresh new growth in fall as well. By the time the summer people arrive, many edible wild plants are forming seeds, but the second-cycle leaves produced from them will lack the succulence of the early ones that thrived in the Island's cool, damp spring. Dandelions, watercress (a delicacy raw but also good in soup), wild mustard, lamb's-quarters, and sorrel are some of the most familiar wild greens. Dock, peppergrass, pigweed, purslane, and chicory are less well known but can be found in any wildflower guide.

All are prepared in more or less the same way. Young leaves should be washed, trimmed, and cooked like spinach in a small amount of water, with salt added to taste. Dandelion, chicory, and other bitter leaves will be more palatable if cooked in several waters. Greens are usually better in combination, in true "potherb" style. A bit of bacon or salt pork may be put in the pot and the mess simmered a long time, southern fashion. Or, like their cultivated counterparts, cooked wild greens can be eaten hot or cold dressed up with bits of browned bacon, slices of hard-boiled egg or lemon, a pitcher of vinegar, some sour cream or mayonnaise. Or they may be added to soup. The best way to tell when they are done is to keep tasting them. Cooking times vary as do tastes.

Do not under any circumstances gather whatever wild greenery takes your fancy. Some are acutely poisonous; many can cause severe stomach disorders. Pick and use only what you are sure of. Even poison ivy looks delectable at some stages of growth.

Dandelion-Bud Omelet

12 dandelion buds
About 3 tablespoons butter
4 eggs
½ teaspoon salt
Freshly ground black pepper

Pick dandelion buds just about to open; wash them if necessary, and toss in paper towels to dry. Melt 2 tablespoons butter in small skillet or omelet pan, add dandelion buds, and cook them slowly 2 or 3 minutes, stirring carefully so they will cook on all sides. Remove pan from heat. Take out dandelion buds and reserve. Beat eggs gently only until mixed; stir in salt. Heat pan with remaining butter (about 1 tablespoon) over moderate heat until butter foams. Pour eggs into pan and cook slowly, lifting around edges to allow uncooked mixture to run under omelet. When eggs are almost done, spoon dandelion buds onto one half of omelet. Fold omelet. Dust lightly with pepper and serve at once.

Makes 2 portions.

Black Walnut and Pumpkin Muffins

Black walnuts are one of several native American nut trees—two others being hazelnuts and hickories—that grow well on the Vineyard. They are very hard shelled, so lay something like an old towel over them before you start whacking or the shells will fly all over. Be sure to remove all the bits of shell or you may crack a tooth as you chew on a muffin.

1½ cups all-purpose flour

2 teaspoons baking powder

1 teaspoon baking soda

1½ teaspoons ground cinnamon

½ teaspoon ground nutmeg

½ teaspoon salt

2 large eggs

½ cup brown sugar

¼ cup pure maple syrup

1½ cups fresh cooked pumpkin puree

5 tablespoons melted butter

½ cup black walnuts

Preheat oven to 400°F.

Position a rack in the center of the oven. Grease a standard 12-muffin tin or line with paper muffin cups.

Mix together thoroughly flour, baking powder, baking soda, cinnamon, nutmeg, and salt. In a large bowl whisk together eggs, brown sugar, maple syrup, and pumpkin puree. Let stand 10 minutes.

Stir melted butter and black walnuts into pumpkin mixture. Add flour mixture, folding in just until dry ingredients are moistened. Do not overmix. Using a ⅓-cup measuring cup, spoon mixture into muffin tin.

Bake 15 to 20 minutes, until toothpick or cake tester comes out clean. Let rest on cake rack for 5 minutes.

The muffins are equally good with 1½ cups of grated, peeled apples in place of the pumpkin puree.

Meadow Tisane

A fascinating lore—and an ancient one—exists that suggests herb tea of one sort or another will cure almost anything. Horsetail is diuretic. Lady's-mantle is "a woman's best friend." Goldenrod is anti-inflammatory; verbena, a sedative; yarrow, a digestive. Be all this as it may—and we like to believe they all do what they're said to do—a pleasant, country, summery sort of leaf tea can easily be made from almost any of the following, used either singly or in whatever combination you fancy or can find to pick. (If you include wild strawberry leaves, be sure that they are well dried before use.) Take along a basket when you stroll through the lovely Up-Island meadows, but pick only things you know. Some leaves—laurel, for instance, and some evergreens—are poisonous enough to make you very ill if you chew up a few. We suggest: yarrow (leaves and flowers), red clover (leaves and flowers), elder flowers, mullein flowers, goldenrod (leaves and flowers), wild strawberry leaves, chicory leaves, sweet fern leaves, and almost any leaves from your herb garden, especially mint, but also borage, sage, chamomile, lemon balm, marjoram, thyme, and lemon verbena. Dry the leaves and flowers well on screens, remove stems and twigs, and store the mixture in a canister. To make the tea, use fresh boiling water and allow 1 teaspoon leaf-flower mixture per cup and 1 teaspoon for the pot. This meadow-herb mixture is an inexpensive and nostalgia-producing memento to take back to your city apartment and enjoy during your months off-Island.

CHAPTER 5

Meat, Game, and Poultry

MEAT

Rev. James Freeman, who visited the Island in 1807, reckoned that there were 15,600 sheep, 400 horses and colts, 2,800 neat cattle and 800 swine. . . . Figures for 1855 are almost identical, but by 1872, they begin to show a decline. . . . The reasons for the gradual abandonment of farming were several: tired land, erosion of salt meadows, falling wool prices, lack of demand for homemade butter and cheese, but most of all, the exodus of farm boys to sea or to jobs on the mainland.

—Eleanor R. Mayhew, ed., *A Short History of Martha's Vineyard* [†]

Our townsman, Mr. David N. Look, has the honor of having the largest herd of cattle in the county, thirty-two head. . . .

—West Tisbury Annual Report, 1894

T he faced stone walls that border so many Vineyard fields were not built for the purpose they so often serve today—to discourage trespassers and enhance the beauty of the high-priced land they outline. Rather, the walls—and hedges, ditches, and miles of post-and-rail fences that have almost entirely disappeared—were meant to

[†]Dukes County Historical Society, Edgartown, Massachusetts, 1956

confine the Island's livestock. As far back as the 1660s there were hogs, horses, and goats; and some of the fine sheep and cattle had bloodlines tracing back to the English animals that were driven down from Boston by the "Bay Path" and ferried across to the Vineyard on sailing ships. So numerous were these creatures that one account reports there were "seventeen gates and twenty-one pairs of bars which had to be opened and closed by the traveler" within a distance of 10 miles. But little by little the pastures were cut up into building lots (as they continue to be today, to the regret of most Island residents), and now only a few dozen head of cattle and some small flocks of sheep remain. Several farmers still slaughter their own sheep and beef cattle; one has a few hogs left. So if you know the right people, you may feast on a roast of Allen Farm lamb or a Vineyard-produced steak some winter night. Island-raised meats are also available now at several local stores and farm stands.

Beefsteak and Oysters

This old-fashioned dish—Victorian and opulent—suggests a hearty midwinter dinner before the fire after a bone-chilling expedition in the gray silence of a Great Pond on a lowering January day. The succulent delicacy of the oysters is balanced by the solid texture and taste of a good hunk of beef. With it you might serve baked potatoes, slices of sweet red onion, a cooked green vegetable, and a bottle of zinfandel or some other light red wine.

Boneless steak (preferably sirloin), weighing about 3 pounds after fat is trimmed
Freshly ground black pepper
½ teaspoon salt

Approximately 1 pint fresh oysters, drained
3 tablespoons melted butter
Maître d'hotel butter
1 teaspoon chopped fresh parsley

Preheat broiler.

Season both sides of the steak with a few grindings of black pepper and the salt. Broil on a greased rack about 3 inches from heat until brown. Turn steak. Remove from broiler about 5 minutes before cooked to your preference. Reduce oven heat to 375°F.

Place steak in a shallow, heatproof baking dish, cover it with the drained oysters, pour the melted butter over the oysters, and bake only until the oysters are plump, about 5 to 10 minutes. Serve immediately with maître d'hotel butter and the chopped parsley sprinkled over all.

Makes 4 generous portions.

Beefsteak-and-Kidney Pie

The whaling wives of days past needed substantial concoctions like this one to send their men off well fortified for the long months—and even years—of eating salt pork and salt beef (called "Salt Horse" by the sailors). It is indeed an old-fashioned dish, but an honorable one, and one that should be brought again into the winter cuisine of the Vineyard. What more auspicious aroma could greet young skaters and iceboaters returning from an afternoon outing on Squibnocket Pond?

The English mother of one author of this book lived in a fairytale "gingerbread" house overlooking Sunset Lake and its swan-dwellers, at the edge of the Oak Bluffs campground. In her tiny kitchen, she concocted a beefsteak-and-kidney pie worthy of one of London's finest chophouses. This is how she made it.

1 beef kidney, trimmed of fat, cut in 1-inch squares
Salt
1½ pounds beef chuck, cut in 1½-inch squares
1 teaspoon salt

½ teaspoon freshly ground black pepper

2 tablespoons butter

2 tablespoons vegetable oil

1 large onion, coarsely chopped

2 cups or more beef stock (or canned beef bouillon)

3 or 4 small carrots, peeled and cut in ½-inch circles

1 tablespoon flour mixed to a smooth paste with 2 tablespoons water

Pastry crust (see page 110)

Soak the kidney squares for 1 hour in water to cover, adding 1 tablespoon salt per quart of water, then drain and dry them thoroughly with paper towels. Season beef and kidney with salt and pepper. In a heavy kettle or flameproof casserole, heat butter and oil until almost smoking, and quickly cook the beef and kidney pieces until brown on all sides. Do not overcrowd pan; if necessary, do a few pieces at a time and set aside.

Reducing heat to moderate, cook onion until golden and transparent. Add beef stock to onion in kettle; cook, stirring and scraping up coagulated juices until dissolved. Simmer a few more moments. Add beef and kidney squares. The liquid should almost cover the meat; if it doesn't, add additional beef stock. Cover tightly and cook at a gentle simmer about 1½ hours.

Add the sliced carrots and cook an additional ½ hour, or until the carrots are done and the beef is tender. With a slotted spoon transfer beef, kidneys, and vegetables to a casserole or baking dish of sufficient size to hold all ingredients. Over high heat bring liquid in kettle to a full boil, then add the flour-and-water paste, stirring constantly, using only enough paste to achieve the proper thickness. The sauce should coat the spoon lightly. Adjust seasonings if necessary. Pour the sauce over the beef and kidney mixture.

Preheat oven to 450°F.

Prepare pastry crust as follows:

Pastry Crust

2 cups sifted flour   *¼ cup milk*
1 teaspoon salt   *1 egg lightly beaten with*
½ cup vegetable oil   *1 tablespoon milk*

Resift the flour with the salt into a mixing bowl. Combine oil and milk without stirring and add all at once to flour. With a fork, stir lightly until well mixed. Form into a smooth ball. Roll out between two 12-inch squares of wax paper. (The paper will not slide during the rolling-out process if the work counter is slightly dampened.) Use short, very gentle strokes until circle reaches appropriate size for baking dish; the pastry should be approximately ½ inch thick. Carefully peel off top paper. Position the circle carefully over the pan, paper side up, then peel off remaining paper. Crimp the edges of the pastry onto the dish to seal the casserole. Cut three or four slits in the pastry so steam can escape, brush with the egg-and-milk mixture to glaze (using about 2 tablespoons), and bake 15 minutes, or until crust is lightly browned. Reduce heat to 350°F and bake 20 to 25 minutes more. Serve immediately.

Makes 4 generous portions.

Brisket of Beef with Barbecue Sauce Louise

2–3 pound brisket, flat cut
Salt
Freshly ground black pepper
Thyme
1 tablespoon olive oil
1 medium onion, sliced
1 large carrot, sliced

2 celery stalks, sliced
2 cloves garlic, sliced
1 12-ounce can of beer
1 can of condensed beef broth or
    1½ cups of beef broth
2 bay leaves
Water, if necessary

Preheat oven to 325°F.

Rub lean side of brisket with salt, pepper, and thyme. Do not remove fat from other side. In a heavy ovenproof casserole or cast-iron skillet, brown both sides of meat in oil. Remove meat from pan, and lightly brown vegetables in remaining fat. Return meat to pan, arranging vegetables over and around meat. On low heat, add beer, broth, and bay leaves. Add water as necessary to just cover meat. Bring to a boil. Cover and place in oven for 2 hours. Turn meat over after 1 hour. Turn off oven and leave for ½ hour. Slice thinly, and put on warmed platter. Serve with pan juices and traditional horseradish cream or with the wonderful barbecue sauce on page 112.

Barbecue Sauce Louise

After selling her Edgartown restaurant, Louise Tate King conducted a very successful catering business from her house in North Tisbury. This barbecue sauce was very popular when used on beef, pork, or chicken as a marinade, basting liquid, or sauce.

1 cup ketchup
1 cup molasses
1 medium onion, minced
2 garlic cloves, minced
2 tablespoons A-1 sauce
2 tablespoons Tabasco sauce
1 tablespoon Worcestershire
    sauce
1 tablespoon vinegar

4 or 5 whole cloves
½ teaspoon salt
½ teaspoon freshly ground
    black pepper
1 tablespoon salad oil
Zest and juice from 1 large
    orange
1½ tablespoons Dijon mustard
2–3 tablespoons butter

Combine all ingredients except butter in a heavy saucepan. Stir well. Add butter and bring to a boil. Simmer, covered, about 30 minutes, stirring occasionally. This sauce keeps very well if covered and refrigerated.

Makes about 4 cups.

Braised Oxtails
[Oxtail Ragout]

Until only a few years ago, it was possible for the day tourist visiting Gay Head to cross the road from his parked bus and have his picture snapped with a yoke of oxen and their Indian owner. In the more glorious days of the Vineyard's history, this visitor's grandfather might have docked in the *Monohansett,* a paddle-wheel steamer that used to tie up at the Lobsterville wharf, and been driven to the top of the famed Gay Head clay cliffs in an ox cart, hanging tightly to his bowler as he jolted along.

Although many people tend to think of the ox as a rather bizarre creature often mentioned in the Bible, an ox is not born an ox but is an "adult castrated male bovine"; and as a mode of conveyance, he has long since been superseded, though there are still two yokes on the Vineyard, handsome animals that can usually be seen at the annual Agricultural Fair. One pair of these is still used by their West Tisbury owner to work the fields. Male bovines are more profitably left to grow up as bulls these days, or killed and sold as food before they reach maturity.

Oxtail, therefore, is merely beef tail, but as it is hardly a best-seller at the meat counter, food purveyors have wisely stuck to the old name in offering this item to the housewives who do search it out. Whatever one calls it, oxtail is one of several specialty meats that deserve to be used more often.

3 pounds oxtails, cut into joints
Flour for dredging
1 teaspoon salt
¼ teaspoon freshly ground black
　pepper
2 tablespoons butter
2 tablespoons vegetable oil
1 small onion, chopped coarsely
2 cloves garlic, minced
2 cups red wine
1 cup beef stock or canned beef

bouillon, or more
Additional salt and pepper, if
　needed
8–12 small whole white onions,
　peeled
½ cup diced carrots
¼ cup diced celery
1 tablespoon chopped fresh
　parsley
2 tablespoons flour (optional)
3 tablespoons water (optional)

Preheat oven to 300°F.

Roll the oxtail sections in flour seasoned with the salt and pepper. In a heavy skillet, heat butter and oil over high heat until butter foam subsides. Add the oxtail pieces, reduce heat to moderate, and brown them thoroughly on all sides. Remove them from pan. Add to the pan the chopped onion and garlic and cook until lightly browned. Add the red wine and 1 cup beef stock to the pan, stirring well; allow it to come to a full rolling boil. Add additional salt and pepper at this time, if required. Reduce heat and allow liquids to simmer for 10 minutes. Transfer oxtail pieces to an ovenproof casserole; pour liquids from skillet over them. The liquid should just barely cover the meat; it may be necessary to add a little more beef stock. Cover tightly and place in the preheated oven; bake approximately 3 to 4 hours, or until meat is fork-tender. Add, for the last ½ hour of cooking, the onions, carrots, and celery. Serve with a garnish of chopped parsley.

If desired, the sauce may be thickened slightly by carefully stirring in a smooth paste of 2 tablespoons flour mixed with 3 tablespoons water, a little at a time, until the proper consistency is reached.

Makes 4 portions.

Roast Leg of Vineyard Lamb
with Fruit Glaze

Vineyard lambs—and a few farmers still raise them—used to be fed for a time during their rearing on salt hay; they were taken to the salt meadows, and there they grazed. The flesh acquired an indefinable flavor, much like the French lamb *pré salé*. Such lamb provided a memorable meal. The following recipe is suggested as a somewhat sophisticated treatment; though it is simple to prepare, the results are singular.

1 teaspoon salt
¼ teaspoon freshly ground black
*   pepper*
Small leg of lamb, 5–6 pounds
*   preferably*
1 cup orange juice
1 cup apricot puree (combine
*   syrup with*

pitted apricots from a small
*   can and*
whisk in electric blender or put
*   through a food mill)*
4 tablespoons cognac
Sliced oranges (optional)
Whole canned apricots (optional)

Preheat oven to 300°F.

Rub salt and pepper thoroughly over surface of meat. Place meat in a roasting pan, using a rack if desired. Pour the juice, puree, and cognac over it. Roast, uncovered, about 30 minutes per pound, or, if a meat thermometer is used, until internal heat reads 175° to 180°F. Baste occasionally with the pan juices while meat is roasting.

Remove pan from oven and set oven to broil position. Broil lamb sufficiently for surface to be nicely glazed, basting during the process.

If a fruit garnish is desired, add slices of orange and whole canned apricots to the pan before the broiling process, then garnish with these fruits at serving time.

Makes 6 to 8 portions.

Allen Farm Stuffed Lamb Shoulder

Early settlers fed their sheep on native grasses and salt-marsh hay, giving their flesh a unique flavor. But gradually farmers began to graze their flocks on the imported European grasses that today cover most of the meadows of Island farms.

In the low, rolling hills of Chilmark, one of the Island's oldest working farms, the historic Allen homestead, sprawls over one hundred acres of meadow traversed by several miles of the Island's most beautiful stone walls. Living in the recently renovated 1773 farmhouse, the present owner turns her 200-odd sheep out to pastures her forebears were using 250 years ago.

Meat from her lambs is available all year, but only at the farmhouse. It is understandably expensive but also unforgettably delectable. The following recipe was devised by this hardworking lady to take to a party, where it was a great success. We are privileged to be able to pass it on.

2–3 pound boned shoulder of lamb
(a boned leg may also be used)
Salt
Freshly ground black pepper
One large bunch of spinach, stems
removed, washed, and briefly
steamed, or a 10-ounce, fresh
package
1 package of Boursin herb cheese

3 tablespoons good olive oil
2–3 medium onions, roughly
chopped
3–4 cloves of garlic, chopped
1 cup of white wine
1 teaspoon chopped fresh rose-
mary, or ½ teaspoon dried
1 teaspoon chopped fresh thyme,
or ½ teaspoon dried

Preheat oven to 375°F.

Unroll roast, cut out all fat and sinewy material. Flatten meat, sprinkle with salt and pepper, and cover surface with drained spinach and cheese. Retie roast. Braise in a heavy, ovenproof casserole in the olive oil until all sides are nicely browned. Remove roast. Sauté onions and garlic in the casserole, add wine, and stir, scraping up any browned bits from the bottom. Return meat to the casserole, add the herbs, and sprinkle with more salt and pepper. Bring to a simmer on top of the stove, cover, and place in oven. Roast about 1 hour.

Note: If boned leg is used, increase amounts of spinach and cheese by one half, and add 15 to 20 minutes to cooking time.

Makes about 4 portions (shoulder) and 6 portions (leg).

Roast Loin of Pork
with Beach-Plum-Jelly Glaze

4–5 pounds center cut of pork loin (a fresh ham or pork
shoulder may be used instead)
Salt and freshly ground black pepper
1 cup Beach-Plum Jelly (see page 81)
1 tablespoon flour (or 1½ teaspoons cornstarch)
1 cup stock (or water with a beef or chicken bouillon cube dissolved in it)

Preheat oven to 350°F.

Rub pork (which should be removed from refrigerator at least ½ hour before cooking) with salt and pepper. It may be necessary to trim surplus fat before seasoning the meat. Place meat, fat side up, on a rack in a roasting pan and cook it approximately 30 to 35 minutes to the pound, or until it reaches an internal heat of 185°F if using a meat thermometer.

While meat is roasting, melt the beach-plum jelly over low heat in a small pan. Remove from heat. When the roast is thoroughly cooked, skim off all but several tablespoons of the fat in the roasting pan. Carefully coat the roast with most of the beach-plum jelly and return it to the oven, basting every 10 minutes with the pan juices. The remaining jelly may be used as additional basting liquid. When the roast is nicely glazed, after 20 to 30 minutes, remove it from the roasting pan and keep it in a warm place on a heatproof platter.

Carefully blend flour or cornstarch into the pan juices and jelly remaining in the roasting pan. Gradually add stock, stirring constantly. Strain into a sauce boat and serve with the sliced roast pork.

Makes 4 to 6 portions.

Pork Chops with Barley and Rutabaga

¾ cup barley
2½ cups sliced, peeled rutabaga,
  cut into ½-inch cubes
¾ cup dried apricots, cut into
  chunks
1 teaspoon dried marjoram
½ teaspoon dried oregano

½ teaspoon salt
Freshly ground black pepper
4 thick pork chops
1 tablespoon vegetable oil
½ cup dry white wine
2 cups beef broth (may be made
  from bouillon cubes)

Preheat oven to 375°F.

Grease baking dish large enough to hold chops in one layer. Combine barley, rutabaga, apricots, herbs, salt, and pepper to taste. Spread over bottom of baking dish. Sprinkle chops with salt and pepper. Heat oil in a large, heavy skillet and brown chops about 5 minutes over moderately high heat, turning once. Transfer chops to baking dish. Pour out any extra fat in skillet and add the wine. Deglaze the pan over medium heat, scraping up browned bits. Remove skillet from heat, add beef broth and stir well. Bring liquid to boil, pour over chops in baking dish, cover, and bake 1¼ hours.

Makes 4 portions.

Kidney "Strew"

From a summering Chilmark cook, born and reared in China, came a recipe devised by her family's Chinese cook and proudly copied out by hand in his new English. As set down by Chou Lin on a now stained and faded half sheet of rice paper, here are the instructions:

½ lb. kidneys   sat pepper   ¼ lb. mushroom   1 cup stook
½ ib. onion   ¼ butter   green pepper   1 tablespoon flour

Clean the kidneys frist and cut to slices, fried them in butter with flour. Put the onion, green pepper, sat, pepper, mushroom and stook in, strew them in every slowly fire about one hour.

The Chilmarker who donated the recipe has noted at the bottom: "Any sort of wine improves this. Also garlic."

We would amend Chou Lin's instructions as follows:

2 tablespoons butter
2 small veal kidneys, trimmed
  of fat and filament
1 medium onion, sliced
¼ pound fresh mushrooms, sliced
½ small green pepper, coarsely
  chopped
1 clove garlic, minced

Butter, if needed
1 tablespoon flour
½ cup beef stock (or canned beef
  bouillon)
4 tablespoons good dry red wine
Salt
Freshly ground black pepper
1 teaspoon chopped fresh parsley

In a heavy skillet over moderately high heat, melt butter. When foam subsides, brown the whole kidneys quickly on both sides, about 10 minutes. Remove them from pan and keep warm. Reduce heat; cook onion in same skillet until transparent. Add mushrooms, green pepper, and garlic; cook 5 minutes or so. Add a little butter if needed. Stir in the flour, blending it in well. Gradually stir in the beef stock and the red wine, stirring constantly. Let this mixture simmer over low heat. Meantime, cut kidneys into ½-inch slices. Add salt and pepper to taste to the skillet liquids, then add the kidney slices. Stir carefully only long enough to reheat the kidneys and serve immediately with a garnish of chopped parsley.

Note: After fat and filament are removed, kidneys should be wiped clean with a damp, clean cloth, never washed. Nor do we believe in sautéing them sliced because they tend to toughen.

Makes 2 portions.

GAME

The rest of the day was spent in trading with them for furs, "which are Beavers, Luzernes, Marterns, Otters, Wild-Cat skinnes . . . blacke foxes, Conie skinnes . . . Deere skinnes very large, Seale skinnes, and other beast skinnes to us unknowen."

—Brereton, quoted in Banks, *History of Martha's Vineyard*

You aren't likely to encounter a marten or a wildcat as you drive around Martha's Vineyard nowadays, but one motorist did count thirty-four conies (or Eastern Cottontails) on the 3- or 4-mile stretch of road between the youth hostel and the airport during a misty, nighttime drive. Through September and October the squirrels frenziedly stock up on acorns and hickory nuts, and a bird-watcher making his way through the brush surrounding a quiet inland pond may startle an otter sunning himself on the warm mud. Both red and fallow deer are numerous, often materializing magically out of the dark woods, leaping stiff-legged across the road in front of an oncoming car, and disappearing before the driver even slows down.

Game animals find the Vineyard a tranquil haven during most of the year, though during official seasons deer, rabbits, ducks, pheasants, quail, and other potentially delectable wild animals are hunted and killed to be used for food as they have been since the Island was first settled. Other creatures, understandably, are less popular than their edible brethren. The rats that frequent the wharfs and forage in compost piles are highly unwelcome. And newer residents, skunks and coons, both introduced to the Island around 1960, have proliferated and become serious nuisances. Skunks uproot plants, wreck garbage cans, and douse many an unwary dog. Coons are even more destructive during their nocturnal forays, often wiping out whole flocks of chickens, one or two per night, despite their owners' frantic safety precautions. Nests crowded with fledgling birds are also favored quarries.

Roast Leg of Venison

Authorities differ about the length of time required to age venison, assuming, that is, there is a hunter in the family who proudly brings home a deer. Consensus seems to be that at least a week is required for aging and that the carcass should be hung in a cool, airy place with temperatures ranging between 38° and 43°F.

Cuts from the hindquarter—in this case the leg—don't really require tenderizing in a marinade. This recipe suggests it, nevertheless, for the marinade conveys a subtle flavor to the meat, and the addition of a small quantity of the reserved marinade to the finished pan juices is a splendid enhancement.

MARINADE

3 cups good red Burgundy or claret

½ cup vegetable oil

1 cup each celery and carrots, diced

1 small onion, chopped

2 cloves garlic, minced

2 teaspoons chopped fresh herbs, mixed (parsley, basil, tarragon, chives, etc.), or 1 teaspoon dried herbs

1 teaspoon salt

½ teaspoon freshly ground black pepper

1 bay leaf (optional)

Combine marinade ingredients. Place half the marinade in a container of sufficient size to hold the meat. Place the meat in the marinade, then ladle the rest of the marinade over the meat, including the vegetables and herbs. Cover and let stand at least 6 hours. Turn the meat every 2 hours. If the meat is refrigerated, it may marinate 12 to 24 hours.

Leg of venison, properly larded (see below)
½ teaspoon salt
¼ teaspoon (or a little more) freshly ground black pepper
¼ pound salt pork, thinly sliced

Preheat oven to 325°F.

Remove meat from marinade; pat it thoroughly dry with a paper towel. Rub the salt in (not too much salt; the salt-pork slices, if used, contribute saltiness). Dust with the black pepper. Reserve the marinade.

Most cooks agree that venison requires larding before it is cooked to preserve its juiciness. Ideally, lardoons (thin strips of salt pork) cut ½ inch thick and 3 to 4 inches long are inserted in the meat at 2- or 3-inch intervals. If you lack a larding needle, an ice pick or a thin-pointed knife will force the lardoons into the meat. Or thin strips of salt pork or bacon may be placed over the top of the roast so that each slice nearly overlaps its neighbor.

Cook in an uncovered roasting pan 15 to 20 minutes to the pound or to an internal temperature of 140°F for rare, if a meat thermometer is used.

Remove the finished roast to a heated platter and keep warm. Pour or skim off all fat from roasting pan except for about 2 tablespoons, and proceed with the following sauce:

1 tablespoon flour
1 cup of the reserved marinade
1 cup beef stock (or canned beef bouillon)
Salt
Freshly ground black pepper
¼ cup sour cream (optional)

Add the flour to the remaining fat and juices in the roasting pan, place over moderate heat and blend thoroughly; then add the marinade and the beef stock, stirring constantly, scraping up all the coagulated juices. At this point additional salt and pepper may be added, if needed. Strain the sauce into a serving bowl. Serve very hot.

Optional: The sour cream, if it is to be used, is stirred slowly into the sauce over gentle heat. Do not let sauce boil, or the sour cream will curdle.

Makes 6 to 10 portions, depending on size of roast.

Venison Pot Roast

Before using the less tender cuts of venison—any portion of the forequarter, for instance—it is almost essential that the meat be marinated overnight in the refrigerator (or at least 4 to 6 hours at room temperature) for maximum flavor and tenderness. The marinade tenderizes and adds an additional dimension of flavor as well.

Marinade (see page 123)
4–5-pound piece of venison
2 tablespoons butter and 2 tablespoons vegetable oil (or ¼ pound
    salt pork, cut into ½-inch dice)
½ teaspoon salt, or more
¼ teaspoon freshly ground black pepper, or more
2 medium onions, coarsely chopped
2 small garlic cloves, minced
2 teaspoons flour
1½ cups beef stock (or canned beef bouillon), more if needed
About 1 tablespoon Beach-Plum Jelly (see page 81), (optional)

Marinate venison 4 to 6 hours at room temperature or overnight in the refrigerator, turning it occasionally.

Remove meat from marinade; dry with paper towels. Reserve the marinade.

Heat butter and oil over moderate heat in a heavy 6-quart kettle or a flame-proof casserole until butter foam subsides. If using salt pork, cook over moderate heat until crisp and golden; remove pork bits, drain them on paper towel, and reserve. Brown meat on all sides in the hot fat, remove it from pan, and sprinkle with the salt and pepper.

Add onions to the pan and cook slowly until transparent and golden. Add garlic and cook a minute or two longer. If using salt pork, drain off all but 2 to 3 tablespoons of the fat. Add the flour to the pan, blending it in thoroughly with the fat, onions, and garlic. Add the beef stock and ½ cup of the reserved marinade and allow the liquids to come to a simmer over moderate heat. If using salt pork, add the reserved cooked dice. Place the meat in the pot, cover tightly, and cook at a gentle simmer until the meat is tender. Cooking time will vary considerably according to the age of the animal. If you prefer, the pot roast may cook in a 275°F oven. If additional liquid is required, add a little more beef stock. Turn the meat at least once during the cooking period.

When tender, remove meat from pan, transferring it to a heated platter.

If necessary, add more salt and pepper to the liquids in the pot or casserole. Stir in the beach-plum jelly, if desired. Then strain and pour into a heated sauce boat.

Slice the meat, spoon a little of the sauce over the meat slices, and serve with the additional sauce.

Note: Lean meat such as venison is improved by larding. See comments about this contained in recipe for Roast Leg of Venison (see page 123).

Makes 6 to 8 portions.

Venison Meat Loaf

Here on Martha's Vineyard, the hunters, in the proper season (and a few in the improper season), stock their freezers with venison roasts, steaks, and chops, but just as important a freezer item is the ground meat obtained from the trimmings and from the shoulder and neck. The ground venison makes such a deliciously different meat loaf that some of us rank it in importance with the venison roasts and steaks.

2 slices white bread, crusts removed

½ cup beef stock (or canned beef bouillon)

3 pounds ground venison (or 2 pounds ground venison and
    1 pound ground beef, preferably chuck)

¼ pound salt pork, ground (optional)

1 small onion, chopped fine

1 small clove garlic, minced

½ teaspoon salt (if ground salt pork is used, omit salt)

¼ teaspoon freshly ground black pepper

1 tablespoon chopped fresh parsley (or 1 teaspoon dried parsley)

2 tablespoons ketchup (or 1 teaspoon tomato paste)

1 teaspoon prepared mustard (preferably Dijon type)

1 teaspoon Worcestershire sauce

3 or 4 thin slices salt pork or bacon (optional)

Preheat oven to 350°F.

Soak bread in the beef stock. Combine all other ingredients except whole slices of salt pork or bacon, then add the soaked bread. Stir everything thoroughly, being sure that the bread combines completely with the other ingredients. Shape into a loaf and place in a shallow baking pan. A black iron skillet is recommended. If desired, place slices of salt pork or bacon on top of the loaf. Bake for approximately 1½ hours, basting occasionally with pan juices.

Note: A little additional beef stock, about ½ cup, may be added to the pan juices after removing the cooked meat loaf. (If using salt pork, pour off excess fat before adding stock.) Stir the added stock thoroughly over moderate heat, then simmer for about 10 minutes, strain, and pour over the meat loaf.

Makes 6 to 8 portions.

Rabbit Stifle

1 or 2 rabbits (2½–3 pounds net weight), skinned, cleaned, and cut
    into serving-size pieces
Salt
¼ teaspoon freshly ground black pepper
Flour for dredging
2 tablespoons butter and 2 tablespoons vegetable oil (or ¼ pound
    salt pork, cut in ½-inch dice)
4 medium onions, cut in ½-inch slices
2 cups beef stock (or canned beef bouillon)
1 teaspoon tomato paste
1 tablespoon flour mixed to a smooth paste with 2 tablespoons water
¼ cup sour cream (optional)
1 tablespoon chopped fresh parsley
1 teaspoon chopped fresh dill (or ½ teaspoon dried dill weed)

Soak rabbit for 2 hours in water to cover, adding 1 tablespoon salt per quart of water (recommended for freshly killed rabbit as an aid in extracting any traces of blood). Dry thoroughly with paper towels. Rub the rabbit pieces with ½ teaspoon salt and the pepper; dust thoroughly with flour, shaking off the excess.

Melt the butter and oil in a heavy 5- or 6-quart kettle or flameproof casserole over moderate heat. If using salt pork, cook the diced bits until crisp and golden; remove them and drain on a paper towel. Reserve them. Brown the rabbit pieces on all sides in the hot fat. Remove the rabbit pieces, reduce heat, and cook the onion slices until golden and transparent.

Pour off excess fat, then add beef stock to pan, and bring to a full boil over high heat; cook for 5 minutes, stirring occasionally. Reduce heat to low; add the tomato paste, continuing to stir for a moment or two. Additional salt and pepper may be required at this point.

Add the rabbit pieces and salt-pork bits to the pan, cover tightly, and cook at a very gentle simmer until rabbit is tender. Cooking time will vary depending on the age of the creature; it should take approximately 1 hour. The kettle—or casserole—may also be placed in a slow oven, 250° to 275°F.

Transfer rabbit pieces to a heated serving bowl; keep warm. Add the flour-and-water paste to the liquids in the pan, stirring constantly over moderate heat until the mixture thickens and bubbles. Turn off heat and carefully stir in the sour cream, if used.

Pour a little of the sauce—about ¾ cup—over the rabbit pieces, sprinkle with the parsley and dill. Serve the remainder of the sauce in a separate bowl.

Makes 3 to 4 portions.

Roast Pheasant with Apricot Sauce

F ew connoisseurs of game agree about the length of time game birds should be
cooked. Nor is there an area of agreement concerning the length of time wild
birds should be hung. Pheasant, for example, is hung, incredibly enough, for as long as
six months by some. For the average palate, two or three days should be enough. Hang
the birds in a cool, dry place (38° to 48°F) before they are drawn or plucked. Wild
duck and pheasant—birds with dark meat—are usually served rare; white-fleshed birds
such as partridge or quail are usually served well done. Wild birds have little fat, and
this lack must be supplemented by the addition of butter, bacon, salt pork, or larding.

1 ready-to-cook pheasant,
weighing 2½–3 pounds
(reserve liver)
1 tablespoon melted butter
Salt
Freshly ground pepper
½ cup celery leaves

1 small whole apple
1 small whole onion, peeled
1 slice lemon
1 clove garlic (optional)
4 slices salt pork, cut thin
Apricot Sauce (see page 131)

Preheat oven to 350°F.
Rub the cavity of the bird with the melted butter, then with a little salt and pepper. Place the celery leaves, apple, onion, lemon slice, and garlic clove (if used) inside
the bird. Truss the bird, place the salt-pork slices over the breast, and roast, uncovered,
from 15 to 30 minutes per pound, depending on your preference. Baste the bird frequently with the pan juices while it is cooking.
Remove bird from its baking pan. Discard string and salt-pork slices. Strain or

pour off fat in roasting pan. Set pan aside. Transfer bird to heated platter and keep warm.

Serve with Apricot Sauce.

Makes 2 to 3 portions.

APRICOT SAUCE

1½ cups chicken stock (or canned chicken broth)
1 cup canned pitted apricots, drained (reserve juice)
1 teaspoon grated orange rind, orange part only
¼ cup port or sherry
½ cup apricot juice
Liver from the pheasant, coarsely chopped (uncooked)
Salt
Freshly ground black pepper
1 teaspoon cornstarch or arrowroot mixed with 2 teaspoons
    water (optional)

Add stock to roasting pan. Stir over moderate heat, scraping up all coagulated juices until dissolved. Cook down until about ¾ cup liquid remains. Rub apricots through a coarse sieve or food mill; add to roasting pan with the orange rind, port or sherry, apricot juice, chopped liver, salt, and pepper. Reduce heat and simmer 5 minutes. Spoon a little of the sauce over the pheasant and pass the remainder in a pitcher or bowl.

The sauce may be thickened very slightly by mixing the cornstarch or arrowroot with water to a smooth paste and adding it gradually to the simmering sauce until the desired thickness is achieved.

Makes 4 to 6 portions.

Roast Wild Duck

2 wild ducks, weighing approximately 2½ pounds each, ready to
  cook (reserve livers)
2 tablespoons melted butter
1 teaspoon salt
½ cup celery leaves
2 small whole apples
2 small whole onions, peeled
2 slices lemon
2 cloves garlic (optional)
¼ teaspoon freshly ground pepper
6 slices salt pork, cut thin, or additional melted butter
Madeira Sauce (see page 133)

Preheat oven to 350°F.

Rub cavities of birds with melted butter, then with about ½ teaspoon of the salt. Place the celery leaves, apples, onions, lemon slices, and garlic cloves (if used) inside the birds. Sprinkle on remaining salt; dust with the pepper. Truss the birds, place the salt-pork slices over the breasts (or rub with additional melted butter), and roast them in an uncovered roasting pan from 15 to 30 minutes per pound, depending on your preference. Baste the birds frequently with the pan juices while they are cooking.

Transfer birds to a heated platter, discarding trussing string and salt-pork slices. Strain or pour off fat in roasting pan. Set pan aside. Serve a half duckling per person.

Serve with Madeira Sauce.

Makes 4 portions.

MADEIRA SAUCE

2 cups chicken stock (or canned chicken broth)
½ cup Madeira or port
2 duck livers (uncooked), coarsely chopped
Salt
Freshly ground black pepper
1 tablespoon cornstarch or arrowroot
2 tablespoons water

Add stock to roasting pan; stir over moderate heat, scraping up all coagulated juices until dissolved. Add the Madeira or port and cook until liquids are reduced to about 1½ cups. Add the chopped livers and simmer over reduced heat another 5 minutes. Add salt and pepper if needed. Make a smooth paste with the cornstarch or arrowroot and water; mix into sauce a little at a time until desired thickness is achieved. The sauce should coat the spoon lightly.

Makes 4 to 6 portions.

Roast Wild Goose with Chestnut Stuffing

6–8-pound young wild goose, ready to cook (reserve liver)

Juice of 1 lemon

1 teaspoon salt

¼ teaspoon freshly ground black pepper

4 tablespoons melted butter (or 6 slices salt pork, cut thin)

Chestnut Stuffing (see page 135)

2 or 3 juniper berries

½ cup gin

1¼ cups water

Preheat oven to 350°F.

Sprinkle the cavity of the goose with half the lemon juice and half the salt and pepper. Rub the melted butter, if used, over the goose, sprinkle it with the remainder of the lemon juice, then with remainder of the salt and pepper. Fill the cavity lightly with Chestnut Stuffing, close the opening with small skewers, and truss the bird. If using salt pork instead of melted butter, cover the breast with the salt-pork slices. Roast, breast side up, in an uncovered roasting pan, until tender, 2 to 3 hours. Combine juniper berries, gin, and ¾ cup water and baste the bird frequently with this mixture.

Transfer goose to a heated platter. Spoon or pour off accumulated fat in roasting pan, add ½ cup water to pan juices, and cook over moderate heat, stirring frequently, until coagulated pan juices are dissolved. Strain, then spoon some of this sauce over the goose just before serving and put the remainder in a pitcher or bowl.

Makes 6 to 8 portions.

Chestnut Stuffing

2 pounds chestnuts
½ cup melted butter
½ cup finely chopped onion
Goose liver
3 cups soft bread crumbs (from day-old French or Italian type)
½ cup cream (or chicken stock)
2 tablespoons chopped fresh parsley
1 teaspoon salt
½ teaspoon powdered ginger
¼ teaspoon freshly ground black pepper

With a small paring knife, cut slits in flat side of each chestnut. Place in a saucepan of cold water; bring to a boil. Cook several minutes, then remove pan from heat. Peel the outer shell and the inner skin from chestnuts. Remove only a few from the water at one time—chestnuts peel a bit better while they are warm. Return the peeled chestnuts to the saucepan of water; cook 10 minutes longer, or until they are tender. Put them through a coarse sieve or a food mill.

In a heavy skillet, heat a little of the melted butter and cook the onion and the goose liver for about 5 minutes. Chop the liver coarsely. Combine all ingredients, including remaining butter and chestnuts, tossing lightly with a fork until well mixed.

POULTRY

Be kind to poor hens in every way, and not let them suffer with hunger and cold; cruelty not in any way. . . . Hens must not have fish, it physics them. Hens must not have anything relaxing. . . . Be clever to them. They must not be affrighted. They can never get over it.

Hen's Gravestone

Poor little heart, ADA, QUEETIE,

O my heart is consumed

In the coffin underground,

O how I feel for her,

She and I could never part,

She was my own heart within me,

She had more than common love,

And more than common wit.

—The Works of Nancy Luce, 1888

Though few people become as enamored of hens as Miss Luce did,[†] those of us who have raised, known, and loved hens can never think of them as mindless and uninteresting. Like people, hens can be stupid or smart, curious and affectionate, or ill-tempered and unmanageable. They love to help with the gardening, and will murmur to you incessantly while laying their eggs, if there is a rapport between the two of you. Fortunately for hen lovers, no such nonsense

---

[†] For more on this incredible, hen-loving woman, consult the West Tisbury library, or see the material about her in Walter M. Teller's *Cape Cod and the Off-Shore Islands* (New York: Prentice Hall, 1970).

precedes the selection of a plump roasting chicken or tender broiler at the meat counter, for there is no denying that chicken is one of the most satisfactory meats we can eat. Relatively inexpensive, endlessly adaptable, delicious plain or fancy, hot or cold, chicken appears frequently on most American tables and is one food that almost everybody loves to eat.

Roast Chicken with Herbs and Lemon

4-pound roasting chicken (remove from refrigerator 1 hour
  before roasting)
1½ lemons
½ teaspoon salt
¼ teaspoon freshly ground black pepper
2 tablespoons butter, melted
1 teaspoon chopped fresh tarragon (or ½ teaspoon dried)
1 teaspoon chopped fresh parsley
½ teaspoon dill weed (dried may be used)
¼ teaspoon crushed coriander seed
⅛ teaspoon powdered ginger
½ cup chicken stock (or canned chicken broth)
½ teaspoon grated lemon rind
½ cup sour cream

Preheat oven to 350°F.

Rub inside of chicken with juice from ½ lemon and some of the salt and pepper. Rub the melted butter over the chicken; sprinkle with remaining salt and pepper. Truss the bird. Mix the herbs and spices and sprinkle over the chicken. Place in roasting pan, uncovered. Roast until the leg bone turns easily in its socket, or about 1 hour and 15 minutes; baste occasionally with pan juices. Remove chicken to a heated platter.

To the pan juices add the chicken stock and the juice from the remaining lemon. Cook over moderate heat, stirring thoroughly, scraping up the coagulated roasting juices to incorporate into liquids in pan. Add additional salt and pepper if necessary. Cook 5 to 10 minutes. Add the lemon rind. Turn off heat and blend in the sour cream. Pour into a sauce boat and serve immediately with the chicken.

Note: Paper-thin slices of lemon, about eight of them, may be substituted for the lemon rind. Add the slices to the sauce just before blending in the sour cream.

Makes 4 portions.

Roast Chicken with Pasta Stuffing

4–5 pound roasting chicken
6 medium mushrooms, chopped
1 tablespoon vegetable oil
6 scallions, chopped
6 ounces tube-type pasta
1 red pepper, roasted and
   chopped
½ cup Four-Basil Pesto (page 295)
½ cup chopped Italian parsley

½ cup freshly grated Parmesan
   cheese
Salt
Freshly ground black pepper
2 tablespoons butter or ½ tablespoon butter and ½ tablespoon
   garlic oil
½ teaspoon honey or corn syrup
1 teaspoon lemon zest

Preheat oven to 425°F.

Remove chicken from refrigerator while preparing stuffing.

Put mushrooms in unheated nonstick frying pan. Cook, stirring, on high heat until they begin to sizzle. Turn heat to low and cook until they release their moisture (about 3 minutes). Stir frequently. Add vegetable oil and scallions, raise heat to medium, and sauté 1 minute.

Cook pasta in salted boiling water until al dente. Drain, cool slightly, and combine in large bowl with scallion and mushroom mixture, red pepper, pesto, parsley, grated cheese, salt, and pepper. Mix well.

Stuff chicken with pasta mix and close opening with a heel of bread. Leftover stuffing can be inserted below skin at neck end. Combine butter, honey or corn syrup, and lemon zest, and heat enough to melt butter. Whisk to mix. Place chicken breast side up in roasting pan, pour half butter mixture over it, and put in preheated oven. After 15 minutes, lower the oven temperature to 350°F and baste with remaining butter mixture. Cook for a total of 1 to 1½ hours, or until leg moves easily in socket. Remove from oven and let sit for 10 minutes before serving.

Makes 6 to 8 portions.

Chicken Baked with Rum and Honey

Rum, a sugarcane product distilled chiefly in the semitropical West Indian islands, has long figured in the Vineyard scene. Clipper ships carried the "red rum of St. Thomas" home to New England; later, during prohibition, rum running was a lively business, and Vineyard seamen who knew their way around the local bays and channels were in great demand.

This recipe was developed by Louise Tate King some years ago when she was in charge of a mountainside restaurant in Charlotte Amalie, St. Thomas, during the winter months.

2 broiler chickens, about 2¼ pounds each, split, backs and
*   necks removed*
2 tablespoons butter, melted
1 teaspoon salt
¼ teaspoon freshly ground black pepper
½ cup rum—any kind, although the New England type is best
½ cup chicken stock (the stock may be made by simmering the backs,
*   necks, etc., with 1 carrot, ½ small onion, 1 small stalk of celery in*
*   a little water until chicken pieces are tender)*
½ cup honey

Preheat oven to 400°F.

Rub the chicken pieces with the melted butter; sprinkle with salt and pepper. Place them, skin side down, in a shallow roasting pan or flameproof baking dish of the appropriate size. Bake 20 to 25 minutes, or until skin is golden. Turn them and bake another 20 minutes.

Combine rum, chicken stock, and honey; baste the chicken with this mixture at frequent intervals for about another 20 minutes. The chicken is done when the leg turns easily in its socket. Transfer chicken to a heated serving dish and keep warm.

Place the roasting pan over direct heat and simmer the sauce slowly, scraping up the coagulated pan juices until dissolved. Continue to cook, stirring, until the sauce is reduced to about 1 cup. Strain the sauce, pour over broilers, and serve.

Note: Brandy, about ¼ cup, may be gently heated for a few moments, ignited, and poured over the chicken just before serving, either at table or in the kitchen, depending on one's flair for the dramatic.

Makes 4 portions.

Breast of Chicken with Artichoke Hearts

This dish can be prepared in the morning and refrigerated until an hour before cooking time. It is so simple to put together that it makes an uncomplicated choice for the cook. It is suggested that two casseroles be prepared. Freeze one to serve at a later time.

½ pound mushrooms, sliced

1 tablespoon fresh lemon juice

1 10-ounce can artichoke hearts, rinsed and well drained, then cut into quarters

1 tablespoon minced fresh ginger root

2 single chicken breasts, skinless and boneless, cut into 1½-inch chunks

2 tablespoons dry sherry or dry white wine

1 10¾-ounce can cream of chicken soup

2 tablespoons cornstarch

1 tablespoon water

½ cup fresh bread crumbs

½ cup freshly grated Parmesan cheese

In a large bowl, combine the mushrooms and lemon juice, then add the artichoke hearts and the minced ginger. Mix slightly, then add the chicken breasts. Mix gently. In a smaller bowl, place the sherry or white wine, the chicken soup, and the cornstarch, mixed to a smooth paste with the water. Mix these ingredients thoroughly, then combine carefully with the contents of the larger bowl.

Place all ingredients in a shallow casserole with a tight-fitting cover. Just before baking, combine the bread crumbs and the Parmesan cheese and sprinkle over the top of the casserole. Cover and bake on the middle shelf of a preheated 350°F oven for 20 minutes. Remove cover and bake another 10 minutes, or until brown and bubbly.

Nice to serve with your favorite green salad.

Makes 4 generous portions.

Chicken and Eggplant Casserole

This is an excellent casserole to prepare the day before you plan to spend a day at the beach. It can be reheated for a one-dish dinner when you get home. If you are in a hurry when making it, you need not brown the chicken pieces first; in that event, bake the casserole at a higher oven temperature.

1 cup flour
1 tablespoon salt
½ teaspoon freshly ground black pepper
4–5-pound roasting chicken, cut into 10 pieces (remove skin if desired)
2 tablespoons butter
2 tablespoons vegetable oil
Medium eggplant, unpeeled, cut into ¾-inch half circles
1 large can Italian tomatoes, drained (or 3 cups fresh tomatoes, cut in chunks)
2 cloves garlic, minced

1 green pepper, coarsely chopped
1 large onion, coarsely chopped
¼ pound fresh mushrooms, sliced
½ teaspoon dried oregano
½ teaspoon dried basil
4 tablespoons chopped fresh parsley
Additional salt and freshly ground black pepper, if desired
2 to 3 tablespoons grated Parmesan or Romano cheese (optional)
4 tablespoons olive oil, vegetable oil, or melted butter (optional)

Preheat oven to 325°F.

Put the flour, salt, and pepper in a heavy brown paper bag, drop in the chicken pieces, and shake vigorously until each piece is well coated with flour. Remove chicken from bag and shake off excess flour.

In a large, heavy skillet melt butter with the oil over moderate heat. When the butter foam subsides, brown the chicken pieces, skin side down first if unskinned; don't overcrowd the skillet. Set chicken aside. Transfer half the chicken to a heavy ovenproof casserole, about 4-quart capacity. Arrange half the eggplant, tomatoes, garlic, green pepper, onion, mushrooms, dried herbs, and parsley over the chicken. Sprinkle with additional salt and pepper, if desired.

Repeat, reserving remaining tomatoes and chopped parsley. Arrange the tomatoes and parsley on top; sprinkle with additional salt and pepper, and grated cheese if desired.

Bake, covered, for 2 hours. To reheat, remove from refrigerator 1 hour before serving. Place in preheated 300°F oven 25 to 30 minutes, until casserole is bubbling.

If you elect to eliminate browning the chicken pieces, bake the casserole, covered, for 1½ hours in a preheated 425°F oven, pouring the optional 4 tablespoons oil or melted butter over all ingredients.

The grated cheese topping (optional) will produce a golden-brown crust if the hot casserole is placed in a moderately hot broiler for a moment or two.

Makes 4 to 6 portions.

Chickeny Chicken

Somewhere in the process of mechanizing and "improving" poultry production, the flavor of chicken seems to have disappeared. If you are cooking an Island-raised, honest-to-God hen, allow it to generate its innate flavor by cooking it simply, without embellishments or camouflage. This recipe is for the chain store's weekend special.

Chickeny Chicken was developed by a partially blind octogenarian cook in West Tisbury who could no longer see well enough to make anything fancy but still set an enviable table. In other circumstances, in earlier days, she disdained "prepared" foods such as canned soups. Forced to use them, she did so with a flourish.

A big pot of this chicken was often ready when her family arrived on a late-night ferry for an out-of-season visit (they began anticipating dinner as far away as Providence). Simple and delicious, it delights everyone and is practically foolproof. The leftover liquid, cooled and skimmed of fat, can be used in various ways—in soup, or in cooking rice or barley, for instance.

4-pound roasting chicken, cut up (skin removed if preferred)
1 can cream of chicken soup (concentrated type)
1 teaspoon mustard, preferably Dijon type
¼ teaspoon freshly ground pepper

Wash chicken pieces well and remove extraneous fat. Place pieces directly in a large, heavy saucepan or flameproof casserole without preliminary browning. Combine soup and mustard. Pour over chicken. Sprinkle pepper over chicken pieces. Cover saucepan or casserole and cook chicken over very low heat for about 2 hours, until meat is almost falling off the bones. Lift and turn the pieces once or twice during the first 10 minutes to prevent their sticking to the pan.

This dish may also be cooked in a 300°F oven for about 2 hours. Prepare it the same way, using an ovenproof casserole with a good, tight cover.

Makes 4 to 6 portions.

Picnic Chicken

[Chicken Baked with Crumbs and Herbs]

Here is a splendid chicken recipe, good either hot or cold, and admirable because it can be done ahead of serving time. Cooled, it may be taken to the beach for a picnic supper or served on the patio. If it is to be presented hot, it is a simple matter to reheat it in the oven. In that case, remove dish from refrigerator 1 hour before serving. Allow 20 to 25 minutes in a preheated 350°F oven to reheat chicken.

2 broiler chickens, 2¼ pounds each, split, backs and necks removed
  (use the latter to make a little chicken stock)

8 tablespoons melted butter

½ teaspoon salt

4 tablespoons strong prepared mustard (Dijon type, preferably)

½ cup chicken stock (or canned chicken broth)

Pinch of cayenne pepper

1 teaspoon Worcestershire sauce

⅛ teaspoon Tabasco sauce

3 cups fresh bread crumbs (use day-old French or Italian type, preferably)

1 tablespoon chopped fresh parsley (or 1 teaspoon dried parsley)

½ teaspoon chopped fresh tarragon (or ¼ teaspoon dried tarragon)

¼ teaspoon chopped fresh basil (or a pinch of dried basil)

4 tablespoons finely chopped scallions (use some of the green tops, too)

¼ teaspoon freshly ground black pepper

Preheat oven to 450°F.

Brush the chicken halves with 3 to 4 tablespoons of the melted butter (or use half butter and half vegetable oil). Sprinkle with the salt. Bake in a shallow flameproof baking pan, skin side down, about 20 to 25 minutes, or until skin is golden. Baste several times. Turn the halves and continue to bake another 20 to 25 minutes; baste occasionally. The chicken is done when the leg turns easily in its socket. Remove chicken from pan; set aside.

To juices in baking pan add remaining butter, the mustard, chicken stock, cayenne, Worcestershire sauce, and Tabasco sauce. Cook over moderate heat until the mixture comes to a simmer, stirring and scraping up the coagulated pan juices until they are dissolved. Cook another few minutes. Remove from heat.

Preheat oven broiler to moderately hot.

Combine remaining ingredients in a mixing bowl, mixing thoroughly, then add to the liquids in the baking pan, lifting and stirring with a fork to allow the crumbs to absorb the liquids evenly.

Pat and press the crumb mixture onto the chicken halves so that the flavored crumbs adhere to both sides.

Brown the chicken halves in the broiler, 5 to 6 inches from the heat source. Watch carefully; the crumbs will brown quickly.

Remove chickens from broiler and cool them. If the chickens are to be eaten within an hour or so, it is not necessary to refrigerate them.

Note: If you prefer to serve the chicken hot but wish to do your cooking in advance, prepare it up to and including the crumb-coating process. Refrigerate until an hour before serving. About 15 minutes before serving time, place in a preheated 450°F oven, allowing chicken to reach serving temperature. Regulate the oven heat, if necessary, to avoid overbrowning the crumb coating.

Makes 4 to 6 portions.

Chicken Livers with Sherry and Cream

Featured at Louise Tate King's former restaurant, this recipe is useful because it is simple to prepare and it can be made an hour or so before dinner.

1 pound chicken livers, preferably fresh

Flour

½ teaspoon salt

¼ teaspoon freshly ground black pepper

2 tablespoons butter

2 tablespoons vegetable oil

½ pound fresh, firm mushrooms, sliced

1 tablespoon flour

¼ cup dry sherry

¼ cup chicken stock (canned chicken broth may be substituted)

½ cup cream

½ teaspoon fresh thyme, chopped (or ¼ teaspoon dried thyme)

Wipe the chicken livers dry. Cut large ones in two. Roll them in flour seasoned with the salt and pepper.

In a heavy skillet over moderate heat melt the butter with the oil. When the butter foam subsides, add the livers and cook until brown on one side, then turn them, but do not overcook—5 to 8 minutes in all is sufficient. Remove from skillet. Cook the mushrooms in the same skillet about 5 minutes. Remove them from skillet.

To the pan juices add the 1 tablespoon flour and blend carefully. Let simmer a few moments, then add sherry, chicken stock, and cream, and simmer until thickened. If sauce seems a trifle thick, dilute with a little additional chicken stock or cream.

Just before serving, return livers to the sherry sauce and reheat briefly without allowing the sauce to boil.

Sprinkle with the thyme and serve.

Makes 4 portions.

CHAPTER 6

Vegetables and Salads

The vegetable departments were well represented, comprehending every variety and size to be found in the category. It is useless to waste adjectives in vainly attempting to portray the enormity of the squashes, the stupendity of the pumpkins and the giganticity and general outrageousness of the turnips and beets.

—From the account of the first Dukes County Agricultural Fair, *Vineyard Gazette*, October 21, 1870

Vegetables grown on the Vineyard seem, at least to Vineyarders, to taste better than vegetables brought over on the ferry. Traditional upon arrival for many summer people is a visit to Morningside Farm in Edgartown or one of the other flourishing farm stands. Here they may pick up a box of gigantic, luscious strawberries or tiny new potatoes, or perhaps some fresh-pulled corn to roast while the swordfish broils, or a head of ruby lettuce almost too beautiful to eat.

Spring is the Vineyard's least appealing season—many residents, in fact, say there is none, we just go from winter into summer. A garden record for May 9 notes: "Cold! Snow in Boston! Afraid may lose our fruit," and for May 31: "Still windy and chilly every day—nothing up yet but lettuce." Yet slowly the icy waters warm, the wind softens, and the sun and the soft sea air nurture the crops all over the Island. And each August, as they have since 1870, gardeners and homemakers bring their finest, their ripest, their biggest—whether it be fifteen carefully matched string beans or two quarts of garden relish—to the West Tisbury Agricultural Fair to compete for the blue ribbons.

Though Vineyard gardens are slow to come up, they bear on and on and on into the bright, bracing days of October. A few sturdy plots are still producing in November—some nubbins of broccoli, a few handfuls of stunted but tasty beans, some hard-skinned, sweet-fleshed cherry tomatoes, and of course the important fall crops of squashes, rutabagas, turnips, and various hardy greens, to be eaten on into winter and even spring.

Green Beans in Cream

This recipe comes from a Nebraska cook, but since Vineyard gardens, like mainland ones, tend to produce masses and masses of green beans—until cooks grow tired of cooking them and diners tire of eating them—here is a slightly different preparation that might be welcome in bean season.

> *1 quart green beans*
> *1 cup medium cream or evaporated milk*
> *1 teaspoon salt*

Prepare beans for cooking—leave whole or cut up. Place in saucepan and add cream or evaporated milk and salt. Over moderate heat bring to a simmer, then lower heat at once and simmer for about ¾ hour, until most of the liquid has boiled away. Stir occasionally. Beans will be "cooked to death" but delicious.
Makes 4 portions.

Baby Beets

[With Dill and Sour Cream]

The Indian Hill section of West Tisbury is now all private property, with the exception of a mile-square area in Christiantown, where the tiny chapel and graveyard of the "praying Indians" are located, memorial land that now belongs to the county. Farmland, small ponds, early homesteads, and lovely lichen-covered stone walls that ramble way back into the woodlots characterize this charming area.

An Indian Hill resident with a good old Vineyard name, Mrs. Charles Norton, who once lived way down past Norton Circle, told us of an interesting way to prepare the tiny baby beets you can pull out of the row in your garden or buy from your local farm stand each summer season.

*12–16 baby beets, depending on
size (or 4 or 5 medium beets)*
1 teaspoon salt, or more
2 tablespoons butter
1 tablespoon flour
1 tablespoon honey
1 teaspoon vinegar

1 teaspoon lemon juice
½ teaspoon grated lemon rind
⅓ cup sour cream
*2 or 3 flowerets of fresh dill (if
not available, use ½ teaspoon
dill seed—or dill weed, if preferred)*

Cook beets, unpeeled, with the salt in water barely to cover until beets are tender. (Cooking time will vary with size and freshness of beets.) Drain them, reserving ½ cup of the beet liquor, and slip off skins. If tiny, leave whole; otherwise, cut in slices or chunks. Set prepared beets aside.

In a small saucepan melt the butter, add flour, and stir to a smooth paste. Simmer over low heat for 2 to 3 minutes. Add honey, vinegar, reserved beet liquor, lemon juice, and lemon rind. Bring to a simmer and cook for several minutes. If additional salt is needed, add it at this point. Return beets to this sauce (which will be quite thick) and simmer only long enough to bring up to serving temperature. Remove saucepan from heat; stir in the sour cream and the dill. Serve immediately.

Makes 4 portions.

Broccoli with Black-Olive Sauce

16 firm black olives, pitted and roughly chopped (about ¾ cup)
1 medium garlic clove, crushed and minced
3 tablespoons olive oil
½ teaspoon dried oregano
4 cups bite-size broccoli pieces
Freshly ground black pepper

Combine olive chunks, garlic, olive oil, and oregano in a mini food processor and pulse five or six times to blend. Or put in a small bowl and chop the mixture by hand. Cook broccoli about 5 minutes in large amount of boiling water. It should be bright green and still slightly crisp. Drain broccoli, return to pan, and stir in olive sauce. Mix well and serve. Freshly ground pepper will add to flavor, but salt is not needed because of the salty olives.

Note: This recipe works well with the small side shoots broccoli plants produce after the main head has been cut. Broccoli rabe could also be used.

Makes 4 to 6 portions.

Green Corn Pudding

This recipe appeared in the Martha's Vineyard Hospital cookbook, *Vineyard Fare;* it has also been printed in *Yankee* magazine and in Imogene Wolcott's delightful *Yankee Cookbook*. It is so delicious that it bears constant repetition.

Fresh ears of corn are urgently recommended. The starchy liquids vary according to the freshness and type of the corn used; therefore, the exact amount of milk to be added to the custard cannot be specified. The consistency, when the dish is ready for the oven, should resemble that of a cornbread mixture. For stripping the kernels from the cob, follow the procedure suggested in the Corn Chowder recipe (see page 11).

12–18 ears of corn (about 6 cups kernels—frozen corn may be used)

3 eggs, well beaten

2 tablespoons melted butter

1 tablespoon sugar (more if desired)

1 teaspoon salt

Milk or cream

2 teaspoons additional butter (optional)

Preheat oven to 250°F.

Strip kernels from corn ears; combine with all other ingredients except milk or cream and additional butter. Then add milk or cream until the mixture is the consistency of a cornbread or corn-muffin batter. Pour into a greased large, shallow baking dish. If desired, dot the top of the batter with 2 teaspoons additional butter. Bake 2 to 3 hours. The pudding should be nicely set and browned on top, and dry enough to cut easily into squares.

Note: Vineyarders sometimes serve this dish as a dessert. Additional sweetening may then be used. Also, the eggs should be separated, yolks and whites well beaten, and the stiff egg whites folded into the batter as the final addition.

Makes 8 portions as a main course or 10 portions as a dessert.

Eggplant Casserole

This recipe was developed by a summer Vineyard cook as a low-calorie version of a more elegant (but fattening) dish.

1 medium eggplant (unpeeled), cut in ½-inch slices
½ teaspoon salt
½ cup sliced, pitted ripe olives
6 scallions, cut fine
2 tablespoons olive oil
2½ cups tomato or mixed vegetable juice (more may be needed)
½ teaspoon oregano
¾ cup grated Parmesan cheese

Preheat oven to 325°F.

Wash and slice eggplant, discarding stem end. Salt slices and arrange them in one layer in a large, shallow ovenproof dish. Do not overlap. Scatter sliced olives over eggplant. In a large skillet, sauté cut-up scallions in olive oil for about 2 minutes over moderate heat. Add tomato or vegetable juice and oregano, lower heat, and simmer for about 20 minutes. Pour sauce over eggplant slices. If it doesn't quite cover them, add a bit more tomato juice. Sprinkle grated cheese over the top of the sauce and bake 35 to 45 minutes, or until most of sauce has been absorbed.

Makes 4 portions.

Baked Potato Chips

Only a step away from plain baked potatoes that are scrubbed, sometimes oiled, and popped in a hot oven, this variation takes only minutes to prepare and should please everyone, especially children, who may quarrel over who gets the crispiest, brownest, puffiest chips on the plate. Allow one good-sized potato for each person. Baking potatoes have the best texture, though any type can be used.

Preheat oven to 400°F. Scrub potatoes, then slice them lengthwise anywhere from ¼- to ½-inch thick. Place slices on lightly oiled baking sheet and bake about 30 minutes. The oven heat and baking time are flexible. If you are baking something else at anything above 300°F, adjust the potatoes' cooking period accordingly. If they are cooked but not browned when done at a lower temperature, slide them under a hot broiler for a few seconds to brown on top. Potatoes are cooked if soft when pierced with a fork. Thin slices tend to puff up more than thick ones; the hotter oven temperature also increases puffiness.

Note: There are several more elaborate versions of this recipe—slices oiled and herbed, spread with pesto, topped with cheese before baking. This one celebrates the goodness of the potato itself, not its trimmings.

New Potatoes with Herbs

Several local farmers sacrifice quantity for quality each summer by rooting around their still-growing potato plants and detaching tiny new potatoes, the size of large marbles, to sell to their customers. At the summer Farmers' Market, tiny fingerling potatoes bring premium prices. Baby potatoes have a delicate, fresh flavor and are marvelous just steamed until tender, dipped in salt, and popped into the mouth. Some people boil them in chicken broth with fresh peas. A cream sauce may be added for enrichment. This is another suggestion.

3 cups tiny new potatoes

1 cup chicken stock (or 1 cup water and 1 chicken bouillon cube)

1 teaspoon chopped fresh chives (optional)

*1 tablespoon chopped fresh herbs (almost any combination of dill,
    parsley, chervil, summer savory, thyme; or dill or chervil alone)*

2 tablespoons butter

Salt to taste (if needed)

Freshly ground black pepper

Wash and scrub potatoes gently but do not peel. Put chicken stock or water and bouillon cube in a saucepan; if using the latter, heat until cube is dissolved. Add potatoes and bring to a boil, then cover and cook over moderate heat 10 to 15 minutes, until potatoes are tender. Shake pan several times to move potatoes around so they will cook evenly (if stirred with a spoon or fork, their skins may be torn). Remove from heat, drain, and add chives, if desired, other herbs, butter, salt if needed, and pepper. Shake or mix gently; replace over low heat until butter is melted and potatoes are well coated.

Makes 4 portions.

Arrowhead Summer Squash

[Two versions]

In the service shed at Arrowhead Farm, along with the artistically laid-out young vegetables that were their proud offering, the Fergusons sometimes used to set out a blackboard with a customer's recipe chalked on it—a practice that their young successors continued as long as the farm was in operation. One of the customers carried the instructions for cooking yellow summer squash home in her head and happily made it with basil for several years, until a dinner guest who had taken the time to copy the recipe down advised her it was supposed to be made with mint. We think it is delectable either way.

8–10 yellow summer squash,
   3–4 inches long
1/2 teaspoon salt
1 tablespoon butter
1/2 cup sour cream

1/4–1/2 cup chopped fresh basil or
   mint leaves
Freshly ground black pepper
   (if desired)

Wash squash, cut off stem and blossom ends. If a vegetable steamer is used, place it in a large saucepan and add 1 inch water. Add whole squash and steam over moderate heat until fork tender, 10 to 15 minutes. If preferred, squash may be placed in large saucepan with sufficient water to cover bottom of pan, covered tightly, and cooked 10 to 15 minutes, until fork tender. Try not to overcook, as this destroys much of their delicate flavor. Remove squash and steamer; discard water. Replace squash in saucepan, slice with fork and knife or mash lightly with masher. Sprinkle with salt; stir in butter and sour cream; stir in basil or mint. Add pepper if desired (however, this recipe is good without it). If necessary, heat just enough to warm to serving temperature. Do not simmer or sour cream will curdle.

Makes 6 portions.

Summer Squash Casserole

4 small summer squash, one variety or mixed
1 small onion
2½ tablespoons butter
1 teaspoon chicken broth powder
Salt
Freshly ground black pepper
2 eggs
¾ cup light cream
½ cup grated cheese, cheddar or qruyere
1 tablespoon freshly grated Parmesan cheese

Preheat oven to 350°F.

Slice squash and onion. Sauté briefly in butter. Stir in chicken broth powder. Put in greased casserole and add salt and pepper to taste. Beat eggs, then mix in cream. Pour mixture over squash. Sprinkle with cheese. Bake until lightly browned and set, about ½ hour.

Makes 4 portions.

Butternut Squash or Pumpkin Casserole

Local farmers begin bringing these hefty vegetables in from the fields about mid-October, and by Halloween most Vineyard households have a butternut squash or two on hand for dinner and at least one bright orange pumpkin on display outside. Rather than leave these seasonal decorations out to freeze and rot, try bringing them in and using them as an alternative choice in this delectable casserole, one variation of many modest vegetable casseroles developed among the peasantry of Provençe.

4-pound butternut squash or pumpkin
Flour for dusting (about ⅓ cup)
1 or 2 tablespoons white or brown sugar (optional)
1 teaspoon dried marjoram

4 garlic cloves, minced
¼ cup freshly grated Parmesan cheese
½ teaspoon salt
Freshly ground black pepper
⅓ cup extra virgin olive oil

Preheat oven to 400°F.

Slice, seed, and peel squash or pumpkin, and cut into 1-inch chunks. Oil shallow baking dish large enough to hold chunks in one layer, and fill with cut-up vegetable. In small bowl, mix all remaining ingredients except olive oil and sprinkle evenly over vegetable. Dribble olive oil on top, place dish in oven, and bake about 35 minutes, or until top is well crisped.

Makes 4 portions.

Squash Blossoms and Scrambled Eggs

2 tablespoons butter
1 green pepper, minced
½ medium onion, minced
6 eggs, beaten
1 cup minced squash blossoms
½ teaspoon chopped fresh basil (or ⅛ teaspoon dried basil)
Salt to taste
Freshly ground black pepper to taste

Melt butter in a heavy skillet over moderate heat. Sauté green pepper and onions 3 or 4 minutes, then add remaining ingredients and scramble in the usual manner. Additional butter may be needed in pan before eggs are added.

Makes 3 portions.

Succotash

The Vineyard's early settlers discovered the pleasures of this vegetable combination from the Indians. The Indian name for the dish seems to have been *m'sickquatash* (meaning "the grains are whole," thus distinguishing this use of corn from the more common meal form). It is a delight when made from fresh corn, cut from the cob, and freshly shelled baby lima beans. Try cooking the vegetables with a small chunk of salt pork.

½ cup water
2 tablespoons butter (or about ⅛ pound salt pork)
2 cups hulled baby lima beans
1 teaspoon salt (less if salt pork is used)
Freshly ground black pepper
½ teaspoon sugar
2 cups fresh corn, cut from cob
⅓ cup whole milk or light cream

Bring water and butter or salt pork to a simmer in a saucepan, then add beans (frozen beans—and frozen corn—may be used, but their flavor is inferior), salt, pepper, and sugar. Simmer until beans are tender, about 10 minutes. Add corn and simmer another 5 minutes. Stir in the milk or cream (the water should have been absorbed by now; if not, pour it off first). Heat but do not allow to boil. Check seasonings and serve immediately. If salt pork is used, remove it before serving the succotash.

Makes 6 portions.

Tomato Pie

1 frozen 9-inch pastry shell
4 medium-size ripe tomatoes, sliced ½-inch thick
¼ cup chopped chives, or scallion stalks
1 teaspoon chopped fresh basil (or ¼ teaspoon dried basil, crumbled)
¼ teaspoon salt, or to taste
¼ teaspoon freshly ground black pepper
1 cup grated Swiss cheese
¼ cup mayonnaise

Preheat oven to 425°F.

Bake pastry shell for 5 minutes. Remove from oven. Reduce heat to 400°F. Cut tomato slices in half and place them on bottom of shell. Sprinkle them with the chives or scallions, basil, salt, and pepper. Combine cheese and mayonnaise, then carefully spread mixture evenly over tomatoes, making sure it reaches the edges of the pie crust and seals in the tomatoes completely.

Bake pie 35 minutes or until brown and bubbly. Allow it to sit outside the oven 5 or 10 minutes before serving.

Note: This is a lovely dish. It is most enjoyable as a summer luncheon, when ripe tomatoes come right from the vine. Its success is uncertain when it is prepared with out-of-season tomatoes.

Makes 6 portions.

Summer Spaghetti Sauce

1 quart stewed fresh tomatoes (or 1 large can Italian tomatoes)
1 6-ounce can tomato paste
½ cup olive oil
6–8 good-sized garlic cloves, minced or put through press
1 large green pepper, coarsely chopped
1 cup chopped parsley, loosely packed
1 teaspoon salt
Freshly grated Parmesan or Romano cheese

Combine all ingredients in a 3- or 4-quart kettle (a large one is needed because sauce will splatter). Stir to mix, bring to a boil over high heat, then lower heat and cook sauce slowly for at least 1 hour, stirring occasionally to prevent sticking. It is important to use the full amount of both garlic and parsley; the more garlic, the better the sauce (a French chicken recipe calls for 40 cloves). This sauce keeps well; in fact, it is better if allowed to sit in the refrigerator a day or two before use. Or make a large batch with vegetables from your own garden, freeze in small containers, and enjoy this fresh-tasting sauce right through the winter. Serve hot over hot, freshly cooked spaghetti; sprinkle with freshly grated Parmesan or Romano cheese before serving.

Makes 6 to 8 portions.

Pasta with Fennel and Tomatoes

1 medium-size fennel bulb (no
    stalk), cut into short slices
    about ⅛-inch thick
½ teaspoon fennel seeds
2 cloves garlic, minced
½ teaspoon salt, or to taste
Dash chili powder or crushed red
    pepper
1 cup pureed canned tomatoes

Freshly ground black pepper
2 tablespoons extra virgin olive
    oil
⅓ pound spaghetti or linguine
¼ cup small mozzarella cubes
2 tablespoons freshly grated
    Parmesan cheese
2 tablespoons chopped fresh basil
    (or 1 teaspoon dried basil)

Preheat oven to 450°F.

Oil a standard 8-inch pie pan. Combine sliced fennel, fennel seeds, and minced garlic in small bowl, then spread evenly over bottom of pie pan. Mix salt and chili powder or crushed red pepper, and stir into pureed tomatoes. Spread evenly over fennel (a spatula is useful for this). Grind black pepper over top, then dribble with olive oil. Place in oven and bake uncovered for about 30 minutes.

Meanwhile, cook and drain pasta. Remove sauce from oven, combine two cheeses and basil, and mix into sauce. Serve over hot pasta.

Makes 2 generous portions.

A Garden Casserole

This is a marvelous dish—a simplified version of the famed Mediterranean concoction, ratatouille. Once the ingredients are assembled, it can be prepared for the oven in 5 minutes; it can be cooked at one time and warmed up sometime later; eaten cold; or left, ready to cook, all day on top of the stove and popped in the oven in late afternoon. It is delicious with both fish and meat; served with either and followed by a green salad and cheese or fruit, it makes a nourishing meal. It is equally good at subsequent meals. Proportions of the vegetables can be adjusted to accommodate whatever the gardener brings in; and people who think they don't like eggplant eat it with murmurs of delight. Made in a handsome white or bright-colored serving dish, this casserole is beautiful to look upon both before and after it is cooked.

1 large eggplant, unpeeled
4 zucchini, about 5 inches long
2 medium onions, peeled
4 large, ripe tomatoes, unpeeled
  (a large can of Italian toma-
  toes, drained of excess juice,
  may be substituted but is not
  as good)
1 large green pepper, with seeds

and membranes removed
3 cloves garlic, chopped
1 tablespoon salt
½ teaspoon cracked black pepper,
  more if desired (or a pinch
  cayenne pepper)
4 sprigs parsley, chopped
½ cup olive oil

Preheat oven to 300°F.

Cut the eggplant into ½-inch circles, the other vegetables a bit thinner, and arrange them more or less in layers in a 2-quart ovenproof casserole. Sprinkle some of the salt and whichever pepper you use on the sliced vegetables as you go along.

Arrangement is not too important, but do try to make the vegetables look pretty. When the vegetables (including the garlic, which need not be chopped too fine) are all used up, sprinkle the rest of the salt and pepper and the chopped parsley over the top, and pour the olive oil over everything. Bake, covered, for 1½ hours, or until all vegetables are soft when pierced with a fork. Let cool a bit before serving. If time is short, you may cook the casserole at 425°F for ½ hour, then lower heat to 300°F, and cook another ½ hour or so.

Makes 8 portions.

Roast Vegetable Mélange

This simple vegetarian dinner needs only a green salad and a dessert to complete it. Vegetables may be used in almost any combination, but the results are more satisfactory if at least five are included.

Preparation is as follows: Oil one large baking sheet or several small ones. Preheat oven to 400°F as you work. Slice all vegetables, cutting slow-cookers like carrots and winter squash thinner than quick-cooking ones like tomatoes and summer squash. Most of the winter vegetables could be steamed briefly before going on the baking sheet, if desired. To avoid having leftover cut vegetables, arrange them in the pan or pans as you go along. Put in a bit of everything, then repeat until pan is full. Do not overlap. Sprinkle herbs and other seasonings (see *note* below) over the top of sliced vegetables. Dribble a generous amount of extra virgin olive oil over everything and place pan in oven. Bake summer vegetables about 35 minutes, winter ones 45 minutes to 1 hour. Check with fork for doneness. Serve hot or at room temperature.

Recommended vegetables for winter mélange: carrots, leeks, butternut or other winter squash, potatoes, red peppers, fennel, brussels sprouts. Other suggestions: parsnips, celeriac, portabello mushrooms, eggplant, rutabaga, cauliflower, Vidalia onions. A choice of seasonings: garlic, marjoram, oregano, rosemary, sage, paprika, curry powder, crushed red pepper flakes, dried sage.

Recommended vegetables for summer mélange: plum tomatoes, green peppers, scallions, eggplant, new potatoes, zucchini, yellow squash, okra. Other suggestions: mushrooms, broccoli, jalapeño peppers, green beans. A choice of seasonings: garlic, crushed red pepper flakes, herbs such as fresh coriander, parsley, rosemary, basil, dill, and tarragon.

Note: The fresh herbs are used to best advantage if snipped over the vegetables after they are cooked.

Summery Salad

Wash, dry, and tear into bite-size pieces an assortment of lettuces, allowing about two handfuls per serving if you are big salad eaters. Include some red-leaf lettuce if possible. Place lettuce in a salad bowl, add about ½ cup sliced sweet onions, and mix. Red onions add attraction. Add to ½ cup vinaigrette dressing 1 teaspoon orange juice and ½ teaspoon grated orange rind. Mix well.

Gather about 1 cup of edible flowers from your garden. Do not pick any whose edibility is not established, no matter how pretty they are. And avoid those which, though edible, are too strongly flavored for this delicate salad (goldenrod and thyme, for instance). Here are some suggestions: nasturtiums, bachelor's buttons, calendulas, dandelions, pinks, chives, roses, day lilies, violets, pansies, lavender, and borage, one of the prettiest. Gently remove stems from petals and tear or shred flowers into small pieces. Restir dressing, pour over green salad, and mix well. Scatter the flowers over the top. Mix flowers in at the table just before serving.

Note: When this salad was tried out on friends, the six-year-old delegated to mix in the flowers peered in the bowl and exclaimed, "A Japanese beetle!" Watch out for these nasty pests if you are picking your flowers when they are around.

Makes 4 portions.

Zucchini with Fresh Mint and Feta Cheese

A French friend now living on Martha's Vineyard discovered this recipe in a French culinary magazine, happily for us.

8–10 zucchini, about 4 inches
 long
2 medium onions
⅓ cup olive oil
2 lemons
14 coriander seeds, lightly
 crushed

Freshly ground black pepper
Salt
1 cup feta cheese
Handful of fresh mint, stems
 removed

Wash and trim zucchini but do not peel. Cut into bite-size pieces. Peel and mince onions. Squeeze the lemons and mix half the juice with the olive oil.

Combine zucchini, onions, and coriander seeds in a heavy saucepan. Pour over them the lemon juice and oil mixture. Add freshly ground pepper to taste and a restrained pinch of salt (the feta will add more salt). Stir to mix ingredients, cover, and cook over moderate heat 8 to 10 minutes or until zucchini is crisp tender. Remove from heat, uncover, and let cool.

Meanwhile, chop feta cheese into small bits. Wash, dry, and chop the mint, reserving six or seven sprigs for garnish. When the zucchini mixture is lukewarm, stir in feta cheese, mix gently, and add as much of the remaining lemon juice as desired. Transfer to a serving dish and garnish with the mint sprigs. Serve at room temperature or chilled.

Makes 6 portions.

Squeezed Cucumber Salad

A simple way to enhance this delicately flavored vegetable.

5 cucumbers of equal size
1 tablespoon salt, preferably coarse
Sugar
White vinegar
Chopped fresh dill (optional)

Peel cucumbers and slice them very thin. Place the slices in a bowl and sprinkle them with the salt. Mix well, transfer to a colander, set colander over the bowl, and allow cucumbers to drain for several hours.

Squeeze the cucumbers, a handful at a time, place slices in a bowl, and add sugar and white vinegar to taste. Aim for a sweet-sour balance.

Transfer cucumbers to a pretty serving dish and refrigerate until ready to serve. Sprinkle with chopped fresh dill, if desired.

Note: An interesting sauce for cold poached salmon can be made by adding yogurt, chopped dill, and chopped scallions to the cucumbers. Spoon the sauce over the fish at serving time.

Makes 4 to 5 cups.

Arugula, Tomato, and Feta Cheese Salad

Italians have been growing arugula for years. Now we, too, know it as a delicious salad. It is peppery, crisp, and refreshing, and there are many of us who are addicted to it. Grow it in your garden. It likes cool weather, so plant it early in the spring and again in August for a fall crop.

3 large handfuls or 3 bunches of arugula, coarse stems removed
6 small tomatoes (about 1½ pounds), sliced, or 12 cherry
*   tomatoes, sliced in half*
¼ pound feta cheese, coarsely crumbled (about 1 cup)
2 tablespoons finely chopped fresh basil or oregano
Dressing (see below)

Wash the arugula leaves and dry them well. Divide them among six salad plates and arrange the sliced tomatoes on them. Divide the feta cheese among the plates and sprinkle the basil or oregano on top. Dressing may be applied at serving time or served separately at the table.

DRESSING
2 tablespoons red wine vinegar
⅓ cup olive oil
1 garlic clove, finely minced
½ teaspoon Dijon-type mustard
½ teaspoon salt (omit if feta is salty)

In a blender combine all ingredients and whiz until well emulsified.

Note: Dried basil is not recommended; it loses its perfume in the drying process. Dried oregano is a satisfactory substitute, but use less of it than of the fresh herb.

Makes 6 portions.

Christmas Eve Salad

Certain menus are often traditional at family meals on various holidays. Christmas Eve supper for one Island family is always the same: A big bowl of oyster stew, made by simply dropping lots of plump native oysters into a pot of simmering milk enriched with cream and a dab of butter, then generously peppered. A basket of toasted and lightly buttered English muffins. And a huge platter of this colorful salad that can be constructed in whatever proportions tastes dictate (this family favors lots of avocado and orange).

Assemble as needed ripe avocados, big sweet slicing onions, Belgian endive, red and yellow peppers, temple or California oranges (or you might try some of the specialty oranges that show up around the holidays). Slice the vegetables and fruits as neatly as possible and arrange them on your prettiest platter either in separate piles or mixed together. Bits of parsley or watercress can be added for garnish, or the whole salad can be arranged atop a bed of red lettuce and curly endive. An elegant touch—nontraditional, full of calories, but delicious—would be a generous sprinkling of nuts. Pecans, walnuts, cashews, or macadamias would all be good. Mix up an appropriate amount of a good vinaigrette dressing to which has been added a teaspoon or so of orange juice, some grated orange peel, and a little brown sugar or honey, and pour this over the salad. Or, if preferred, serve the dressing separately in a small pitcher and allow each diner to help himself. Provide a small utensil for mixing, as some of the dressing ingredients tend to settle.

Grapefruit and Red Onion Salad

A variation on the popular combination of orange and onion with salad greens, this version is nicely refreshing in winter, when the palate appreciates the pairing of citrus and onion and the tang of these two salad greens.

2 small seedless grapefruit
2 small red onions
3 cups bite-size pieces of curly endive (sometimes sold as frizée)
3 cups bite-size pieces of watercress, stems removed
Vinaigrette dressing
1 teaspoon grated orange rind (optional)

Peel grapefruit, divide into sections, and carefully remove all white membranes and pulp. A sharp knife is helpful in separating membranes from the fruit, and you may want to work over a small bowl to catch the juice. Try to keep sections as intact as possible. Slice onions into very thin pieces. Gently wash and dry the two greens, then combine grapefruit, onions, and greens. Mix gently, then toss with 6 tablespoons vinaigrette dressing, or more if desired. A teaspoon of grated orange rind may be added to the dressing to intensify the citrus flavor.

Note: Ingredients may be prepared in advance and stored in separate bags in the refrigerator until shortly before serving time.

Makes 6 portions.

Spinach, Fennel, and Walnut Salad

5 ounces fresh spinach (½ of 10-ounce package)
4–5 leaves radicchio
¾ pound fennel, bulb only
½ cup walnuts, chopped and lightly toasted
½ cup crumbled gorgonzola cheese
2 tablespoons canola or other vegetable oil
1 tablespoon walnut oil
1 tablespoon wine vinegar
Salt
Freshly ground black pepper

Wash and spin dry spinach (use fresh young leaves only) and radicchio. Tear into bite-size pieces. Quarter fennel bulb lengthwise, cut in half, then slice into thin strips.

Place greens and fennel in salad bowl, add walnuts and cheese, and toss to mix. Combine oils, vinegar, salt, and pepper to taste, and whisk until well blended. Pour over salad and toss again.

Makes 4 generous portions.

Tricolored Salsa

M ulticolored vegetables and a unique method of preparation distinguish this salsa from most others.

2 tablespoons butter
3 large yellow tomatoes
3 large red tomatoes
3 large purple or pink tomatoes
    (or 3 more either red or yel-
    low)
1 large green pepper
1 large red pepper

1 large yellow pepper
4 jalapeño peppers
2 cloves garlic, minced
¼ teaspoon salt
¼ teaspoon white pepper
1 tablespoon lime juice
1 large handful fresh cilantro,
    chopped

Peel and chop all the tomatoes. Chop green, red, and yellow peppers. Chop jalapeño peppers after removing seeds and white linings, unless you want your salsa *very* hot.

Place all vegetables and all other ingredients in a large mixing bowl and combine well. Portion into several freezer containers and freeze 8 to 10 hours or overnight to blend the flavors. About 2 hours before serving, remove desired amount of salsa from freezer and place in colander to thaw and drain (this will reduce the bulk by almost half). Serve at room temperature.

Note: Fresh, ripe vegetables, preferably homegrown, are important in this recipe. Its author uses her own heirloom tomatoes in her salsa, which is especially savory. For an out-of-season version, cherry or plum tomatoes and imported yellow and red peppers could be used. A purple pepper could be added for an additional dash of color.

Makes about 3 cups when finished.

Turkey and Barley Salad

¾ cup chopped scallions

1 large stalk celery, chopped (use some leaves)

2 tablespoons peanut oil

2 cups bite-size turkey meat, at least half dark

1 cup cooked barley

1 cup cooked wild rice

1 tablespoon soy sauce

2 teaspoons hoisin sauce

½ cup chopped oil-cured black olives

1 teaspoon dark sesame oil

2 tablespoons fresh lemon juice

½ cup coarsely chopped dry-roasted peanuts

Salt (optional)

Freshly ground black pepper

3 tablespoons chopped parsley

In a small skillet, sauté the scallions and celery briefly in the peanut oil (about 2 minutes). In a large mixing bowl combine all remaining ingredients and mix well. Stir in scallions and celery when cool. Refrigerate salad several hours before serving. Serve at room temperature.

Note: An additional cup of cooked barley may be substituted for the wild rice, but the taste and texture of the salad will not be quite as interesting. Also, the peanuts and parsley can be added just before the salad is served to preserve their texture.

Makes 4 to 6 portions.

Couscous Salad

An important event in the national horticultural world and a momentous occasion on the Vineyard was the opening, on a sparkling June day in 1998, of the new Polly Hill Arboretum, one of the most important plant collections in the country. A scrumptious luncheon for about 150 people was prepared and served under a huge yellow tent. The menu included a delectable chicken salad, strawberry shortcake topped with dead-ripe local strawberries, and this unusual couscous salad. We liked it so much we jotted down as many of the ingredients as we could recognize and devised this version.

2½ cups water
1 cup regular or whole wheat couscous
⅓ cup golden raisins
¾ cup cooked wild rice
¾ cup cooked corn kernels
⅓ cup chopped sun-dried tomatoes
4 tablespoons chopped Kalamata olives
¼ cup olive oil

3 tablespoons lime juice
Zest of 1½ limes
½ teaspoon salt
Freshly ground black pepper to taste
3 tablespoons chopped cilantro
3 scallions, chopped
¾ cup sliced, toasted almonds or pecans

Bring water to boil in medium saucepan. Remove from heat and stir in couscous and raisins. Mix well and let stand for 10 minutes, then fluff. Mix in rice, corn, tomatoes, and olives, then spoon into medium-size bowl. In small bowl, whisk together olive oil, lime juice, zest, salt, and pepper. Pour over couscous and mix gently. Stir in cilantro, scallions, and nuts, using fork to mix. Let sit briefly to blend. Serve at room temperature.

Makes 10 portions.

CHAPTER 7

Blueberries and Cranberries

BLUEBERRIES

The small bush creepeth along upon the ground, scarce rising half a yard high, with divers small dark green leaves set in the green branches . . . [the flowers] pass into small round berries . . . of a purple, sweetish, sharp taste; the juice of them give a purplish colour to the hands and lips that eat and handle them. . . .

—*Culpeper's Complete Herbal,* 1640

Whatever name you call them—high-bush, low-bush, early sweet, late low, or sour-top blueberries, whortleberries, huckleberries, dangleberries, whorts, hurts, bilberries—the fruit of the twenty or more species of *Vaccinium* and *Gaylussacia* are popped into almost every mouth on the Vineyard during blueberrying time. Discriminating pickers tend to seek out one variety and pass up the others, but most of us just drop anything that's ripe and within reach into our pans and serve them all up together. The black huckleberries—the dark-colored berries that lack that lovely dusting of soft blue—have tiny, hard seeds, but their spicy flavor overbalances this slight flaw. High-bush blueberries in full fruit are a spectacular sight—ten feet high and laden with ripe berries. There are acres of them on the Vineyard, but don't expect a berry picker to tell you where they are. He probably guards his secret jealously, because there is a sort of magic about blueberrying alone or with one special friend in a high, rock-studded Vineyard meadow on a blue-skied summer afternoon that is too precious to share at random.

Blueberry Puddings

[One old, one adaptation]

From *The Dinner Cookbook,* published by Scribner's in 1878 and reproduced here from its reprint in the *Vineyard Gazette* some years later, comes this intriguing recipe for a blueberry dessert. (See page 184 for the contemporary version.)

BLUEBERRY PUDDING WITH SWEET SAUCE

1 pint of milk

2 eggs

*1 quart of flour (or enough for
    thick batter)*

1 gill baker's yeast

1 saltspoonful of salt

*1 teaspoon soda dissolved in
    boiling water*

*1 quart of blueberries, dredged
    in flour*

Make the batter and let it rise in a warm place for four hours. When very light, stir in the berries lightly and quickly; pour into a buttered dish and bake one hour, covering with paper should it "crust" over too fast. Turn out and eat with Sweet Sauce.

SWEET SAUCE

3 tablespoons of powdered sugar

2 cups of cream

2 teaspoons of rosewater

Sift sugar into cream and add the rosewater.

Confusions arise when one starts to prepare this dish. "1 gill of baker's yeast" becomes ½ cup; if today's dried yeast were used, the batter would rise to heroic proportions. How much boiling water is needed to "dissolve the teaspoon of soda"—enough to make a paste, or more? And how is the gill of yeast treated? If it is dissolved with the soda, the boiling water would of course destroy the leavening capacities of the yeast organisms. How much is a "saltspoonful of salt"? And, most important of all, if one were to "stir in the quart of berries dredged in flour" four hours after preparing the yeast-risen batter, the berries would be a sodden, pasty mess, a sad aftermath to the pleasant time spent picking them in a breeze-swept Vineyard pasture.

Today's recipes, formulated in more precise terms for the busy cook, promise successful results. Here is a contemporary version of a blueberry pudding that should please any cook, whether novice or expert.

STEAMED BLUEBERRY PUDDING

2 cups sifted flour

4 teaspoons baking powder

½ teaspoon salt

3 tablespoons sugar

3 tablespoons butter

1 tablespoon lemon juice

2 tablespoons molasses
   (optional but very good)

⅞ cup milk

2 tablespoons flour

1½ cups blueberries, leaves
   and stems removed

Vanilla ice cream or whipped
   cream

Resift the 2 cups flour with baking powder, salt, and sugar. Work in the butter with a pastry blender or the fingertips. Combine lemon juice, molasses if used, and milk and add to flour mixture. Sift the 2 tablespoons flour over the blueberries and add them to other ingredients. Avoid overmixing. Grease a 1-quart mold or a 1-quart earthenware bowl and fill it two-thirds full with the pudding mixture. If your pudding mold has no cover or an earthenware bowl is used, cover with foil or a clean dish towel and tie to the sides with string. Place either mold or bowl in a large pot; pour in enough boiling water to come three-quarters of the way up the mold or bowl. Cover the pot tightly and cook over low heat 1½ to 2 hours. Replenish the water as needed. A small rack or trivet may be used to support the mold while it is steaming.

Turn out the pudding on a serving platter. Serve with vanilla ice cream or whipped cream.

Makes 4 generous portions.

Blueberry Grunt
[Sometimes called Blueberry Pot Pie or Blueberry Slump]

BLUEBERRY SAUCE

2 cups fresh blueberries

½ cup sugar

1 cup water

1 tablespoon lemon juice

Remove stems and leaves from berries, if any. Wash the berries. Combine them with sugar, water, and lemon juice in a heavy 4-quart saucepan, cover tightly, and cook several minutes over moderate heat until the berries are barely tender. (They will finish cooking with the dumplings.) Remove from heat.

DUMPLINGS

1 cup sifted all-purpose flour

2 teaspoons baking powder

¼ teaspoon salt

1 teaspoon sugar (optional)

½–¾ cup milk

Heavy cream or whipped cream

 (optional)

Resift the flour with the baking powder, salt, and sugar, if used. Stir in sufficient milk so that the dumpling dough will drop readily from a spoon.

Return blueberry sauce to stove; over low heat bring to a gentle simmer. Drop the dough from a tablespoon over the blueberry sauce—the dumplings should measure 1½ to 2 inches. Cover pan tightly and cook about 15 to 20 minutes.

Spoon the dumplings into shallow soup plates, covering them with the berry sauce. Serve with heavy cream or slightly sweetened whipped cream, if desired.

A salty Chilmark acquaintance remarks that the dumplings are to be "bailed out of the pot" at serving time.

Makes 4 generous portions.

Blueberry Crisp

3 cups blueberries (if frozen or
    canned are used, drain well)

½ cup sugar

¼ teaspoon mace or nutmeg

¼ teaspoon cinnamon

1 tablespoon lemon juice

½ teaspoon grated lemon rind

¾ cup sifted all-purpose flour

½ cup sugar (brown sugar may
    be substituted)

6 tablespoons butter, softened

¼ teaspoon salt

¼ cup nut meats, chopped
    (optional but recommended)

Whipped cream or vanilla ice
    cream (optional)

Preheat oven to 350°F.

Remove stems and leaves, if any, from blueberries. Wash and drain the berries and place in a mixing bowl. Add sugar, spices, lemon juice, and rind; mix lightly. Place the mixture in a shallow 1- to 2-quart casserole or baking dish.

Prepare the crumb topping as follows:

Combine in a mixing bowl the flour, sugar, butter, and salt. With the fingers or a pastry blender, work these ingredients to a crumbly consistency. Sprinkle over the berry mixture, adding the nut meats, if they are used.

Bake 30 minutes, or until the topping is nicely browned and the fruit is tender. Serve with sweetened whipped cream or a scoop of vanilla ice cream, if you wish.

Makes about 6 portions.

Lemon-Blueberry Pie

2 eggs, separated
1 cup sugar
4 teaspoons flour
⅛ teaspoon salt
Grated rind of 1 lemon
Juice of 1 lemon

1 teaspoon melted butter
¾ cup milk, scalded
9-inch unbaked pie shell (see
    page 304)
1½ cups fresh blueberries

Preheat oven to 450°F.

Beat the egg yolks until light and thick. Combine sugar, flour, and salt; add the egg yolks, lemon rind, lemon juice, and butter. Beat well. Gradually beat in the scalded milk. Beat the egg whites stiff and fold them in. Pour the mixture into the unbaked pie shell and sprinkle the blueberries on top. Bake 10 minutes on middle shelf of oven. Reduce heat to 350°F and bake an additional 30 minutes. Let pie cool; then chill it thoroughly and serve very cold. A little egg white brushed on the pie shell before filling it will help to prevent sogginess.

Note: Thinly sliced fresh peaches or rhubarb, or raspberries or strawberries could be used instead of blueberries. The mixture may also be baked as a fruit pudding, without the pastry.

Blueberry–Cottage Cheese Pie

GRAHAM-CRACKER CRUST

1½ cups graham-cracker crumbs

¼ cup sugar

½ cup melted butter

⅛ teaspoon nutmeg

Preheat oven to 350°F.

Mix graham-cracker crumbs, sugar, melted butter, and nutmeg thoroughly in a bowl, pressing with a fork to blend well. Put mixture into a 9-inch pie plate and shape into crust. Chill in refrigerator while preparing filling.

FILLING

½ cup light cream or evaporated milk

1 pound dry-curd cottage cheese

⅓ cup sugar

½ teaspoon salt

3 eggs, well beaten

Juice and grated rind of 1 lemon

2 tablespoons melted butter

1 cup blueberries (if using frozen or canned, drain well)

Blend cream or milk, cottage cheese, sugar, and salt in a blender until thoroughly combined (do only half of mixture at a time). Put blended cheese mixture in a large bowl and add beaten eggs, lemon juice and rind, and melted butter. Mix well, then fold in blueberries. Pour mixture into chilled crust. Allow pie plate to warm slightly before putting in oven if using ovenproof glass. Bake for 1 hour.

Blueberry Pancakes with Orange Sauce

1½ cups sifted all-purpose flour

1 teaspoon salt

3 tablespoons sugar

2 teaspoons baking powder

1 cup milk

2 eggs, lightly beaten (you may separate them, adding the lightly beaten
*   yolks to the milk; the stiffly beaten whites then are folded into the*
*   batter just before baking)*

3 tablespoons melted butter

1 cup blueberries (if using frozen or canned, drain well)

Orange Sauce (see page 190)

Preheat a griddle or heavy skillet over moderate heat; it will be ready for use when a few drops of water sprinkled over it sputter, bounce around, and evaporate almost instantly. When the cakes are ready for the griddle, brush it lightly with an oiled brush. Repeat the oiling as necessary.

Resift the flour with the salt, sugar, and baking powder in a mixing bowl. Make a well in the center of these ingredients; pour into it the milk and beaten eggs (or only the yolks if the whites are to be folded in later). Stir these ingredients only long enough to blend them, then add the melted butter and blend briefly. Ignore the lumps in the batter; the cakes will be lighter if the batter is not overmixed. Fold the stiffly beaten egg whites, if used, into the batter only until no white streaks appear.

Pour the batter onto preheated griddle, forming 4-inch cakes. (A pitcher or ladle is best for pouring.) Immediately sprinkle a tablespoon or so of the blueberries onto the cakes. Bake until a number of bubbles appear on the surface—about 3 minutes. Immediately turn the cakes with a pancake turner or spatula; bake another minute or two.

Transfer to a heated platter and proceed with next batch. The platter may be kept in a 150° to 200°F oven, but these cakes are best when served promptly and as successive batches leave the griddle. Serve with Orange Sauce.

Note: It is not desirable to fold the fruit into the batter before baking; the berries are liable to stick to the griddle.

Makes about 1 dozen pancakes.

ORANGE SAUCE

½ cup softened butter

1 cup sifted confectioners' sugar

1 teaspoon grated orange rind

¼ cup orange juice

Beat the butter until it is very soft. An electric mixer is best for this. Add the confectioners' sugar gradually; continue beating at high speed until the mixture is light and fluffy. Add orange rind and orange juice and continue to beat until well blended.

Makes about 1½ cups.

Blueberry Muffins

Home from a berrying expedition, a lovely conflict arises. What shall be done with these fruits of the summer? Shall it be blueberry pancakes served with orange sauce, blueberry pie, a steamed or baked pudding? Or blueberry muffins, bursting with fruit, made with the following recipe?

2 cups sifted all-purpose flour
1 teaspoon salt
4 teaspoons baking powder
½ cup sugar, sifted
2 eggs, well beaten
¾ cup milk

⅓ cup melted butter
⅓ cup flour
1 cup blueberries (if frozen or canned, drain well)
1 teaspoon cinnamon

Preheat oven to 425°F.

Butter muffin tins or insert paper liners.

Resift the 2 cups flour with the salt, baking powder, and ¼ cup of the sugar. Combine the beaten eggs, milk, and melted butter; stir quickly into the dry ingredients only until ingredients are moistened. Unnecessary handling of the mixture results in tough, grainy muffins. Do not try to smooth out the lumps.

Sprinkle the ⅓ cup flour over the berries and combine quickly and lightly; stir immediately into the batter, lifting and mixing just long enough so that the berries combine with the batter. (If using frozen or canned berries, after draining them, sprinkle the flour over them, making sure they do not stand long enough for the flour coating to become pasty.) Fill muffin cups about ⅔ full. Combine the remaining ¼ cup sugar and the cinnamon and sprinkle a little over each muffin.

Bake 20 to 25 minutes. Let muffins cool slightly before removing from tins.

Makes about 2 dozen muffins.

Durgin-Park's Blueberry Tea Cake

3 cups sifted all-purpose flour
¾ teaspoon salt
4 teaspoons baking powder
¾ cup sugar
2 eggs, well beaten

2 tablespoons melted butter
1½ cups milk
¼–⅓ cup flour
1½ cups blueberries (if frozen or
    canned, drain them well)

Preheat oven to 400°F.

Butter a 9- by 14- by 3-inch baking dish; flour it lightly and tap off excess flour. Resift the 3 cups flour with the salt and baking powder.

Mix sugar with the eggs, combining well. Add dry ingredients and the melted butter and milk. Mix only long enough to moisten all ingredients. Ignore any lumps; they will smooth out while baking.

Sprinkle the ¼ to ⅓ cup flour over the blueberries, less if using frozen or canned berries. Immediately add the floured berries to the batter; mix lightly, lifting and stirring only long enough to combine the berries in the batter.

Pour the batter into the baking pan, spreading it evenly. Bake about 30 minutes, or until a cake tester or toothpick inserted in center of cake emerges clean.

Note: Some minor liberties have been taken with this famous restaurant's recipe. More berries, for instance, are used, assuming that one's berrying expedition to Chappaquiddick or elsewhere was a rewarding one. (A Chappaquiddick friend, when asked to elaborate on that island's status regarding blueberries, replied: "Loaded! High-bush, low-bush, home-canned, home-frozen!")

Makes 15 to 20 squares.

Hallie's Blueberries

1 quart blueberries

1½ cups sour cream, or ¾ cup
    sour cream and ¾ cup low-fat
    yogurt, mixed

½ cup brown sugar, lightly packed

Grated nutmeg

Fresh raspberries

Pick over blueberries, removing bits of stems and leaves. Do not wash unless berries are store-bought. If washed, dry gently on a clean towel before using. Pour berries into a decorative pie plate or other flat, nonmetal dish and spread sour cream or sour cream–yogurt mix over them as evenly as possible. (The yogurt mix is easier to spread as well as lower in calories.) Sprinkle the brown sugar evenly across the top and set the dish in the refrigerator for several hours to allow sugar to dissolve into topping. Remove in time for berries to reach room temperature before serving. Grate a little nutmeg over the top. Decorated with a handful of fresh raspberries, the dessert is perfect for the Fourth of July.

Makes 4 to 6 portions.

CRANBERRIES

Tuesday was Cranberry Day in the town of Gay Head and the majority of inhabitants turned out, visiting the wild bogs to harvest the berries after the manner of their Indian ancestors. . . . The berries grow on common land, for Gay Head is the only Island town to preserve its "common," and all inhabitants have rights to the crop, and even descendants of Gay Head people who live elsewhere are granted whatever rights that may be theirs by inheritance.

—*Vineyard Gazette*, October 16, 1953

Cranberries, like blueberries, are another long-used fruit with somewhat confusing early appellations. The herbalist John Josselyn referred to cranberries as "bear berries" because bears "use much to feed upon [them]." The true bearberry, however, is an entirely different plant, whose bright red berries are of no use as food but were recommended by Gerard, the best known of the early writers on folk medicine, as good for "burning agues."

On the western end of the Island, in the low-lying land behind the towering Gay Head cliffs, wild cranberry bogs still thrive on the peat beds formed by remains of the preglacial forests that once covered the Vineyard. The low-growing evergreen plants blanket the spongy soil, dwarfed and protected from the sweep of the sea winds by thickets of beach plum, bayberry, and bush poison ivy.

The rich-red berries have been used as food for hundreds of years; a local record from 1755 refers to their use by the early settlers, and of course the Indians gathered cranberries long before that. There is still token celebration of Cranberry Day in Gay Head, and though cranberries are no longer grown commercially on the Island, the industry is still enormously important on Cape Cod and is credited with rescuing that entire area from economic disaster in the lean years following the Civil War.

Long associated with Thanksgiving and other festive occasions, the cranberry is actually widely adaptable for use in cakes, muffins, stews, pies, and puddings; and cranberry juice is a tart and delightful beverage.

There is also a high-bush "cranberry" that flourishes on the Vineyard. This is no relation to the true cranberry, but a species of viburnum and more closely related to the elderberry. Though not included in this book as a food source, high-bush cranberries have long been used medicinally, and quite acceptable jelly and juice can be made from its clusters of brilliant red fruits.

Spiced Cranberries

1 cup water

1½ cups brown sugar

½ teaspoon ground cinnamon

½ teaspoon ground allspice

½ teaspoon ground cloves

½ teaspoon ground ginger

1 pound cranberries, washed

Combine all ingredients except cranberries in a heavy saucepan. Bring to a boil, then simmer over low heat for 20 minutes. Add cranberries (discard imperfect fruit). Cook over very low heat for 2 hours, stirring occasionally. Pack immediately into hot, sterilized jars, seal, and process 5 minutes in a hot-water bath. The spiced berries may also be kept in a covered container in the refrigerator.

Recommended as a relish for roast pork or cold meats.

Makes about 3 cups.

Steamed Cranberry Pudding
with Lemon Sauce

1 cup sifted all-purpose flour
½ teaspoon salt
2 teaspoons baking powder
⅓ cup brown sugar, lightly packed
  in cup
½ cup fresh bread crumbs
⅔ cup finely chopped suet (may

be put through food chopper)
1 cup coarsely chopped
  cranberries
1 egg, lightly beaten
⅓ cup milk
Lemon Sauce (see page 197)

Grease a 1-quart pudding mold with lid or a 1-quart earthenware bowl (or even a 1-pound coffee can).

Sift the flour again with the salt and baking powder. Combine in a mixing bowl with the brown sugar, bread crumbs, suet, and chopped cranberries. Combine the beaten egg and milk, and add. Stir just enough to moisten and combine all ingredients. Turn into the greased mold. Mold should not be more than three-quarters full. If lacking a lid, cover tightly with a piece of foil or a clean dish towel and tie securely.

Place the mold on a rack in a kettle of sufficient size. Fill kettle with boiling water until water comes three-quarters of the way up the sides of the mold; place over high heat until steam forms, then reduce heat to a simmer, cover, and cook 2 hours. Add more water to kettle as needed.

Unmold pudding onto a heated platter, spoon a little Lemon Sauce over the pudding and pass remainder of sauce in a separate bowl.

Makes 6 to 8 portions.

LEMON SAUCE

⅓–½ cup sugar

1 heaping teaspoon cornstarch

1 cup water

4 teaspoons fresh lemon juice

3 teaspoons butter or margarine

1 teaspoon grated lemon rind

In a small bowl combine ⅓ cup sugar, the cornstarch, and the water. Transfer mixture to a small saucepan and stir briskly until ingredients are well blended. Cook over moderate heat, stirring constantly until thickened. Add the lemon juice, butter or margarine, and grated lemon rind. Continue to stir and cook another 1 or 2 minutes, then remove from heat. Gradually stir in remaining sugar to taste. Serve the sauce warm.

Makes about 1 cup.

Cranberry Upside-Down Cake

6 tablespoons butter

2¼ cups sugar, sifted

2 cups cranberries, washed

1 cup sifted cake flour

1½ teaspoons baking powder

¼ teaspoon salt

4 egg yolks

1 teaspoon vanilla

4 egg whites

Whipped cream

Preheat oven to 350°F.

In a 9- or 10-inch skillet with ovenproof handle, melt 4 tablespoons of the butter over moderate heat, add 1¼ cups of the sugar, and stir the mixture well. Add the washed cranberries (discard imperfect fruit). Cook slowly about 5 minutes, stirring frequently. Remove skillet from heat.

In a small saucepan melt remaining 2 tablespoons butter over moderate heat and set aside to cool.

Resift the flour with the baking powder and salt. Beat egg yolks until thick and pale yellow, gradually adding all but 2 tablespoons of the remaining sugar. Continue beating until mixture is very thick. Beat in the vanilla.

In another bowl beat the egg whites until they form soft peaks, then beat in remaining 2 tablespoons sugar until egg whites form stiff peaks. Spoon half the egg-white mixture over the egg-yolk mixture, sift on about half of the flour mixture and delicately fold in until partly blended. Add remaining egg-white mixture, sift on remainder of flour mixture, repeat folding-in process, and just before mixture is fully blended, gradually add remaining 2 tablespoons melted butter. Avoid overmixing or the egg whites will collapse.

Spoon the mixture over the prepared berries in the skillet. Bake 30 to 40 minutes. Cool slightly. Cover skillet with a plate of proper size, invert, and turn out cake. Serve with whipped cream.

Cranberry Conserve

4 cups cranberries

1½ cups water

3 cups sugar

½ cup seeded raisins (the plump, muscat type)

2 apples, preferably tart ones, coarsely chopped (cored but not peeled)

1 orange, put through largest blade of food chopper (reserve juice)

1 lemon, put through largest blade of food chopper (reserve juice)

2–4 tablespoons crystallized ginger, coarsely chopped

1 cup walnut meats, coarsely chopped

½ cup brandy

In a large kettle, at least 8-quart capacity, cook the cranberries in the water over moderately high heat until their skins pop open. Add the sugar, raisins, apples, chopped orange and juice, and chopped lemon and juice. Stir and mix all ingredients thoroughly. Bring to a boil and cook over moderately high heat, stirring frequently, until the mixture is thick and clear. (Cooking times vary. As the mixture thickens, place a small amount in a spoon, cool it slightly, and let it drop back in the pan from the side of the spoon. When two large drops form on the edge of the spoon, one on each side, the conserve may be removed from the heat.)

Add 2 to 4 tablespoons of the crystallized ginger, depending on your taste, plus the walnuts and the brandy.

Pack in hot, sterilized jars, seal, and process 5 minutes in a hot-water bath.

Makes about five 8-ounce glasses.

Cranberry-Apple Relish

*1 large apple, cored and chopped (may be put through medium blade
   of food grinder)*
*1 cup cranberries, chopped (may also be put through medium blade
   of food grinder)*
¾ cup sugar
Pinch of salt
1 tablespoon crystallized ginger, chopped (optional but very good)

Combine all ingredients thoroughly. Let stand at least 1 hour before serving to allow flavors to develop.

Makes about 2 to 3 cups.

Cranberry Pudding

In a Victorian house set high on a Chappaquiddick knoll, surrounded by blueberry bushes and with a long view across the Katama sandspit and the ocean, Virginia and Vance Packard used to spend many pleasant months each year. While he wrote, she worked on her paintings (for some years a professional artist, she had many canvases exhibited at shows), beachcombed, decorated the house, planned dinner parties, and did other enjoyable, creative things.

Cooking was one of her many pleasures; and this dessert was a favorite at Packard dinner parties. Described as one of her "treasured recipes," it was given to her by a very special friend. The finished pudding has a cakelike bottom and a crisp, meringue-type topping.

2 cups fresh cranberries, washed and picked over

¾ cup sugar

¼ cup coarsely chopped walnuts

6 tablespoons melted butter

1 egg, well beaten

½ cup flour

Vanilla ice cream (optional)

Preheat oven to 350°F.

Place cranberries in a well-buttered 8-inch pie plate. Mix ¼ cup of the sugar with the nuts and 4 tablespoons of the melted butter and pour over the cranberries. To the beaten egg add the remaining ½ cup sugar combined with the flour, then add the remaining 2 tablespoons melted butter. Beat a bit more. Pour over berry mixture. Bake 45 minutes.

The pudding is at its best when served warm with a scoop of vanilla ice cream on top of each serving.

Makes 6 portions.

Ethel's Cranberry Conserve

While she rested on her sofa in her tiny, snug West Tisbury cottage under a handsome striped blanket woven many years ago out of wool from Farmer Whiting's sheep, the elderly lady who made this delicious preparation described it as "sort of rehashed Fanny Farmer." She studied her tattered and bespattered 1924 edition of that most venerable of cookbooks and then read out her version of this excellent conserve. The main change is the addition of extra raisins and the omission of nuts because they get "all gooey."

1 quart cranberries, washed
⅔ cup water
1 scant cup seeded raisins
3¼ cups sugar

1 California orange, thinly sliced
*   and chopped into tiny pieces*
⅔ cup boiling water

Combine cranberries and water in a saucepan, bring to a boil over moderate heat, and cook until the skins split. Allow to cool slightly, then put cranberries and cooking liquid through a food mill. Replace in saucepan and add all other ingredients. Bring to a boil, then reduce heat to a simmer and cook about 25 minutes, or until quite thick. Pour or spoon into hot, sterilized jars, seal, and process 5 minutes in a hot-water bath.

Makes about 8 standard jelly jars.

CHAPTER 8

Cakes, Cookies, and Breads

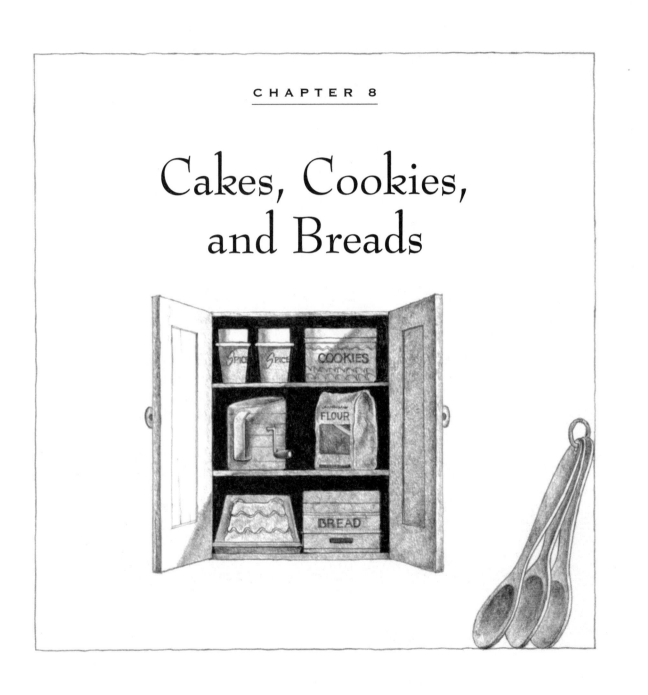

General Directions for Making a Cake: Do not use the hand to make a cake, but a wooden spoon or spad. Earthern is best to make a cake in. In receipts where milk is used, never mix sweet and sour milk . . . even when either alone would not do it. . . . Try whether cake is done by piercing it with a broom splinter and if nothing adheres it is done.

—*Vineyard Gazette,* June 29, 1848

Baking seems to have been a favorite occupation of early Vineyard housewives, as it was of most New England homemakers. Cakes in particular—along with pies, of course—have long lured the ungodly as well as the godly to church suppers and other community affairs. And, for several decades, various groups of civic-minded ladies set up tables several times each summer under the magnificent linden tree that stood on Vineyard Haven's Main Street and raised funds for worthy causes by selling to vulnerable passersby cakes oozing with rich-brown chocolate or similarly irresistible home-baked goodies. Bake shops flourished, as they do now. In 1945 the Meiklehams' little shop in Edgartown, the Seagull and the Whale, advertised "Delicious FFV [Finest Food Value] Cake Squares, Penoches, MV Square Deals, Crisp Cookies, Nutritious Date Nut Bread." One of this book's authors remembers nostalgically a summertime experience of long standing—the first trip of the season to Argie Humphries's North Tisbury bakery, where one could munch on a freshly baked, still-warm date square and savor the air while waiting for Argie to count out the cookies.

Cookbooks—old ones and new ones—seem stuffed with recipes for baked goods, many traditional, some relying on mixes and other shortcuts. This being so, we have chosen only a few recipes to represent the cakes, cookies, and breads of the Vineyard. Most are special favorites, family favorites, from local cooks. One or two, however, will look—and taste—familiar to the summer people who like to stop in the little local bake shops and choose a bag of goodies for the weekend.

Chilmark Chocolate Cake

This true chocolate fudge cake, rich and delicious, has long been popular at ladies' gatherings Up-Island. It should satisfy, at least temporarily, the most rabid chocolate addicts. Don't be alarmed if the batter seems too thin. This is characteristic of the cake.

4 squares unsweetened baking chocolate	1¾ cups milk
2 tablespoons butter	¾ teaspoon salt
2 cups sifted sugar	1 teaspoon vanilla
4 egg yolks, beaten until light	1 teaspoon baking soda
	2 cups sifted cake flour

Preheat oven to 350°F.

Grease and flour two 9-inch round cake pans.

In a heavy saucepan, melt chocolate and butter over low heat. Pour into mixing bowl and add sugar, egg yolks, and 1 cup of the milk, then beat until smooth. Add salt, vanilla, ½ cup of the milk, and soda dissolved in the remaining ¼ cup milk and beat some more. Then add, about ⅔ cup at a time, the sifted cake flour. Beat slowly while adding the flour (use low speed if using an electric mixer). Bake 30 to 35 minutes. Cool cakes in pans for 5 minutes, on racks. Run a knife around sides of pan, invert each on a plate, then turn right side up on a rack. Cool completely before frosting.

Frost with Soft Chocolate Frosting (see page 250).

English Lemon Cake

The grandmother of a Vineyard cook used to serve this cake in England; it is now prepared as a special treat in several Island and off-Island households. It is as lemony as the Chilmark Chocolate Cake is chocolatey.

1 cup sugar
1 scant cup butter, softened
2 eggs
1½ cups flour
½ teaspoon salt

1 teaspoon baking powder
½ cup milk
1 teaspoon poppy seeds
2 tablespoons lemon juice
Grated rind of ½ lemon

Preheat oven to 350°F.

Grease and flour a standard-size loaf pan.

Cream ⅔ cup sugar and the butter together. Add eggs, one at a time, beating in well until mixture is light and fluffy. Resift flour with salt and baking powder; add to first mixture alternately with milk, beating in well. Pour into the pan, sprinkle with poppy seeds, and bake 45 minutes.

Mix the remaining ⅓ cup sugar, lemon juice, and lemon rind in a small saucepan, heat until sugar is dissolved, and pour over cake in pan while cake is still hot. Let cool to room temperature before removing cake from pan.

Makes 1 loaf.

Orange Kiss-Me Cake

There must have been good reason for tacking such a ridiculous name onto such a delectable concoction as this old-time favorite cake. Whatever it is, we failed to uncover it. But the cake was the topic of a good deal of pleasant banter in one of Louise Bugbee's *Gazette* columns some years ago, and since one of this book's authors also "grew up on it," we include it in spite of its name.

Orange Kiss-Me Cake, by the way, is even better the second day after baking than it is when freshly baked, if one can resist cutting into it that long.

THE CAKE

1 large navel orange
1 cup seeded raisins (muscat type)
2 cups sifted flour
1½ teaspoons baking soda
1 teaspoon salt

½ cup shortening (half butter, half margarine is suggested)
1 cup of sugar, sifted
2 eggs
1 cup milk
⅓ cup walnuts, coarsely chopped

Preheat oven to 350°F.

Grease a standard-size loaf pan.

Squeeze the orange, reserving the juice for the topping. Put the orange (rind and pulp) and the raisins through medium blade of a food chopper. Set those ingredients aside.

Resift the flour with the baking soda and salt. Beat the shortening (an electric mixer is recommended) until softened; gradually add the sugar and continue to beat until the mixture is fluffy. Add the eggs, one at a time, beating well after each addition. At low mixer speed, or stirring by hand, add half the flour mixture and half the milk. Mix only enough to moisten ingredients. Add the reserved chopped orange and raisins; blend briefly. Add remainder of flour mixture and milk. Blend only enough to moisten. Add the walnuts. Pour the batter into the loaf pan and bake approximately 1 hour. Cake is done when a cake tester or a toothpick inserted in center of cake comes out clean. Leave in pan while preparing the topping.

THE TOPPING

Orange juice (reserved from cake recipe)
⅓ cup brown sugar, lightly packed
½ teaspoon cinnamon
⅓ cup walnuts, coarsely chopped

Combine the reserved orange juice, the brown sugar mixed with the cinnamon, and the ⅓ cup of walnuts. Pour this mixture over the finished cake in pan while the cake is still hot. Let stand until cool. This cake should be sliced in its pan.

Note: The cake the author grew up on was made without the topping. The orange juice went into the cake. If you make your cake this way, reduce the milk content by ¼ cup.

Santa Claus Cakes

Another old family recipe, this one was devised in England more than a hundred years ago by the grandmother of a contemporary Vineyard cook, who passed it along to her son's bride. These chewy confections keep well when stored in an airtight container, if you can hide them from the family until you are ready to put them out during the holidays. Traditionally, in their family of origin, two were left on the hearth on Christmas Eve for Santa (he always managed to find them, assisted, perhaps, by one of the family poodles).

2 cups dates, cut in small pieces
   (or buy precut ones)
3 egg yolks, beaten
1 scant cup sugar
½ cup sifted flour
1 tablespoon baking powder

½ teaspoon salt
1 cup coarsely chopped English
walnuts (black walnuts are far
   better, if available)
3 egg whites, beaten stiff
½ cup sugar (more if needed)

Preheat oven to 375°F.

Grease a baking pan (about 10 by 14 by 2 inches).

Cut dates in small pieces (kitchen shears work fairly well). If they are stuck together and hard to cut, sprinkle them with a bit of the flour or dip scissors in hot water. Beat egg yolks until light yellow. Beat in the 1 scant cup sugar. Resift flour with baking powder and salt. Put dates and nuts into a fairly large bowl, sift flour mixture over them, mix well with a fork, coating them as well as possible. Add egg-yolk-and-sugar mixture; stir well. Beat egg whites until stiff; mix gently into fruit-nut mixture. Spoon out into the baking pan and spread evenly over bottom. Bake 5 minutes at 375°F; lower heat to 325°F and bake 20 minutes more. Cut with a silver knife into bars, four strips lengthwise and ten strips crosswise. Cool in pan 15 minutes. Remove carefully with a pancake turner and roll each bar in the ½ cup granulated sugar while warm. Cool to room temperature before storing.

Makes 40 bars.

Two-Layer Cookies
[Brown-Sugar Nut Squares]

These scrumptious cookies, best-sellers for years at an Up-Island bake shop, were one of the first things put down as essential when the plan for this cookbook was conceived. But how to get the recipe? Even before then we had long tried to steal or cajole the secret from their maker. Then, to our joy, we found it in *Vineyard Fare,* the useful—and, fortunately for us, not copyrighted—collection of recipes published in 1963 by the Martha's Vineyard Hospital Auxiliary. So here it is.

COOKIE BASE

2 egg yolks

1 cup brown sugar, lightly packed

½ cup softened butter (or half
   butter, half margarine)

1½ cups sifted flour

1 teaspoon baking powder

½ teaspoon salt

1 teaspoon vanilla

¾ cup chopped pecans or walnuts

Preheat oven to 275°F.

Grease a baking pan (about 10 by 14 by 2 inches).

Beat egg yolks until light yellow, then combine with the brown sugar and butter. Beat well. Resift the flour with the baking powder and salt and gradually add to the egg-yolk mixture. Add the vanilla and blend well. Spread the mixture in the baking pan and sprinkle with the chopped nuts.

MERINGUE TOPPING

2 egg whites

¼ teaspoon cream of tartar

1 cup brown sugar, lightly packed

Beat egg whites with cream of tartar until stiff peaks form. Lightly fold in brown sugar. Carefully spread this mixture over the cookie base and bake 1 hour. Let cool, then cut into squares.

Makes about 2 dozen 2-inch squares.

Fruit Pastry Squares

PASTRY

Double recipe for 2-crust pastry (or double recipe for Suzanne's Pie Crust, page 304), chilled

FRUIT FILLING

3–4 cups applesauce seasoned with cinnamon and nutmeg (or 3–4 cups mincemeat, or any favorite jam, with 1 or more tablespoons lemon juice added to reduce sweetness)

1 egg yolk mixed with 1 tablespoon water

Preheat oven to 450°F.

A rimmed, 12- by 16-inch cookie sheet will be required.

Divide chilled pastry in half. Roll it on floured surface and fit one piece in bottom of cookie sheet. It should be about ¼ inch thick. Spread it with the applesauce, mincemeat, or jam. Roll the second piece of dough, fold it in half, and place fold in middle of pan. Unfold and adjust it to fit. Trim edges with a sharp knife and press together to seal. Make small slits in the pastry to allow steam to escape during baking.

Brush the crust with the egg-yolk mixture and bake 15 minutes or until crust is golden brown. Reduce heat to 350°F and bake until pastry is done, a total cooking time of approximately 45 minutes to 1 hour.

Cool, then cut into squares or rectangles.

Makes about 2 dozen squares.

Togus Bread

We found this bread listed in an early book of Vineyard recipes and were intrigued by its name. Investigations made us suspect a typographical error in this earlier printing, for though "togus" was nowhere to be found, *togue,* especially interesting to us, is an Algonquian Indian word for the even more euphonious word (also of Indian origin) *namaycush,* the name of a particular kind of large trout. Since the Vineyard Indians are a branch of the Algonquians, we think this should be called Togue Bread, and feel that the Gay Head Indians used to eat it with their togue, or namaycush. We made some and had it with baked fish, but recommend it also with such dishes as baked beans, since it strongly resembles—and may be a precursor of—Boston brown bread. Though the bread takes a long time to steam, it takes only a few minutes to mix up and is a comforting sort of thing to have bubbling on the stove on a winter morning.

1½ cups whole milk

½ cup sour milk or buttermilk

¼ cup molasses

1½ cups sifted Indian meal (yellow cornmeal)

½ cup sifted white flour

½ teaspoon soda

¾ teaspoon salt

Grease a tall 1-pound coffee can.

Mix whole and sour milk; warm molasses slightly in measuring utensil (so it will pour and mix more easily) and add to milk. Stir in well. Resift cornmeal and flour with soda and salt. Add milk-molasses mixture, a little at a time, to prevent lumping. Mix thoroughly; or put into a shaker and shake well to mix. Pour into the coffee can and seal top tightly with foil. (Be sure to leave a space of half an inch or so at the top of the can, since the bread will expand.) A heavy rubber band may be used to fasten the foil securely; also good is the paper-covered wire used for tying up garden plants. Place sealed, filled can on a rack in a kettle of boiling water deep enough to immerse about 90 percent of the can. Weight can with a plate to prevent floating, cover kettle, and steam in boiling-water bath for 4 hours. Add hot water when needed to maintain original level. Let bread cool somewhat in can, then unmold and allow to cool to room temperature before slicing.

Note: This bread tends to mold, so keep it in a plastic bag in the refrigerator if it is to be kept more than a day or so. Allow to warm to room temperature before eating.

Makes 1 round loaf.

Mary Alley's Banana Bread

The general store has been, as it should be, the social center of West Tisbury for many generations. "Dealers in Almost Everything" proclaims the sign that for many years has swung from the porch, and anyone in the neighborhood who ever has needed anything, from a piece of sandpaper to a pint of chocolate swirl ice cream, has taken the sign at Alley's Store quite literally.

One thing that Alley's doesn't deal in is this banana bread that used to be made in Mrs. Alley's kitchen in the big, old white house across the street and down a bit from the store. Its fame reached us from one of the Alleys' neighbors, who was given a loaf of it every Christmas. Its source, Mary Alley told us, was not a cookbook but a long-ago friend in New Hampshire. She stressed that this is not cakelike, but breadlike, and thus very good for sandwiches. A filling of cream cheese and ground nuts should be especially good.

1¾ cups flour, sifted
½ teaspoon salt
1 level teaspoon soda
⅓ cup butter, softened

1 scant cup sugar
2 eggs, lightly beaten
3 large bananas, mashed

Preheat oven to 350°F.

Oil a 9- by 5- by 3-inch loaf pan. (Mrs. Alley used a piece of wax paper on the bottom of her pan to facilitate removal of bread.)

Resift flour with salt and baking soda. Cream the butter and sugar until light and fluffy; add eggs and mix well. Stir in bananas. Sift flour mixture into banana mixture about ½ cup at a time, mixing well but gently between additions. Do not beat batter. Pour bread batter into pan. Bake 1 hour; cool slightly. Remove from pan and cool on rack. Let loaf cool completely before storing away.

Makes 1 loaf.

Ellie's Zucchini Bread

The donor of this recipe used to fly in from Arizona every summer to help her daughter at her Farmers' Market stand. Faced with the usual summer excess of zucchini, she began making this bread that contains lots of spices but only about half the usual amount of oil.

2 generous cups grated zucchini
Unseasoned commercial bread
   crumbs
3 cups all-purpose white flour
1 teaspoon baking soda
½ teaspoon baking powder

3 generous tablespoons cinnamon
2 eggs
2 cups sugar
1 cup vegetable oil
1½ teaspoons vanilla
¼ cup water, or more as needed

Preheat oven to 350°F.

If large zucchini are used, remove seeds and pulp, pare skin if tough, and grate only firm flesh. Generously grease bottoms and sides of two standard-size loaf pans or three 3-cup loaf pans and coat with bread crumbs. Sift together into large bowl the flour, baking soda, baking powder, and cinnamon. In another large mixing bowl, beat eggs until yellow. Stir in sugar, oil, and vanilla. Beat until smooth. Add flour mixture, beating in about 1 cup at a time until well blended. Add grated zucchini and enough water to produce a thick but fluid batter. Pour evenly into loaf pans. Bake approximately 1 hour or until metal skewer inserted into center of loaf comes out clean.

Remove from oven immediately, set on wire rack to cool about 10 minutes, then turn out of pans onto rack, and let cool 8 hours or so or overnight. Then wrap well in cellophane or plastic wrap. The bread keeps well in the refrigerator for at least a week. It also freezes well.

Makes 2 large loaves or 3 small ones.

Edith Foote's Oatmeal Bread

This remarkable West Tisbury lady was widely known for her community spirit on both a small scale and a large one. When new neighbors moved in next door, she appeared with a basket of sandwiches and fruit. And in 1962 when the Martha's Vineyard Community Services was being organized and a thrift shop was suggested as a way of raising money, Mrs. Foote said, "Give me $150 and I'll start one." In the 1998 fiscal year, the thrift shop's donation to the organization was nearly $105,000.

This delicious, crunchy crusted bread, attributed to Edith Foote's grandmother, is one of many good things she used to produce in her kitchen between meetings. Note that the dough is refrigerated overnight.

1 tablespoon sugar
½ cup warm water
2 packages of yeast
1½ cups boiling water
1¼ cups rolled oats
½ cup dark molasses

⅓ cup vegetable oil or melted
butter
½ teaspoon salt
5½–6 cups unbleached flour
2 eggs, beaten

In a small bowl, mix sugar into warm water. Sprinkle yeast on top to proof. Combine boiling water, rolled oats, molasses, oil or butter, and salt in a large bowl. Let cool until lukewarm. Stir in 2 cups of flour. Add eggs and yeast mixture and beat well. Add enough of remaining flour to make a soft dough (it will be sticky). Brush top with oil, cover tightly, and refrigerate overnight.

Preheat oven to 375°F.

Punch dough down, turn onto floured board, and knead for 8 minutes. Add flour as needed. Grease two standard-size loaf pans, form loaves, and place in pans. Let rise in warm place until nearly doubled. Bake for 40 to 50 minutes. Butter tops of loaves for softer top crust. Let cool before slicing.

Note: Bread rises in pans rather slowly because dough is cold. It will rise more as it bakes.

Makes 2 loaves.

CHAPTER 9

Pies, Puddings, and Other Desserts

PIES

In Colonial days New England housewives often baked as many as 100 pies at a time, stacked them in big jars, and stored them in a shed where they'd freeze. When a pie was wanted it was placed in the pie cupboard in the fireplace chimney and thawed out.

—Imogene Wolcott, *The Yankee Cookbook*[†]

P ies," says the *Columbia-Viking Desk Encyclopedia,* "were known to Romans, and were common in England by 14th cent.; mince pie early became a festive Christmas dish." Webster thinks perhaps the word derived from *magpie,* which brings to mind the "four and twenty blackbirds" that met such an inopportune end beneath a pastry crust. New Englanders—including Vineyarders—have never concerned themselves about how pies originated; they just originated their own with whatever was at hand or took their fancy—bits of cooked meat and vegetables, leftover fish or shellfish, any sort of fresh, dried, or preserved fruit, or almost any of these in seemingly ungastronomic combinations. Who first decided, for instance, that an apt mixture of roasting beef, molasses, lemon rind, beef fat, salt, raisins, and a dozen or so other things, including a good dollop of brandy, would produce mincemeat? Some ingenious English

[†]New York: Coward, McCann, Inc., 1963

kitchen lady of the Middle Ages, it seems, who might be pleased to know that her invention was brought to a new world centuries later and carried out with whatever of the standard ingredients were available in the snowbound kitchens of the New England settlements.

Pies have always been—and still are—traditional fare at Island gatherings. *Gazette* accounts of long-ago church suppers, Grange meetings, benevolent-society dinners, and golden wedding celebrations almost always include the word "pie." Nowadays, however, far too many pies arrive in the kitchen via the grocery bag, done up and ready to defrost, brown and serve, or merely take out of the bakery box and slice. We don't disdain all ready-made pies, and certainly prepared pastry mixes and frozen ready-to-bake crusts are a blessing to those of us who simply can't roll a pie crust out of a wretched little heap of crumbly dough. But any cook who summers or lives year-round on the Vineyard should surely present her family with at least one summer-flavored delight—a fresh-baked rhubarb, blueberry, blackberry, or apple pie.

Brandied Apple Pie

This is the absolute favorite of one of the authors.

Pastry for 9-inch crust (see page 304)
6–8 tart apples, medium size (or large windfall apples)
1 cup brown sugar
½ teaspoon cinnamon
2 tablespoons butter, cut in small pieces or melted
1 tablespoon lemon juice
2 tablespoons brandy
2 tablespoons cream or 1 tablespoon beaten egg yolk

Prepare a single-crust pie dough and chill it. Peel, core, and slice apples; place in a large bowl with brown sugar, cinnamon, butter, lemon juice, and brandy. Mix well and let stand ½ hour.

Preheat oven to 450°F while assembling pie.

Place apple mixture directly in a 9-inch pie pan. Roll out pie crust and place carefully over apple mixture. Flute edges of crust and prick in several places with a fork or cut several slits. Brush crust with cream or with egg yolk combined with a little water. Bake at 450°F for 15 minutes; reduce heat to 350°F and bake another 20 to 30 minutes. (Apples may be tested for doneness by carefully inserting a paring knife into crust.)

Black-and-Blue Pie

Blackberries are often disdained because of their strong flavor and multiple seeds (not to mention the aggravations involved with picking them). True blackberry lovers, however, feel they are the finest of the wild fruits and, conversely, consider blueberries insipid-tasting and textureless. A pie pleasing to both extremes—and everyone in the middle as well—can be constructed by following a regular blueberry-pie recipe, but using half blueberries and half blackberries. A bit more thickening agent (1 tablespoon flour or 1 teaspoon cornstarch or arrowroot) should be added to the sugar to absorb the extra juice released by the blackberries.

Deep-Dish Blackberry Pie

For forty years or more, first in Kentucky, then in North Carolina, and now on Martha's Vineyard, the first blackberries picked every season have been preempted in one particular household by the cook of the family, who gave us this recipe. No complaints come from the berry pickers—only the insistence that she "make plenty of it."

Rather than reformulate what is basically a very simple dessert to prepare, we give you her instructions just as received.

> Freshly picked blackberries. At least one cup per person with more if you can get them. Sprinkle with about one tablespoon flour per cup, tossing lightly with wide fork. Place in pretty, wide, shallow pottery dish. Cover with half as much sugar as berries.
>
> Make a standard pie crust, only roll it a bit thicker than usual. Cover berries and prick top. Bake in moderate oven about three quarters of an hour or until fork finds berries well done and crust is nicely browned. Serve with lots of rich cream or ice cream. Yummy.

An alternate method of preparation, which avoids any possibility of the flour lumping, would be to combine the flour with the sugar and sprinkle the mixture over the top of the berries after they are placed in the dish.

We suggest an oven temperature of 450°F for 10 to 15 minutes, then 350°F for the rest of the baking period. This particular cook likes things sweet; for some tastes, a ratio of one-third as much sugar as berries might be better.

Rhubarb-and-Strawberry Pie

These two springtime fruits, both carefully cultured on the Vineyard, combine delectably in a flaky-crust pie. The fruit is cooked briefly, and eggs are added to create a sort of custard. This delicious filling has been used by Vineyard cooks for generations. (The strawberries, if huge, should be halved or quartered before use.)

9-inch pie shell (see page 304)
2 tablespoons butter
1½ cups sugar
2 cups 1-inch pieces of unpeeled young rhubarb
1 cup strawberries, hulled and washed, if necessary
2 tablespoons flour
2 egg yolks, lightly beaten
2 egg whites

Prepare and bake pie shell. Leave oven on at 300°F. Let pie shell cool while preparing filling. In a heavy saucepan melt butter over moderate heat; add 1 cup of the sugar, the rhubarb, and the strawberries. Mix well and cook until sugar is dissolved. Mix ¼ cup sugar with the flour, add beaten egg yolks, combine thoroughly with fruit. Cook over low heat, stirring frequently, until mixture thickens and rhubarb takes on a slightly transparent look. Remove from heat, cool, then pour into pie shell. Beat egg whites until stiff peaks are formed, then gradually add the remaining ¼ cup sugar, beating constantly. Spread meringue over filled pie shell and brown in oven about 15 minutes.

Green-Tomato–and–Apple Pie

After the first "white" frosts of the autumn (which kill the tenderer crops such as green peppers and eggplant) and before the first "black" frost, dreaded by every vegetable gardener who has gone out one still, chill fall morning to find his beloved garden blackened and devastated by the first true touch of winter—somewhere between these early harbingers, the provident gardener will pick all the unripened tomatoes from his vines and store them in a cool place until he finds time to convert them into pickles, a tart relish, a tasty marmalade, or this unusual pie. (The finest of the green tomatoes can be wrapped in newspapers, stored in a cool dark place and opened and used as they ripen—a process that can sometimes be sustained into early December.)

Pastry for 2-crust pie (see page 304)

3 medium-size tart apples

2 cups sliced green tomatoes

1 cup sugar (half white and half brown is suggested)

· 1 teaspoon cinnamon

¼ teaspoon nutmeg

¼ teaspoon allspice (optional)

2 scant tablespoons flour

1 tablespoon allspice (optional)

1 tablespoon lemon juice

2 tablespoons butter

1 tablespoon cream or melted butter (or 1 tablespoon beaten egg yolk)

Preheat oven to 450°F.

Prepare pastry and use half to line a 9-inch pie pan. Peel and core apples and cut into ½-inch slices. Slice tomatoes to match. In a large bowl combine sugar, spices, and flour. Mix lightly, then gently mix in apples, tomatoes, and lemon juice. Fill pie shell with this mixture; dot with bits of butter. Add top crust. Crimp edges. Brush with cream, melted butter, or egg yolk mixed with a little water. Cut several slits in top crust or prick with fork. Bake about 15 minutes, or until crust is golden brown. Reduce heat to 350°F and bake for a total of about 1 hour.

All-Season Fruit Tart

Almost any combination of fruits or berries can be used separately or in combination for this tart—pears, grapes, kiwis, bananas in winter, berries, peaches, plums in summer. Just make sure the fruit is ripe.

1 cup of flour
¼ pound butter
2 tablespoons confectioners'
* sugar*
8 ounces of cream cheese
¼ cup of sugar

½ cup of heavy cream
3 tablespoons frozen orange
* juice*
⅓ cup currant or apricot jelly
1 teaspoon brandy
2 cups fruits or berries

Combine flour, butter, and confectioners' sugar in a food processor to make dough, and press into a 9-inch tart pan. Bake in 425°F oven for 8 to 10 minutes. Cool before filling. Combine cream cheese, sugar, cream, and frozen orange juice in food processor and blend until very smooth. Spread cream cheese mixture into cooled pie shell. Melt jelly in small saucepan and season with brandy. Slice fruit into thin slices. Overlap in circular pattern over filling. Arrange berries on top of sliced fruit, if used. Glaze with melted currant or apricot jelly. Chill and serve.

Makes 8 servings

PUDDINGS AND OTHER DESSERTS

The puddings which accompanied them . . . were of many varieties ranging from the aristocratic plum-pudding of English vintage to the lowly "Gap and Swallow" with its sauce of thick maple syrup.

Among the jewels of the pudding family were the floating islands, sweetened with rosewater, the flummeries made by turning rich custard over cake and topping it all with the beaten whites of eggs, and the syllabubs with their foundations of good sweet cream. . . .

—Imogene Wolcott, *The Yankee Cookbook*

The mere word *pudding* sounds fattening and delicious, and most puddings are both. Almost anything cooked up with flour, tapioca, eggs, rice, milk, fruits, spices, and—always—some sort of sweetening can be termed a pudding. Through the years, needless to say, puddings and variations of puddings have been developed in numbers that boggle the mind and would certainly incapacitate the stomach, were it suddenly confronted by all of them. Since there are instant puddings and canned puddings and frozen puddings in every food store to tempt the time-conscious cook, we have not included many puddings in this book. For most puddings demand leisure—they need to be sifted, whipped, patted, steamed, baked. Yet in the end, a good homemade pudding is a comforting object to set before your family as the last course of a pleasant evening meal.

Simpler desserts usually involve fruit or fruits, and aside from omitting a last course altogether, nothing is more appropriate after a rich, heavy meal. Many fruits can simply be served raw—washed, sometimes peeled, but often left just as they are. Many respond well to poaching in wine or fruit juice, a bit of lemon juice or peel, a dash of spice. Really good fruit, like really good vegetables, should not be tampered with, or their innate flavor is altered. Experiment, but with discretion.

Blackberry, Huckleberry, or Blueberry Flummery

Flummeries were made in medieval times, as various conglomerations of oatmeal, sugar, flour, eggs, and eventually fruit, something between a gruel and a pudding, it seems. The British were fond of them, and it is very likely that some English lady brought along her favored recipes for flummery when she settled her household on Martha's Vineyard several hundred years ago. Somewhere along the line, the name dropped out of usage, for though we found numerous residents who remembered eating this dish in their childhood—and some housewives who make it still—none of them knew of it as flummery, but simply as a berry pudding. And, as in earlier days, there are still different sorts of flummeries. These two distinctly different preparations are the ones used on the Vineyard. However you make them, and whatever you call them, flummeries are lovely inventions.

FLUMMERY I

1 quart blackberries, huckleber-
    ries, or blueberries (frozen
    may be substituted)
1 cup sugar
1 tablespoon lemon juice

¼ teaspoon ground cinnamon
8 slices (or more) home-style
    white bread, crusts removed
Softened butter
Whipped cream (optional)

Preheat oven to 350°F.

Remove stems and leaves from fruit. Wash and let drain in a colander for a while. Combine berries, sugar, lemon juice, and cinnamon in a 2-quart saucepan and cook over moderate heat only long enough for the mixture to come to a simmer. Remove from heat. Butter the bread slices generously. Cut several slices of bread to fit bottom and sides of a 2-quart bowl or charlotte mold; place in bowl and spoon half the berry mixture over bread slices. Lay additional bread slices over berries; cover with remainder of fruit, and lay bread slices over top. Bake 20 to 25 minutes. Allow to cool, chill thoroughly, and serve with whipped cream if desired.

Note: This dessert may also be served unbaked. Simply prepare the mixture as above, then place a plate and heavy skillet or kitchen weight on the top of bread slices. Allow weighted dessert to remain in the refrigerator overnight before serving.

Makes 4 portions.

Flummery II

2 cups blackberries, huckleberries, or blueberries	*3 tablespoons cornstarch or arrowroot powder*
2 cups water	*¼ cup cold water*
1 tablespoon lemon juice	*Whipped cream (optional)*
½ cup sugar	

Remove stems and leaves from berries, rinse carefully with cold water, and drain. Combine berries with water and lemon juice and cook over low heat, simmering gently, for 10 minutes. Mix sugar and cornstarch or arrowroot, blend in ¼ cup water, and carefully stir into fruit. Simmer another 5 minutes. Cool slightly and pour into glass bowl or individual glass serving dishes. Chill thoroughly and serve very cold. Garnish with whipped cream if desired.

Note: Freshly picked red raspberries—or the rare but delectable black ones—are admirably suited to this recipe in place of the berries specified.

Makes 4 portions.

Queen of Puddings

Small wonder that old-timers were fond of this wonderful dessert—it is handsome to look at and a delight to the palate.

1 cup soft bread crumbs (use
    French, Italian, or home-style
    bread, if possible)
2 cups milk
1 tablespoon butter
¾ cup sugar

Grated rind of ½ lemon
¼ teaspoon salt
3 egg yolks, lightly beaten
½ cup raspberry jam (or ¾ cup
    fresh raspberries)
3 egg whites

Preheat oven to 350°F.

Combine crumbs, milk, butter, ½ cup of the sugar, lemon rind, and salt in a saucepan. Place over low heat and cook only until milk comes to a simmer. Remove from heat, beat in the egg yolks thoroughly, pour into a buttered 8-inch round baking dish, about 2 inches deep. (A deepish pie plate will do.) Set baking dish in a pan of hot water that comes halfway up the sides of the pudding dish and bake about 45 minutes, until it is firm. It is done when a knife inserted in center of pudding comes out clean. Remove dish from oven. Melt jam over low heat; pour over pudding. If using fresh berries, sprinkle on top of pudding.

Beat the egg whites until soft peaks are formed; add the remaining ¼ cup sugar gradually, beating constantly until a firm meringue develops. Spread the meringue over the pudding (or use a pastry bag to pipe the meringue decoratively over the top). Return pudding to oven to brown the meringue delicately, for 10 to 15 minutes.

Makes 6 to 8 portions.

Quince Pudding

The library of the Dukes County Historical Society in Edgartown is an enchanting place to while away a rainy afternoon looking at stereopticon slides of places and people long gone, or reading whaling journals or accounts of the early settlers. In an 1829 householding book from the library's collection, we came across this receipt for a quince pudding. With an added meringue, and baked in a fluted ironstone bowl, it came out of the oven looking so pretty that it seemed a shame to eat it.

A somewhat tart flavor and an unusual texture distinguish this creation from most custard-type baked puddings.

3 medium-size quinces, quartered, peeled, and cored	*¾ cup sugar*
1 cup milk	*½ teaspoon ginger*
1 cup medium cream or evaporated milk	*¼ teaspoon cinnamon*
	¼ teaspoon salt
3 egg yolks	*3 egg whites*
	½ teaspoon cream of tartar

Preheat oven to 350°F.

Put quince pieces in a saucepan and barely cover with water. Bring to a boil and cook gently about 10 minutes, or until fruit is soft enough to puree. Remove from heat and put through a food mill. In same saucepan, combine milk and cream or evaporated milk. Heat to scalding; remove from heat. Beat egg yolks lightly and combine with quince puree, ½ cup of the sugar, spices, and salt; mix well, then add scalded milk. Pour mixture into a 1½- to 2-quart ovenproof bowl (about 3 inches deep), set bowl in a pan of hot water (water should come up sides 1 or 2 inches), place in oven, and bake 30 minutes.

Beat egg whites with cream of tartar until they form stiff peaks, then beat in the remaining 4 tablespoons sugar a little at a time. Remove pudding from oven and spread meringue over top with back of a wooden spoon, spreading to edge of bowl so meringue will not shrink when baked. Replace pudding in oven, raise oven temperature to 400°F, and bake another 10 minutes. Serve pudding either warm or cooled (not cold).

Makes 6 to 8 portions.

Gooseberry Fool
[Or Raspberry or Blackberry]

Although the dictionary defines this use of *fool* as relating to the word *trifle* (also a dessert term) or *surprise,* describing it as a "dish of crushed fruit with whipped cream and sugar," we were unable to find the origin of this entertaining name. Perhaps early cooks considered the dish to be a foolishness. We suggest that it is a delicious foolishness, good enough to be prepared two ways. One variation uses whipped cream, the other has a custard base.

VARIATION I

1 quart fresh, ripe gooseberries (or raspberries or blackberries)

1 cup sugar

3 cups heavy cream, whipped

Remove stems from berries; discard bruised or damaged fruit. In a heavy saucepan combine berries with the sugar and cook over moderate heat until the fruit is tender, about 15 minutes if using gooseberries, 10 minutes for other berries. Stir frequently, pressing down on the berries to extract their juices. Press the cooked fruit through a colander or puree in a blender. Refrigerate until thoroughly chilled. Just before serving, whip the cream and fold it into the chilled fruit.

Makes 6 to 8 portions.

1 quart fresh, ripe gooseberries (or raspberries or blackberries)
2 cups water
1 cup sugar
¼ teaspoon salt
1 tablespoon butter
4 egg yolks, beaten until light
4 egg whites
3 tablespoons confectioners' sugar
½ teaspoon grated lemon rind (optional)

Prepare berries as in Variation I. Put berries and water in a heavy saucepan and cook over moderate heat until tender, about 15 minutes if using gooseberries, 10 minutes for other berries. Press mixture through a colander or puree in a blender. Return mixture to saucepan and add sugar, salt, and butter. Cook over low heat until butter is melted, then fold beaten egg yolks lightly into fruit mixture. Immediately remove from heat. Pour into a serving bowl and refrigerate until thoroughly chilled. Just before serving, beat egg whites until very stiff; beat in confectioners' sugar, beating constantly. Heap the meringue on the fruit mixture and serve immediately.

Optional and attractive: Sprinkle ½ teaspoon grated lemon rind on the meringue.

Makes 6 to 8 portions.

Trudy's Rhubarb Crisp

3 large stalks rhubarb, cut in ½-inch slices
1 tablespoon tapioca
¾ cup sugar
1 navel orange, peeled and cubed (save rind for grating)
1¼ cups cubed white bread
4 tablespoons melted butter
1 teaspoon grated orange rind
¼ cup unsweetened coconut

Preheat oven to 375°F.

Place the rhubarb, tapioca, sugar, cubed orange, ½ cup of the bread cubes, and 2 tablespoons of the melted butter in a mixing bowl. Mix well. Transfer to a 1- to 2-quart shallow baking dish. Sprinkle ½ teaspoon of the grated orange rind over these ingredients.

In the mixing bowl, combine the remaining bread cubes with the remaining melted butter, the coconut, and the remaining ½ teaspoon grated orange rind (more grated rind can be added, if desired). Arrange mixture evenly over the top of the rhubarb mixture.

Bake approximately 40 minutes. If you wish, serve with a little vanilla ice cream atop each portion.

Makes 4 portions.

Rhubarb Fool

1½ cups sugar

1 quart rhubarb, cut in 1-inch
   lengths

1 cup water

1 pint light cream

1½-inch piece stick cinnamon

Peel of ½ lemon, cut in strips

4 whole coriander seeds

4 whole cloves

2 tablespoons flour

4 egg yolks, well beaten

Nutmeg

Combine 1 cup of the sugar with rhubarb in a saucepan, add water, bring to a low boil, and simmer gently for 5 minutes. Let cool while preparing cream mixture.

Place cream in a medium saucepan. Tie cinnamon stick, lemon peel, coriander, and cloves in a small piece of cheesecloth and simmer in cream for 10 minutes. Remove from heat. Discard cheesecloth and contents. Combine remaining ½ cup sugar with flour and stir in beaten egg yolks. Return cream mixture to low heat and stir in egg mixture. Cook slowly on low heat until mixture thickens somewhat, stirring constantly. Do not boil. Pour thickened mixture into large bowl. Cool. Put rhubarb through a food mill or colander. Stir into cooled cream mixture. Mix well. Chill thoroughly. Serve with dash of nutmeg atop each serving.

Makes 6 to 8 portions.

CHAPTER 10

Sundries

Mrs. Mayhew Look, grape sauce, 1st prem., 1.00 . . . Mrs. A. S. Tilton, b'lkberry preserve and chili sauce . . . Mrs. Sarah B. Russell, pickled onions and cucumbers . . . Mrs. Z. A. Athearn, preserves, pickles, chow chow, piccalili, 1.40 . . . Mrs. Edgar West, spiced pears . . .

—From the list of awards, County Agricultural Fair, West Tisbury, September 26, 1895

An adaptable word, *sundries* may be used to refer to various types of miscellaneous collections. It seemed an apt heading for this chapter, which contains recipes for marmalades, herb sandwiches, pickles, sauces, and other good things that don't quite fit into the other sections of this book.

The Vineyard is a delightful place to make many of these sundries—using end-of-summer garden leftovers, a handful of herbs, a basket of gnarled fruit from a deserted farmstead. Some of them can be bottled and sealed in a canner or steam bath, then packed up and carried home at summer's end, along with the beach stones, bits of driftwood, gull feathers, and other flotsam you can't bear to throw away—pleasant ways of taking a little of the Vineyard home with you. A pot of rose-hip jam on Sunday morning, or artichoke relish, zucchini pickles, and pear chutney with your Thanksgiving turkey or Christmas ham can evoke memories of the bright days of your Island vacation and sustain your nostalgia until you return.

Million-Dollar Pickles

An elderly gentleman in West Tisbury who loved to gather and preserve the fruits of his garden gave us this wonderful pickle recipe, which he learned many years ago from an African-American neighbor of his in the South. The directions came to us well annotated with such remarks as "4 or two qts. sliced cukes (original recipe not clear, depends on how much you want)," and, at the bottom of the typewritten page: "(Unfortunately mice (?) had chewed original recipe sheet and amounts are only approx. Determine how much needed by testing by taste)." We appreciate, in principle, this fairly casual approach to cookery; and after both testing and tasting found the proportions given below produce flavorsome and memorable pickles. You may prefer them made with less spices and a bit less sugar.

These pickles, by the way, were sold one summer during pickling season at a small roadside vegetable stand in North Tisbury, and each time they appeared, Theresa Morse, a celebrated cook and cookbook author in her own right, appropriated every quart to serve at her delightful Menemsha guest house, Beach Plum Inn.

4 quarts sliced cucumbers　　　*2 green peppers, chopped*
8–10 small onions, sliced　　　*½ cup salt*

Put cucumbers, onions, and green peppers into a crock or other large receptacle (do not use metal). Mix well with a long wooden spoon; add salt and mix in thoroughly. Add cold water barely to cover cut vegetables. Lay a towel or piece of cheesecloth over top of crock and place in a cool spot overnight. In the morning, remove vegetables a quart or so at a time into a colander, press as much water as possible from them, and transfer them all to a large saucepan (at least 6-quart size). Taste vegetables as you work—if they seem too salty, spray some cold water over one batch or more to remove some of the salt. Prepare syrup.

SYRUP

4 scant cups sugar	2 teaspoons mustard seed
1 quart vinegar	1–3 teaspoons mixed pickling
1 teaspoon celery seed	spices
1 teaspoon turmeric	

In smaller saucepan, combine sugar, vinegar, and spices. Let mixture come to a boil, stir to dissolve sugar thoroughly, then pour syrup over cucumber mixture.

Bring pickles to a boil; cook over moderate heat about 15 to 20 minutes, until vegetables are fairly tender but not soggy. Mix and stir several times during cooking period. A wooden spoon is best for this. If pickles are to be canned, have four hot, sterilized quart jars ready to use, pack well with pickles, and seal. If desired, cook pickles only 10 minutes, pack and seal, and process 5 minutes in boiling-water bath. Pickles may also be put into clean quart jars, allowed to cool, and stored for some months, tightly capped, in the refrigerator or in a very cool part of the basement.

Makes about 4 quarts.

Baby Zucchini Pickles

Enough tiny (3–4-inch) zucchini squash to fill quart jar
1 teaspoon salt
¼ teaspoon cayenne pepper (optional)
2 cloves garlic, peeled and sliced
1 teaspoon olive oil
1 cup vinegar
1 cup water (approximately)
Sprig of fresh tarragon, dill, or basil

Allow two or three extra squash, as they should be well forced into the jar when packed. Wash squash well, remove stems and blossom ends, let soak in a bowl of hot water while you assemble other ingredients, then pack carefully and neatly into clean, hot quart jar. Add salt, cayenne (if used), garlic, and olive oil. Heat vinegar and water almost to boiling and pour over zucchini. Use a knife if necessary to remove any air at bottom of jar. Place sprig of tarragon, dill, or basil on top of squash, seal, and process 10 minutes in hot-water bath.

If pickles are to be eaten soon rather than canned for later use, place squash in saucepan, add seasonings, oil, and herb sprig, and pour on enough of the vinegar-water mixture barely to cover the squash. Bring to a boil, lower heat, and simmer 5 minutes. Squash should be crisp, not tender. Let cool, pour off excess liquid, and store pickles in closed containers in the refrigerator.

Makes 1 quart.

Raw Artichoke Relish

A refreshing raw relish can be made very simply from grated raw unpeeled Jerusalem artichokes and a good vinaigrette dressing. During the fall and winter, when interesting lettuces and other spring and summer delectables are prohibitively expensive or infrequently available, serve this as a salad with your evening meal, if you have been farsighted enough to raise this unique vegetable.

Scrub half a dozen or so raw artichokes, grate on medium grater blade, and add 2 tablespoons vinaigrette dressing to each cupful of raw artichokes. Mix well and allow to marinate for several hours in the refrigerator. Serve chilled but not too cold with a dusting of freshly ground black pepper or cayenne pepper and a sprinkling of chopped fresh parsley.

Note: A tablespoon of grated raw onion may be stirred into this relish to give added tang.

Carolina Artichoke Relish

Like most of the best recipes, this one has been handed down through generations of cooks. It originated many years ago on a South Carolina plantation and came into the family of one of this cookbook's authors from a southern friend, a descendant of the plantation owners. Guests have been known to eat a pint of this relish at one sitting, so try to make a large batch at one time. It is easy to can—merely follow any standard pickling directions, processing the jars 10 minutes in a boiling-water bath.

2 quarts ground unpeeled Jerusalem artichokes (cut up biggest
   ones before grinding)
1 quart cut-up green peppers (or mixed red and green bell peppers)
1 quart cut-up onions
1½ gallons cold water
1½ cups salt
2 tablespoons turmeric
4 tablespoons white mustard seed
4 cups brown sugar, lightly packed
2 quarts cider vinegar

Scrub artichokes well (soak in cold water if necessary to remove dirt). Put through a food chopper, using medium blade, until you have about 2 quarts of ground vegetables. Grind cut-up peppers and onions. Soak ground vegetables in water and salt overnight—use large nonmetallic container for this purpose. In the morning, drain well and taste to be sure vegetables are not too salty (if they are, rinse part of them in a colander under cold water). Mix turmeric and mustard seed into ground vegetables. In a large kettle (at least 6-quart size), mix brown sugar and vinegar. Place kettle over heat; stir until sugar dissolves. Add ground vegetables. Bring mixture to a boil and simmer 3 minutes, stirring constantly.

If relish is to be canned, place in sterilized jars and process 10 minutes in a hot-water bath. If preferred, simmer relish another 8 to 10 minutes, stirring occasionally, cool, and store in glass jars or plastic containers in the refrigerator.

Makes about 4 quarts.

Green-Tomato Marmalade

Barbara Nevin, widow of Edgartown's beloved Dr. Bob Nevin, for years not only managed an enormous house and household but also busied herself in such other areas as politicking for town offices, novel writing, and cooking all manner of delights. All sorts of helpful ideas and suggestions began to arrive from her as soon as she heard this book was being compiled. One recipe she sent us was this version of tomato marmalade, which offers a practical disposal of those green tomatoes you pick off just before the first frost threat and never know what to do with.

6 pounds green tomatoes (about 20, preferably small ones)
2 pounds sugar
6 lemons
1½ teaspoons salt
1 cup water
½ teaspoon whole cloves (optional)
1-inch-piece stick cinnamon (optional)
½ teaspoon whole allspice (optional)

Cut tomatoes into 1-inch chunks and place in a large bowl. Add sugar and stir. Cut lemons into paper-thin slices, sprinkling them with salt as you go. Cook the lemons in the water for 5 minutes, then combine with sugared tomatoes in a large saucepan and cook over very low heat, stirring constantly, until mixture thickens, about 50 minutes. Pack marmalade into hot, sterilized jars, seal, and process 5 minutes in hot-water bath.

If a spiced marmalade is preferred, tie spices in a cheesecloth bag and drop into pot after fruit comes to a boil. Remove spice bag before pouring marmalade into jars.

Makes about 3 quarts.

Quince Honey

Anyone fortunate enough to have a quince tree on the premises usually guards it carefully as quince season approaches, then parcels out some of the hard, knobby yellow-green quinces to special friends and relatives, saving the rest for home use—to be baked whole (sweetened and spiced) and served with cream (plain or whipped), or to be converted into preserves or some other delicious sweetener. A few Vineyarders have quinces, and in mid-October comes the call: "The quinces are ready." Our quinces came from a tree in the yard of a very old farmhouse nestled back in the valley off Lambert's Cove Road and were picked on a bright October morning from an old tree entwined with a scarlet-hued Virginia-creeper vine.

We used them to make up this "honey" from a recipe in an old book of Vineyard recipes. "Honey" seems to have been an old-fashioned New England term for what newer cooking guides call preserves, which is actually what this is since the cooked fruit is not strained out but left in. We just like calling it quince honey.

8 medium-size quinces
Juice from 1 lemon
Sugar

Wash the quinces, quarter them, then core and peel them, saving cores (unless too wormy) and parings. Quinces darken even more rapidly than apples, so if you want a light-colored honey, drop your peeled quinces into a bowl of water to which the juice of a lemon has been added. Put parings and cores into a saucepan, barely cover with water, bring to a boil, lower heat, and simmer 20 minutes. While they cook, grate or finely chop the peeled quince quarters. Cover with wax paper to retard darkening, if desired; or grate just before parings are through cooking. Strain liquid from parings, measure, and add enough water to make 3 cups liquid. Combine this liquid and the grated or chopped quinces in a saucepan, bring to a boil, lower heat, and simmer 15 minutes. Measure cooked quince and add an equal amount of sugar; replace in saucepan, stir well, return to a boil, lower heat, and simmer about 15 minutes, stirring frequently so mixture will not stick. Skim if needed, then pour into hot, sterilized jars, seal, and process 5 minutes in hot-water bath.

Makes 4 jelly glasses.

Pear Chutney

3 large, firm pears
1 chili pepper
½ cup raisins
2 cloves garlic, minced
¼ teaspoon ground allspice
½ teaspoon ground cinnamon
2 tablespoons fresh ginger,
*   minced*

1 tablespoon coriander seeds
½ teaspoon red pepper flakes
½ teaspoon salt
1 cup brown sugar
½ cup vinegar
1 lime, chopped fine (including
*   rind)*
½ cup toasted sliced almonds

Peel, core, and chop pears into ½-inch dice. Seed and mince chili pepper. Combine all the ingredients in a heavy saucepan. Cook over moderate heat, stirring until the sugar dissolves. Bring to a boil and simmer, stirring occasionally until thick, about 30 minutes. Spoon into hot, sterilized jelly jars and seal. May be refrigerated for two to three weeks. Or process 5 minutes in hot-water bath as in Quince Honey recipe (see page 245).

Makes 4 cups.

Herb Sandwiches

English traditions linger in many Vineyard homes, as they do in much of New England. The social life of many elderly Island residents centers on occasional visits from friends who live in another part of the Island. As the tea things are passed around, topics range from the oriole at the feeding station to the defeat of the zoning law at the last town meeting.

Fresh herbs, good white bread, and sweet butter combine exquisitely with tea's delicate flavor, and in summer and fall herb sandwiches at teatime make a nice change from oversweet cakes and other sugary goodies. Collect a handful or two of herb sprigs and cut or chop them as fine as possible. Experiment with combinations and proportions, but don't cut too much of the more overpowering herbs like sage, tarragon, thyme, mint, fennel, and rosemary. Parsley, basil, chives, marjoram, chervil, dill, lovage, and savory are all flavorsome. Two pleasing combinations are equal parts of parsley, basil, chives, and dill; or about one-third each of lovage, parsley, and dill and a small bit of tarragon. Whimsical gardeners could snip in some nasturtium leaves and flowers, scented geranium leaves, or maybe a marigold or two.

Butter one side of both slices of bread, or use a good mayonnaise on one side of the sandwich. This helps keep the herbs in place. White bread is recommended, but oatmeal, pumpernickel, and rye are also quite good. Spread 2 or 3 tablespoons chopped herbs on one buttered slice and top with another. Press slices together lightly to imbed the herbs in the butter. Cut into desired shapes and serve. Don't prepare these sandwiches ahead and refrigerate them—they should be freshly made.

Portuguese Sweet Bread
Luncheon Delight

This is really an assemblage rather than a recipe. Many years ago an Edgartown hostess served a version of this dish containing cooked zucchini and onions, sliced tomatoes, ham, and cheese. Her guests sat on the sunny deck, sipping iced tea and watching the boats sail by, duly impressed with the company and with this pretty and easy concoction. We offer a couple of options, but feel free to create. Fish and vegetable dips like hummus are good ingredients. This is also a great way to use leftover grilled or sautéed vegetables.

VARIATION I

1 loaf of Portuguese sweet bread
8 ounces cream cheese, softened
2 hard-boiled eggs, minced
Capers and fresh dill
Salt and freshly ground black
    pepper to taste
8 ounces sliced smoked salmon
Lemon juice
Mayonnaise as needed
1 peeled, sliced cucumber

VARIATION II

1 loaf of Portuguese sweet bread
2 cups finely chopped cooked
    chicken
3 ounces cream cheese, softened
⅓ cup mayonnaise plus a little
    more as needed
3 green onions, finely chopped
¼ cup toasted slivered almonds
Curry powder, cumin, salt and
    freshly ground black pepper to
    taste
½ cup chutney (see Pear Chutney,
    page 246)

Slice bread horizontally into three equal slices. For particularly liquid ingredients, you may want to lightly toast the rounds of bread.

For Variation I: Combine cream cheese with eggs, capers, and freshly snipped dill. Add salt and pepper to taste. Spread mixture on one of bread slices, and cover with smoked salmon. Sprinkle with lemon juice. Cover bottom of next slice of bread lightly with mayonnaise, and place gently on top of salmon. Spread mayonnaise on top of slice, and cover with overlapping layer of cucumber. Sprinkle with more dill, salt, and pepper. Lightly cover bottom of top layer of bread with mayonnaise and place on top of cucumber slices. Refrigerate bread until ready to use. To serve, slice in wedges like a cake.

For Variation II: Combine the chicken, cream cheese, ⅓ cup mayonnaise, green onions, and almonds. Add curry powder, cumin, salt, and pepper to taste. Spread on one bread slice. Lightly cover remaining cut surfaces of bread slices with mayonnaise. Spread chutney on top of middle bread slice. Reassemble bread and serve as above.

Makes 4 to 6 portions.

Berry Sauce

⅓ cup soft butter
1 cup sifted confectioners' sugar
1 egg white, beaten lightly

⅔ cup blackberries, huckleberries,
 or raspberries

Beat the butter until very soft, add the sugar gradually, beating until well blended and fluffy. Add the egg white and continue beating until completely blended. Crush the berries slightly; fold into the sugar mixture. Chill thoroughly and serve very, very cold. Good on a simple, unfrosted cake such as pound cake.

Makes about 2 cups.

Soft Chocolate Frosting

1½ cups sugar, sifted
4 tablespoons cornstarch
½ teaspoon salt
1½ cups milk

4 squares baking chocolate
 (unsweetened)
3 tablespoons butter
1 teaspoon vanilla

Combine sugar, cornstarch, and salt in a heavy saucepan, then stir in milk and add chocolate squares. Cook over moderate heat, stirring frequently, until chocolate melts and mixture begins to bubble. Cook a few minutes more, stirring constantly (a wire whisk is useful for this). Remove saucepan from heat and stir in butter and vanilla. Cool mixture slightly before spreading on cake.

Makes enough for 1 cake.

Polly's Luncheon Soup

For many years a group of knowledgeable lady gardeners have assembled once or twice a summer with a bring-your-own lunch at the home of one of the members to share seeds, plants, problems, and discoveries. When they meet at the Far Barn of the Polly Hill Arboretum, Polly often serves this simple cold soup that she enhances with a generous amount of curry powder.

2 cans of beef consommé
12 ounces cream cheese
6 tablespoons lemon juice
2½ teaspoons curry powder
Chopped chives
Coarsely chopped black olives

Blend everything but the chives and olives until mixture is smooth and creamy. Chill several hours. Serve garnished with chives and olives.
Makes 6 portions.

Rum Tea

Beach picnics, cookouts, clambakes, or just a sandwich from a fisherman's back pocket—any food enjoyed at the seaside seems enhanced by one's surroundings. The pleasantest beach outing remembered by one Vineyarder took place some years ago at Katama. On the long-anticipated day, it rained; but being primed and prepared, the family voted to go anyhow. It was really only a typical midsummer mizzle, the husband observed. Cold chicken, good garlicky salami, marinated artichoke hearts with capers, cherry tomatoes, homemade dill pickles, Camembert, Italian bread, stuffed eggs, homemade oatmeal cookies, a quart of rich-red strawberries, and two Milkbones for the poodles were laid out along a flat board that had been washed up by the sea, and the rum tea was poured. An Elysian period ensued.

Rum tea came to us from late-fall luncheons at Max Eastman's house, where it was served with the meal in large white cups. It is fine for chilly days at home, but even better on the beach. Prepare large vacuum bottles of good, strong, boiling-hot tea. Use a regular blend, not something fancy, and allow at least a pint of tea per person. Sweeten the tea slightly, and take along extra sugar in case someone wants it. Put the rum (a light Puerto Rican type is good, but you may prefer something else) in an appropriate bottle, allowing for about a tablespoon per cup of tea, and take a small jar of milk. The rum and the milk, if desired, are added to each cup as it is poured.

The concoction is especially recommended for sunless, windy days when you have to eat your lunch while wrapped in a blanket or crouched behind a rock or dune. Also fortifying after a chilling swim in the surf.

Max Eastman's Daiquiris

Sitting outside the hilltop house in East Pasture with Max and Yvette Eastman on an idyllic summer afternoon and sharing their panoramic view of Menemsha Pond, Vineyard Sound, and the Elizabeth Islands is a memory treasured by many of their friends. The daiquiris Max often served us to enhance our pleasure were as inimitably delightful as everything else about this great man. When we began to compile this book, we asked him to tell us how he made them. He credited their invention to his first wife, Eliena, saying that "like all her creations, they were speedy, spontaneous, and very simple."

> *One ounce of light rum,*
> *One ounce of dark rum,*
> *The juice from half a succulent lime.*
> *My mother's sugar-spoon level full of sugar,*
> *A leaf or two of mint,*
> *Mixed in a blender with oodles of ice.*

CHAPTER 11

Portuguese Cookery

Alley's General Store; Ben David Motors, Inc.; Da Rosa's M.V. Printing Co.; De Sorcy Paint Store; Maciel Marine Park; Raul B. Mederios, Jr., Contractor; Pachico Septic Inspection; Sequira Well Drilling.

—From the Martha's Vineyard Telephone Directory

On Vineyard storefronts and mailboxes Portuguese names are almost as common as long-familiar New England ones like Daggett, Luce, Manter, and Mayhew. When whaling ships set sail from the Edgartown wharves two centuries or more ago, they often left without a full crew and stopped by the Azores and the Cape Verde Islands to sign on a complement of Portuguese sailors, renowned for their seafaring skills. Some of these vigorous, industrious men brought their families to the new land of America when their seagoing days were over, and it is fortunate for Martha's Vineyard that they did, as most of the Island's services are owned and run today by the descendants of these sea specialists—men who are as hard-working and as rugged as their forefathers were. The Island's Portuguese are noted also for their friendliness; anyone caught in a snowbank or with a flat tire or an injured animal never has to wait long for aid—and the odds are high that his savior will be a Portuguese-American.

Mingling easily and cordially with their fellow New England neighbors, the Portuguese people of the Island have nonetheless maintained many aspects of their heritage with pride and care. Not the least appealing of these is the Mediterranean-oriented cooking that is the backbone of their cuisine. All the local grocers stock tasty linguica and chorizo sausages, and the Portuguese bakery in Oak Bluffs turns out a delicious massa sovada, the traditional sweet bread. One local Portuguese housewife attributes her family's good health—and that of her people in general—to the ingestion of huge amounts of parsley, both raw and cooked, citing it as one essential of Portuguese cookery, along with mint and, when possible, fresh coriander leaves. The cuisine in the Island's Portuguese households is still traditionally Azorean cooking and differs from the cuisine of mainland Portugal in somewhat the way the Vineyard's food differs from that of the rest of New England. Azorean recipes specify white cornmeal, for instance, whereas most Portuguese recipes use yellow meal. (One of the world's most ubiquitous foods, cornmeal figures importantly in the diet of the Vineyard's three principal cultural families—the British colonists, the Indians, and the Portuguese.)

In general, Portuguese food might be said to be hearty, interesting, and delightful—words that could also describe the people whose cuisine these dishes are drawn from.

Portuguese Chowder

The Mediterranean influence is evident in the fish chowder prepared by some of the Vineyard's Portuguese cooks. The basics are constant—fish, salt pork, onions, potatoes—but the addition of spices and vinegar results in a somewhat piquant dish instead of the more traditional one.

¼ pound salt pork, cut in ½-inch
    dice
2 large onions, chopped medium
    fine
3 medium potatoes, cut in ½-inch
    dice (about 3 cups)
6 cups water
About ½ teaspoon salt
1 tablespoon vinegar

1 teaspoon dried oregano
¼ teaspoon saffron
Freshly ground black pepper to
    taste
About 2 pounds cleaned, boned
    fish (haddock, halibut, cod,
    flounder, in any proportion),
    cut in chunks

Cook salt pork in a heavy aluminum kettle or Dutch oven over moderate heat until golden brown. Remove and drain on a paper towel. Reserve. Add chopped onions to fat and cook slowly until transparent and tender. Add potatoes, water, and seasonings. Bring to a slow boil and cook gently until potatoes are tender. Do not overcook. Add chunks of fish and cook gently about 5 minutes, until fish flakes easily when poked with a fork. Test for seasoning—more salt may be needed. Add browned salt-pork bits just before serving.

Makes 6 portions.

Holy Ghost Soup
[Kale Soup]

A variation of the traditional method of preparing kale soup is offered as a memento of a Vineyard summer festival sponsored by the Portuguese-American community: the Feast of the Holy Ghost. A Vineyard prelate claims no one really knows the origin of Holy Ghost Soup except that it all began back in the old country, some say in honor of a queen who was extremely generous to the poor. In Oak Bluffs the affair is sponsored by St. John's Holy Ghost Society. Most of the people concerned, or their forebears, came from the Azores during old whaling days. "Not shanghaied," the good priest says, "but as honorable crew members and paid."

Hundreds are fed this soup. All they want. And free. The proportions below won't feed hundreds but should satisfy six to eight hungry people.

*2 pounds marrow bones, cut into
    3-inch pieces*
Vegetable oil, if needed
*3 pounds beef chuck, cut in
    1-inch cubes*

*4 medium onions, coarsely
    chopped*
Salt
Freshly ground black pepper
1 bay leaf

4 allspice seeds
3 whole cloves garlic
8–10 cups water
3 or 4 hot Italian sausages
(linguica may be substituted),
sliced ½ inch thick

3 or 4 medium potatoes, peeled
and cut into 1-inch cubes
1 pound kale, coarsely shredded
Loaf of French or Italian bread
Sprigs of fresh mint

Brown the marrow bones in a heavy 8-quart kettle over moderately high heat until the marrow can be extracted. Reserve the bones. Using the marrow (and a little oil if needed), brown the meat and then the onions. Add salt and pepper to taste, the bay leaf, allspice, and garlic. Return the marrow bones to the kettle and add the water, enough to cover all ingredients by at least 2 to 3 inches. Simmer over low heat, covered, until beef is tender, about 2 hours. Add sausages, potatoes, and kale, and simmer another ½ hour.

Slice the bread in 2-inch chunks; crisp them in a preheated 400°F oven about 10 minutes. Place one or two pieces in each bowl, lay several sprigs fresh mint over the bread, and ladle the soup over bread and mint. Serve immediately before bread softens.

Note: An Azorean version of kale soup, also popular among the Vineyard Portuguese community, calls for simmering a large shinbone with chopped onions for 2 hours, then adding kale, linguica, potatoes, a can of kidney beans, and sometimes chopped fresh tomatoes and fresh peas. After these have simmered 20 minutes or so, chopped fresh mint is tossed in and simmered briefly. The meat is removed from the shinbone and cut into small pieces before the soup is served. Flavor is improved if it is allowed to mellow a day or two before being eaten.

Makes 6 to 8 portions.

Marinated Pork Chops

MARINADE

3 cloves garlic, minced

½ cup vinegar (preferably
   white-wine vinegar)

½ cup dry white wine

1 large onion, cut in ½-inch slices

Pinch of cinnamon

1 tablespoon salt

1 hot pepper, coarsely chopped

Combine marinade ingredients in a large glass, ceramic, or stainless-steel bowl.

8 lean pork chops (or 8 slices
   pork loin, cut 1 inch thick)

Marinade

3 tablespoons lard or vegetable oil

1 teaspoon of flour

2 tablespoons water

Lemon wedges

Pimiento slices

Place pork in marinade and refrigerate 24 hours; or marinate 12 hours at room temperature. Turn the meat occasionally.

Remove pork from marinade. Drain it well and dry it with paper towels. Reserve the marinade. Add lard or oil to a heavy skillet; melt over moderately high heat. Brown the pork evenly on both sides. Remove from skillet. Pour off fat from skillet. Strain 1 cup of the marinade and add it to skillet. Bring to a boil over high heat, scraping the brown particles from the bottom and sides of the skillet to incorporate them in the marinade. Return pork to skillet, reduce heat to low, cover tightly, and simmer 30 minutes, or until meat is tender. Sauce may be thickened slightly by slowly stirring in 1 teaspoon flour mixed to a smooth paste with 2 tablespoons water.

Serve with a garnish of lemon wedges and strips of canned pimientos.

Makes 4 portions.

Lima Beans and Linguica

1 cup dried lima beans
1 large onion, coarsely chopped
2–3 tablespoons butter (or half butter, half vegetable oil)
1 pound linguica, cut in 1-inch slices
Salt
Freshly ground black pepper

Soak lima beans overnight in water to cover. Drain, cover with 3 cups fresh cold water, and bring to a boil over high heat. Reduce heat to low and let simmer. In a small, heavy skillet cook onions in butter or butter-oil mixture until golden and transparent. Add linguica slices and brown lightly on both sides, then add onions and linguica to lima beans. Cover tightly and barely simmer until beans are tender (see note below regarding cooking time). Season to taste with salt and pepper. Linguica has a high salt content, so it may not be necessary to add salt to this dish.

Note: Soaking period for dried beans may be hastened as follows: Drop beans into 3 cups rapidly boiling water, bring back to the boil and cook over moderately high heat for 2 minutes. Remove saucepan from heat and let beans soak for 1 hour, then proceed with recipe.

It is nearly impossible to give even an approximate cooking time for dried beans. Too many factors are involved—the length of time the beans have sat on the grocery-store shelf, for instance. Beans soaked overnight will cook up more quickly than those soaked in the method given in the preceding paragraph. Sometimes specially treated beans may be purchased that presumably do not require soaking.

Makes 4 generous portions.

Codfish Cakes

1 pound salt cod (the Canadian fillets are recommended)
2 cups day-old French or Italian bread, coarsely crumbled
¾ cup olive oil (or part olive, part other vegetable oil)
2 tablespoons chopped parsley
2 tablespoons chopped fresh coriander, if available
1 teaspoon chopped fresh mint
Freshly ground black pepper
3 cloves garlic, peeled and cut in half
Parsley sprigs
6 poached eggs (optional)

Freshen the cod by soaking at least 12 hours in cold water to cover. Change water several times during this period. Drain fish, rinse it, place in a saucepan, and add sufficient cold water to cover it by 1 inch. Bring to simmer over moderate heat, and cook over low heat about 20 minutes, or until fish flakes easily when pierced with a fork. Do not let it boil at any time. Drain the fish and let it cool, then shred it fine with the fingers, discarding any bones or skin.

In a large bowl combine bread crumbs, ½ cup of the oil, chopped parsley, coriander, mint, and pepper. Stir vigorously. Add flaked codfish and mix well. Shape mixture into flat, round cakes, about ¾ inch thick. The hands may be lightly moistened with water before shaping fish cakes. Heat the remaining ¼ cup oil in a heavy skillet with the garlic until almost at the smoking point. Add the fish cakes to the pan and cook over moderate heat until golden brown on each side. Drain briefly on a paper towel, then serve on a heated platter with a garnish of parsley sprigs. A poached egg may top each fish cake.

Makes 6 large fish cakes.

Salt Cod with Potatoes

1½ pounds salt cod fillets (the Canadian fillets are excellent)
¾ cup olive oil (or half olive oil, half other vegetable oil)
4 medium onions, peeled and cut into ¼-inch slices
½ teaspoon finely minced garlic
6 medium potatoes, boiled without salt, peeled, and cut into
  ½-inch slices
Salt
Freshly ground black pepper
2 tablespoons finely chopped fresh parsley
4 hard-boiled eggs, cut into 16 wedges
18–20 pitted black olives
Lemon wedges

Freshen the cod by soaking at least 12 hours in cold water to cover. Change the water several times during this period. Drain the fish, rinse it, place in a saucepan, and add enough cold water to cover it by 1 inch. Bring to a simmer over moderate heat, then cook over low heat about 20 minutes, or until fish flakes easily when pierced with a fork. Do not let it boil at any time. Drain the fish; let it cool. Shred fine with the fingers, discarding any bones or skin.

Heat half the oil in a heavy skillet over moderate heat and cook the onions in it until golden and transparent. Stir often. Stir in garlic and immediately remove the skillet from the heat. With a slotted spoon, remove onion-garlic mixture and set aside.

Preheat oven to 375°F.

Place half of the sliced potatoes in a heavy 8- or 9-inch casserole, 4 inches deep. Salt them very lightly. Cover with half of the onion-garlic mixture, then with half of the codfish. Season with a little black pepper. Repeat layering process with remainder of potatoes, onions, cod, and black pepper. Now pour remainder of the oil over the contents of the casserole. Bake about 20 minutes, or until top is lightly browned. Sprinkle with parsley and garnish with egg wedges and olives. Serve immediately.

Offer, as an accompaniment, lemon wedges—and, for those who wish it, coarsely ground black pepper.

Makes 4 to 6 portions.

Steamed Hard-shelled Clams in White Wine and Seasonings

This variation of a classic dish is prepared by a Spanish friend who cooks sublimely in Portuguese as well.

2 tablespoons olive oil
1 tablespoon butter
½ cup finely chopped onions
1 tablespoon minced garlic
½ cup coarsely crumbled day-old
    French or Italian bread,
    crusts removed
¼ cup chopped parsley
¼ cup pine nuts (pignoli), if avail-

able, or ¼ cup slivered
    almonds
24 small hard-shelled clams (little
    necks), scrubbed clean
1 cup dry white wine
Freshly ground black pepper
Salt, if needed
Lemon wedges
Parsley sprigs

Heat oil and butter in a heavy casserole or skillet over moderate heat until foam subsides. Reduce heat to low, add onions and garlic, and cook until onions are golden and transparent. Add bread crumbs, parsley, and nuts; cook about 5 minutes, adding a little additional oil or butter if needed. Add clams and wine. Cover pan tightly and cook over low heat 8 to 10 minutes, or until clam shells open. Remove clams to a heated platter, add pepper and salt (if needed) to sauce, and pour it over clams.

Garnish with lemon wedges and sprigs of parsley.

Makes 2 portions as main course, 4 as appetizer.

Portuguese Cornbread

Traditionally served in Portugal as an accompaniment to Holy Ghost Soup (page 258), this coarse-textured cornbread may be prepared with either white or yellow cornmeal. In the Azores, where a large group of the Portuguese people on Martha's Vineyard originated, the white meal is preferred. Serve it also with any hearty soup or with a good salad. Or serve leftover cornbread at breakfast, warmed, cut into wedges, and generously buttered.

1½ cups white cornmeal (or yellow)

1½ cups boiling water

1½ teaspoons salt

2 tablespoons sugar

2 tablespoons butter

1 package compressed or granulated yeast dissolved in ¼ cup
warm water (water for granulated yeast should be slightly more
than lukewarm)

½ cup milk

3–4 cups (approximately) sifted all-purpose flour (a mixture of 2
parts pastry flour and 1 part all-purpose flour may be used and
will make a softer dough)

Grease a 9-inch round pan, 2 to 3 inches deep.

In a large bowl combine cornmeal, boiling water, salt, sugar, and butter. Stir vigorously until smooth. Cool slightly. Add the yeast mixture and blend well. Add milk and flour, using enough flour to produce a moderately firm dough. Place dough on a lightly floured board and knead by pressing down on it with the heel of the hand, lifting the mass off the board, and then throwing it back onto the board. Continue this process until dough becomes smooth and elastic, about 5 minutes. Avoid overflouring the pastry board. Place dough in a buttered bowl, cover with a clean, dampened towel, and let it rise in a warm, draft-free place. The oven, unheated, is a good spot. Set the bowl over a pan of hot water to hasten rising. When the dough has doubled in bulk, after about 1½ to 2 hours, punch it down in its bowl, then take it out and knead it again two or three times. Shape dough into a ball, place in baking pan, and allow it to rise again until doubled in bulk, about 1 to 1½ hours. Bake in a preheated 350°F oven until the top is golden brown, 45 to 50 minutes.

Note: The cornbread will be lighter in texture if dough is allowed to rise twice in the bowl before final rising in the pan.

Makes 4 to 6 portions.

Portuguese Sweet Bread

[Massa Sovada]

This is the sweet bread for the Sabbath—perfect with hot, freshly brewed coffee. Toasted and accompanied by a firm white cream cheese and jelly—beach plum, especially—it is the purest of pleasures.

Another name for these light and airy loaves is Easter bread. When the bread is made during that season, one hard-cooked egg in the shell for each child in the family is placed in the dough before the second rising.

2 packages granulated or compressed yeast

½ cup warm water

¼ teaspoon sugar

1 cup milk

¼ pound softened butter

1 teaspoon vanilla extract

½ teaspoon powdered mace (optional)

Pinch of powdered saffron (optional)

About 6 cups sifted flour, preferably unbleached (2 parts pastry
*   flour and 1 part all-purpose flour may be used)*

1¼ cups sugar

1 teaspoon salt

5 or 6 eggs, well beaten

1 beaten egg yolk, mixed with 2 tablespoons water (or 2 tablespoons
*   granulated sugar)*

Grease two 9-inch round pans, preferably 2 inches deep.

Combine yeast, warm water, and ¼ teaspoon sugar, and set aside. (If using granulated yeast, water should be slightly hotter than lukewarm.) In a small saucepan heat milk and butter. Add vanilla, mace, and saffron, if used. Remove from heat when butter has melted. Cool slightly. In a large mixing bowl combine 4 cups of the flour, 1¼ cups sugar, and the salt. Make a well in the center and add the cooled milk and yeast mixture. Beat vigorously. The electric mixer works well up to this point. (If your mixer has a dough hook attachment, you can use it to do the rest of the mixing if you wish.) Add beaten eggs and mix well. Add remaining flour, ½ cup at a time, until a firm dough is achieved (additional flour may be needed). Place dough on a lightly floured board or marble slab; knead by pressing down on bread mass with heel of hand, lifting mass off board, then throwing it back. Knead about 5 minutes, or until dough becomes smooth and elastic. Place dough in a buttered bowl and let rise in a warm, draft-free place such as an unheated oven (set bowl over a pan of hot water to hasten rising). When dough has doubled in bulk, turn out onto a floured board and knead again for a few moments. Cut dough into two equal pieces, shape lightly into round balls, and place one ball in each cake pan. Brush loaf tops lightly with beaten egg mixture, or sprinkle a little granulated sugar over the loaves. Let bread rise until doubled in bulk, about 1½ hours. Bake in preheated 350°F oven approximately 1 hour.

Note: Instead of the five or six eggs specified, up to twelve eggs are sometimes used to make this bread, in which case additional flour is required to stiffen the dough.

Makes 2 medium loaves.

Portuguese Bread Pudding

A deliciously different bread pudding that typifies the Portuguese fondness for sweets prepared with many eggs. It is a departure from standard bread puddings using bread slices (this one contains bread crumbs); and the caramel mixture coating the baking dish melts during the process, adding another dimension of flavor.

½ cup sugar, sifted

2 tablespoons water

2 cups milk

6 tablespoons sugar

½ teaspoon grated orange rind

2 tablespoons butter

2 cups fine bread crumbs, made from day-old French or Italian
   bread, crusts removed

5 or 6 beaten eggs (4 whole eggs and 2 egg yolks may be used)

Preheat oven to 350°F.

Combine ½ cup sugar and water in a small, heavy saucepan. Cook over moderate heat, stirring with a wooden spoon, until sugar melts. Continue to cook, swirling the pan now and then, until the liquid turns caramel brown. Immediately remove saucepan from heat and pour the caramel into a 6- to 8-cup baking dish, at least 4 inches deep, or a 1½- to 2-quart charlotte mold. Tilt the baking dish so that the bottom and sides are coated with caramel, which will harden as it cools. In a saucepan combine milk, 6 tablespoons sugar, and orange rind and heat to scalding (the scalding point is reached when tiny beads or bubbles appear around the edges of the pan). Remove from heat. Add the butter and crumbs to the milk mixture. Stir the beaten eggs into this mixture, then pour into the caramel-lined baking dish. Set it in a container holding about 2 inches of boiling water and bake in middle of oven 45 to 50 minutes. Custard is done when a knife inserted in its center comes out clean. Cool thoroughly in mold, then chill in refrigerator for several hours. Unmold by running a knife around the sides of the baking dish, then placing serving plate over pudding and inverting. Spoon some of the caramel over each serving.

Makes 6 to 8 portions.

CHAPTER 12

The Old-Timers

Flour, per barrel	$ .59
Wood, per load	1.00
Potatoes, per bushel	.25
Beef, per pound	.04
Veal, per pound	.03
Pork, per pound	.05
Butter, per pound	.10
Cheese, per pound	.05

—From an 1829 Grocer's Advertisement in the *Vineyard Gazette*

The Vineyard was not only self-supporting but self-sustaining for nigh onto two centuries. Only spices, sugar, tea, coffee, breadstuffs and the rum, which was considered quite essential, were imported. . . . Meat, beef, pork, and mutton; fish, both fresh and cured; vegetables and fodder; the clothes people wore, their shoes . . . all were raised, caught, grown or made on the Island.

—Eleanor R. Mayhew, ed., *A Short History of Martha's Vineyard*

Nostalgia for times past lingers in many sections of the Vineyard. The hazy, halcyon days of summer and fall often evoke the shade of some former Islander, and though you will no longer pass one of the Reverend Mayhews riding his mare along a cowpath on his way to minister to an ailing farmer, you may very well buy your lobsters from a contemporary member of that distinguished family, or chat with another one of them at the airport as he waits for a plane to Boston to attend meetings of the legislature as a state representative. Mayhew, Norton, Athearn, Manter, Luce, Pease, Allen—the old names survive; the families still live here.

Like other New Englanders, Vineyarders settled in for the winter prepared for almost anything. "In those days," says John Daggett (*It Began With a Whale*, privately printed, 1963), "we had no warning that a storm was coming until it practically reached us. However, we never worried but took it in stride because we usually had pork, bacon, chickens, eggs and also vegetables in the cellar. We always had a barrel of flour, another of sugar and usually one or two of apples, as well as 100 pounds of prunes." Travel was precarious during much of the year—and tediously slow because of innumerable sheep and cattle bars across the roads. As a result, an Edgartown lady might see her brother in Chilmark only once or twice a year. On arriving from the mainland by boat, the traveler lodged for the night at a Holmes Hole (now Vineyard Haven) tavern before he "sett forward" on the road to Gay Head.

Food was a vital concern. Remarkable ingenuity was displayed by industrious housewives in both preserving and preparing what foodstuffs they had. A few pecks of oysters, bedded down in sawdust and partially frozen, could be feasted on for weeks. Deer, rabbits, and other small game were easy targets on snow-covered fields and could be drawn and hung in outsheds until needed for food. On good days there was ice fishing in some of the Great Ponds. Pickles and jellies put up on hot summer days added tang to late-winter meals; and when beans and cornmeal, and salt pork, potatoes, and onions were about all there was left, Yankee inventiveness remained as active as ever. Thus a simple combination of three basic ingredients—salt pork, potatoes, and onions—became many things: Potato Bargain, Necessity Mess, Tilton's Glory, or Scootin'-'Long-the-Shore (the latter being the shipboard name because the dish was often prepared in ships' galleys as the fishermen were scooting along the shore). And if you became *very* hungry about the middle of March; there was always Field Mouse Pie, which, however, was not made out of the Vineyard's white-footed mice that crept in from the fields to winter in the basement, but involved sausages and other prosaic ingredients.

Joseph Chase Allen's Dry Beef Stew[†]

Venerable journalist Joseph Chase Allen probably knew more and wrote more about Martha's Vineyard than anyone else, with the exception of his long-time associate at the *Vineyard Gazette,* Henry Beetle Hough. An old-style talespinner and humorist, a fisherman and historian and Yankee to the core, Joe Allen was raised in a beautiful old weatherbeaten farmhouse that still sits tight-built on the earth in a windswept Chilmark meadow, with the rambler roses and grapevines and lilacs of his childhood now gone wild among the grasses.

We reprint this recipe just as he sent it to us some years before his death, feeling it should not be tampered with.

I don't know whether people ever made a "dry" beef stew anywhere save on the Vineyard, but to me it is one of the best ways of serving beef normally too tough for steaks or roasts. My wife turns out a splendid kettle of it, always sufficient for at least two meals for us, because "it's better every time it's warmed over."

[†] Old-timers' stews presumably were prepared like soups; their "dry" stews contained only enough water to braise the meat.

Here's how you do it, regulating your quantities according to the mouths to be fed:

Select beef that has some fat on it and leave it there. Cut it, or have it cut, into pieces that will weigh a quarter of a pound or even more. (Incidentally, it doesn't matter a whoop what part of the animal it comes from; neck to tail it can be used.)

Boil this meat with some salt and onions until you can almost separate it with a fork. Then drop your vegetables into the same kettle, potatoes, white and sweet, if you like them; turnip, more onions, carrots, that's it.

It's a good idea to cut these vegetables into relatively small pieces, say, halve the potatoes, cut the slices of turnip in two. While they are cooking, mix up some flour dumplings, quite stiff, and about the size of a human fist. Drop those into the kettle on top of everything and steam the whole until everything is done.

Then, the dumplings have to come out first, then skim out meat and vegetables and put 'em on a platter. Heat up the liquid in the kettle and thicken it with flour to whatever consistency you like gravy. Your dry stew is ready to serve.

The diner fills his plate with meat, vegetables and a dumpling broken into several pieces and then ladles a cupful of the gravy over the whole.

After that a deep silence falls upon the scene and lasts until the plates are empty.

We should add that Mr. Allen's comments about Vineyard cooking included the following: "The oldest and best cooks always swore that no cooking utensil could impart flavor to food like cast iron. Be it boiled, baked or fried, they insisted that this is true. My grandmother even made her baking powder biscuits in an iron frying pan on top of the stove." For this stew and other such "receipts," we suggest using a cast-iron Dutch oven with a tight-fitting lid.

Chicken and Oyster Stifle

Certain quaint, early-English culinary names occur frequently in old cookbooks, in old newspapers, and in talks with the elderly on Martha's Vineyard. *Flummery* fascinates. So does *fool*. The dictionary defines the former as a "custard of *blanc mange*"; the latter is a "sweet made with heavy cream and stewed fruit." The kitchen-oriented use of *stifle* is not listed under that word as either verb or noun, but *smother*—a good term familiar in southern kitchens—is one synonym. Smothered chicken and chicken stifle are prepared in much the same way: the meat is well browned, then braised in a seasoned, slightly thickened liquid until tender.

Here is an ancient recipe, several hundred years old, using two ingredients with great empathy toward each other—chicken and oysters.

2 tablespoons butter
2 tablespoons cooking oil
2 fresh broiler chickens, quartered
1 teaspoon salt
Freshly ground black pepper

1 tablespoon flour
1 cup milk
1½ cups medium cream
1 quart drained fresh oysters

Preheat oven to 350°F.

In a skillet, heat the butter and oil until foam subsides. Add the chicken pieces, first seasoning them with salt and pepper, and cook over moderate heat until golden on each side. Don't overcrowd the skillet. Remove chicken pieces from skillet and place in a large casserole. Add the flour to the fats in the pan and cook, stirring, until smooth. Add the milk and stir until a smooth sauce is obtained and the mixture comes to a simmer. Strain the sauce over the chicken pieces in the casserole, and bake, covered, for about 1 hour, or until the chicken pieces are tender. Pour in the cream, top with the oysters, and return casserole to the oven for 15 minutes, or until the edges of the oysters curl, then remove casserole immediately.

Place chicken and oysters on a heated platter, pour the sauce over all, and serve. *Makes 6 portions.*

Clam Stifle

From a 1921 issue of the *Vineyard Gazette* come the following instructions:

One quart clams is of course the essential part of the dish. Separate the stomach from the ribs and chop the ribs thoroughly before combining with the stomachs. Strain the juice carefully before using.

Take a baking dish, and put in a layer of potatoes, a layer of scallions, and a layer of clams, and repeat until all the clams are used.

Add at least a half a pint of milk and all the butter, applied in generous dabs, that your conscience will let you use. Put several slices of salt pork over all. This is important. Salt and pepper to taste. Bake for two hours.

These directions, quoted in full, were obviously written by a cook—and we suspect a male one—who feels that anyone who is messing around in the kitchen in the first place should know intuitively about proportions and other mundane technicalities, such as how to distinguish a clam's ribs from its stomach. Agreeing in principle, we give you the recipe just as it appeared.

Potato Bargain

[Also known as Poverty Hash or Necessity Mess]

Quaintly, even forthrightly named, this recipe has persisted for generations, perhaps because today it is as appetizing in taste as it was in other, less affluent times. Its appearance on the menu in those earlier days was dictated by what was left in the food or root cellar along about February or March. There was always the salt-pork barrel to be dipped into, and usually a few rations of potatoes and onions remained. Mrs. Welcome Tilton's great-great-granddaughter supplied this recipe. She said her father, when sailing as a young man on the *Alice B. Wentworth,* claimed it was "better after two or three days but tiresome after a week of being served up daily."

> *4 slices of lean salt pork, cut in ½-inch dice*
> *4 medium onions, sliced thin*
> *4 medium potatoes, pared and sliced thin*
> *Boiling water*
> *Freshly ground pepper to taste*
> *Salt if needed*

In a heavy aluminum pot with a tight-fitting lid or a black iron skillet with a good lid, fry the salt-pork dice until a crisp, golden brown. Remove them from pan and drain on a paper towel. Add the sliced onions to the fat in pan and cook until golden and transparent. Return pork dice to pan, add the sliced potatoes and enough boiling water to cover ingredients. Add freshly ground pepper, and salt, if needed. Cover the pan tightly and cook slowly, turning the food from time to time. The potatoes, when tender, should have absorbed most of the water.

The Tilton recipe, handed down through the years, suggests that "the secret of a good Bargain is not too much water but cook slow and let the steam cook them."

Makes 4 portions.

Red Flannel Hash

The meat and vegetables left over from a New England boiled dinner create this savory dish. It is a delicious dividend and attests to the inventiveness of the old-timers. Its name derives from the brilliant color imparted by the beets.

¼ pound salt pork, cut into ½-inch dice
¾ cup finely chopped onions
3 cups finely chopped cooked corned beef
3 cups coarsely chopped cooked potatoes
1⅓ cups cooked beets, cut into ½-inch dice

1 small clove garlic, minced (optional)
1 tablespoon finely chopped celery leaves (optional)
½ cup cream
Salt
Freshly ground black pepper
6 poached eggs (optional)
1 tablespoon chopped parsley

Brown salt pork in a 10- or 12-inch heavy skillet over moderate heat. Remove dice from pan and drain on a paper towel. Reserve. Pour off all but 2 tablespoons of fat. Reserve extra fat. Add chopped onions, and cook slowly until transparent. Transfer to mixing bowl. Add diced pork, corned beef, potatoes, beets, and if desired, garlic and celery leaves. Then add cream and stir thoroughly to blend. Add salt and pepper to taste.

Return the reserved fat to preheated skillet, add the hash ingredients, press down with spatula to cover the skillet evenly, and cook uncovered over moderate heat until bottom is crusty brown, about 25 minutes. Or place skillet in preheated 425°F oven for 20 to 30 minutes or until browned crust forms.

To remove from skillet, slide spatula or narrow pancake turner along sides and carefully work under the hash. Then fold hash in half as you would an omelet. Transfer to heated platter and top with poached eggs, if desired. Sprinkle with chopped parsley before serving.

Makes 6 generous portions.

Pumpkin Soup

New Englanders—and Vineyarders—seem to have used "pumpkin" and "squash" interchangeably when they spoke of making fall and winter dishes from this or these vegetables. What would be a pumpkin pie in the South would be made with a squash filling in Massachusetts; and many northern cooks disdain pumpkins altogether except as something to set out on the porch as a traditional symbol that fall has arrived and jack-o'-lantern season is approaching.

In a way, everyone is right in this particular culinary issue: the *Cucurbitas* include pumpkins and squashes (as well as gourds), and *C. maxima,* according to Norman Taylor's *Encyclopedia of Gardening,* "includes very large squash that pass for pumpkins."

So here is an old-fashioned recipe for a pumpkin—or squash—soup. Actually, sherry and cream, two of its ingredients, bring it close to the category of *haute cuisine,* and it is doubtful that early New Englanders would have condoned their use. The other ingredients, however, were available in their larders at all times, despite the long, cold winters and dwindling food supplies.

In any case, the soup is a delight served hot or thoroughly chilled and is recommended as an unusual prelude to a Thanksgiving dinner.

2 tablespoons butter
3 tablespoons chopped onion
2 cups chicken stock (or canned chicken broth)
2 cups cooked pumpkin, fresh or canned (or cooked hubbard squash)
2 cups milk
Small pinch each of ground cloves, ground ginger, ground allspice
½ teaspoon salt
½ cup heavy cream

¹/₄ cup dry sherry
Whipped cream for garnish

Melt the butter over moderate heat in a heavy 4-quart saucepan. When the foam subsides, add the onion and cook until transparent and golden. Add chicken stock, pumpkin or squash, milk, spices, and salt. If fresh pumpkin or squash pulp is used, it should be well drained and put through a food mill or strainer before use. Mix ingredients well and bring to a boil, stirring thoroughly. Reduce heat and simmer, stirring from time to time, for 15 or 20 minutes.

Puree the soup in a food mill or force it through a fine strainer. Return puree to saucepan. Add the cream and sherry and heat the soup carefully without allowing it to boil. Taste for seasonings. Garnish each serving with a spoonful of stiffly beaten heavy cream, lightly salted. May be served chilled using the same garnish.

Makes 4 to 6 portions.

Sea Voyage Gingerbread

Mentioned by Henry Beetle Hough in his foreword to this cookbook, here, for the curious, is the recipe for Sea Voyage Gingerbread exactly as it appeared in the *Vineyard Gazette* in an issue dated August 28, 1857.

Sift two pounds of flour into a pan, and cut up in it a pound and a quarter of fresh butter; rub the butter well into the flour and then mix in a pint of West Indian molasses and a pound of the best brown sugar.

Beat eight eggs until very light. Stir into the eggs two glasses or a gill of brandy; add also to the egg a teacup full of ground ginger and a tablespoon of powdered cinnamon, with a teaspoon of soda melted in a little warm water. Wet the flour, etc. with this mixture till it becomes a soft dough.

Sprinkle a little flour on your paste board, and with a broad knife spread portions of the mixture thickly and smoothly upon it. The thickness must be equal all through; therefore spread it carefully and evenly, as the dough will be too soft to roll out. Then with the edge of a tumbler dipped in flour, cut it out into round cakes.

Have ready square pans, slightly buttered; lay the cakes in them sufficiently far apart to prevent their running into each other when baked. Set the pans into a brisk oven and bake the cakes well, seeing that they do not burn.

These cakes will keep during a long voyage and are frequently carried to sea. Many persons find highly spiced gingerbread a preventive to seasickness.

Baked Indian Pudding

[A Durgin-Park Recipe]

The proprietors of Boston's famed Durgin-Park Restaurant, an ancient establishment known to many Vineyarders, supply this recipe in an amusing brochure they offer to their diners. They claim this pudding recipe was taken to sea by clipper-ship captains, who were among their early patrons, and made in ships' galleys from Valparaiso to Hong Kong. In the course of a current year, Durgin-Park claims, they make enough Indian pudding "to float the *Queen Mary*, the *Queen Elizabeth* and one small rowboat."

1½ quarts hot milk
1 cup yellow cornmeal
½ cup black (dark) molasses
¼ cup sugar
¼ cup butter

½ teaspoon salt
¼ teaspoon baking powder
2 eggs, slightly beaten
Heavy cream, whipped cream, or
   vanilla ice cream

Preheat oven to 500°F.

Grease a stone crock (preferably) or a baking dish.

Using half of the hot milk (3 cups), combine and thoroughly mix all ingredients except the cream or ice cream. Pour into the stone crock or baking dish. Bake until the pudding comes to a boil. Then stir in the remaining milk. Reduce oven heat to 200°F and bake the pudding for 5 to 7 hours.

Serve warm with thick, heavy cream, whipped cream, or a scoop of vanilla ice cream.

Makes 12 portions.

Fried Cheese Pancakes

These pan, griddle, or whatever cakes, adapted from a very old New England recipe, are unexpectedly good. Try them for Sunday brunch with crisp bacon slices and broiled garden-fresh tomatoes.

1 cup grated Cheddar cheese
3 tablespoons flour
½ tablespoon grated lemon rind
½ teaspoon salt

⅔ cup sour cream
3 egg yolks, lightly beaten
3 stiffly beaten egg whites
  (optional)

Combine cheese, flour, lemon rind, and salt in a mixing bowl. Stir in sour cream and beaten egg yolks.

Heat a griddle or large heavy skillet over moderate heat. Grease it lightly. When the griddle is hot enough (test with a drop of water; it should sputter on the griddle's surface), spoon the mixture into cakes averaging 3 to 4 inches in diameter. Brown lightly and turn; 2 to 3 minutes a side should cook them properly. Do not overcrowd the griddle. Remove first batch to a heated platter and keep warm. Grease the griddle lightly again if necessary and finish baking the cakes.

Note: If used, the egg whites may be beaten to stiff peaks and folded into the griddle cakes.

Makes 2 portions (8 pancakes, 3 to 4 inches in diameter).

Priscilla Hancock's
Chocolate Nut Fudge

As an only child on her father's chicken farm at Quenames, near South Beach, Priscilla Hancock spent many happy hours in her "kitchen" out under the trees, making splendid concoctions from flour, water, mud, and whatever else was appropriate and at hand. When she grew up, she moved indoors, and for forty years—until she retired in 1956—Miss Hancock turned out in that Quenames kitchen the tastiest confections ever produced on the Vineyard or, some thought, anywhere else. Her success, according to an article on her published in a February 1970 issue of the *Vineyard Gazette,* she attributed largely to "never using anything but the finest ingredients, always taking plenty of time, and thinking up interesting taste combinations. I'd always use sweet chocolate for anything with fruits and nuts in it, but then I'd dip butter creams and peppermints in bittersweet. But there wasn't really anything so remarkable about it all. There's no great secrecy to candy-making except never changing the quality of your ingredients."

Gone now are the long quiet walks down the woodsy road to the candy lady's house; and gone is the West Tisbury general store where Miss Hancock used to "gam" with her friends James Cagney and Clarence Budington Kelland and a former policeman named McNamara, who'd been in the movies and studied voice with Caruso. And Miss Hancock and her friend Lucy Wiig no longer live in a pleasant old West Tisbury house, with a big ginger cat and rooms filled with Victorian antiques. But there are still a few quiet woodsy roads to stroll down, and comfortable country kitchens where a Vineyard dweller can mix up her own batch of one of Miss Hancock's specialties—this luscious fudge.

4 cups sugar

1½ teaspoons salt

1½ cups light cream

2 tablespoons corn syrup

6 squares Baker's unsweetened chocolate

5 or 6 tablespoons butter

2 teaspoons vanilla

1½ to 2 cups coarsely chopped walnuts or pecans

Bring sugar, salt, cream, and corn syrup to boiling point in a large saucepan and cook slowly for several minutes, then add chocolate. Reduce heat and cook without stirring to the soft-ball stage, or 234°F on a candy thermometer. Put butter and vanilla in mixture but do not stir. Cool to lukewarm; beat until creamy, then add nuts. Pour onto a buttered platter and allow to harden before cutting into squares.

Note: In one conversation, Miss Hancock stressed the importance of allowing the fudge to cool sufficiently before beginning to beat it. This prevents graininess in the finished confection.

Makes 4 pounds.

Tea Lane Chutney

Every Christmas for many years, certain favored Up-Island households were the recipients of a jar of this prized apple chutney. A foil-wrapped and beribboned jelly glass always appeared in the mailboxes of this cookbook's authors; but though they tried for years to extract the recipe from its eighty-six-year-old owner, it was only given to them the day before this manuscript was originally sent off to the publisher. With the recipe came the story of its origin on Martha's Vineyard, which we also pass along.

About fifty years ago, a charming Englishwoman appeared at the door of one of the two year-round farmhouses on Tea Lane and asked if she and a friend might pick blueberries on that property. Since the lady of the house was also English, a friendship developed that lasted for many years, and each summer the lady came back to pick blueberries and have a pleasant afternoon tea. Over the tea things, this recipe was shared, copied out, and placed in the recipe box of the house on Tea Lane. That Christmas, the apple chutney was sent around to dear friends, as it has been each subsequent Christmas. But the recipe, invariably sought, was never divulged.

When asked how much the recipe makes, the chutney maker got out a 1942 diary, which was used each year to record brief notes on planting times, first frosts, bird visitors, egg production, and canning records. "Nine containers" was the amount given, but "I always put up big jars for certain people and small ones for the others," the cook said. We filled eight jelly jars with our test batch and had a small amount left over.

One caution: This chutney is extremely hot when made with the full amount of red pepper. Start with half the amount stated; if you want more after testing your chutney, stir in a little more at a time, tasting after each addition.

2 pounds apples
1½ pints vinegar
2 pounds dark brown sugar
1 pound raisins or chopped dates

2 cloves garlic, minced (or 1 large onion, chopped fine)
4 ounces crystallized ginger, chopped fine
1 dessertspoon (about 1½ teaspoons) dry mustard
1 teaspoon salt
1 tablespoon dried red pepper flakes (see caution on page 289)

Peel, quarter, and core apples. Cook them in the vinegar until they are soft and mushy. Add the other ingredients, using only half the red pepper. Mix well. Bring to a boil and cook over moderate heat about 10 minutes. Taste chutney and gradually add remainder of red pepper as desired. Cook about 15 minutes more, stirring occasionally. Pour into hot, sterilized containers and seal. Process in hot-water bath, 10 minutes for pints, 15 minutes for quarts.

Makes about eight 8-ounce jelly glasses.

CHAPTER 13

The Farmers' Market

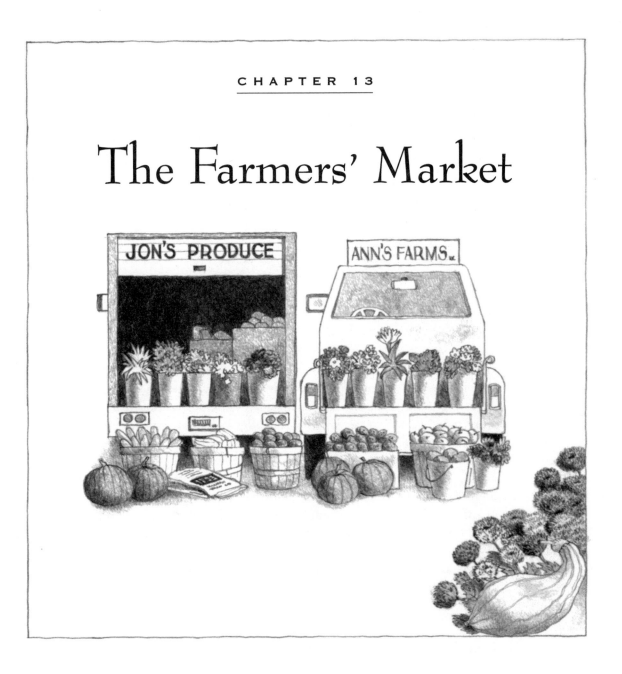

Nothing underscores the recent renaissance of Vineyard agriculture better than the success of the farmers' market. It is an Island institution rooted in the soil of this community, an important symbol of strength and diversity in the Vineyard economy, an economy that requires balance between the shifting rhythms of tourism and other economic enterprises.

—*Vineyard Gazette*, June 14, 1991

Every Saturday morning and Wednesday afternoon from mid-June till mid-October, the quiet town center of West Tisbury becomes for three hours or so a small, crowded metropolis. A town policeman is usually stationed in the middle of State Road directing traffic. Cars sit with turn signals blinking, waiting to slip into a coveted parking space. Music Street lawns sprout No Parking signs; householders emerge shouting and waving their arms when these are disregarded. And hundreds of people, many carrying shopping bags or baskets, swarm toward the grounds of the Old Agricultural Hall, where the weekly Farmers' Market is set up. Arms and receptacles are soon crammed with special favorites—a box of tiny potatoes; huge sun-ripened tomatoes just off the vine; crisp little bundles of arugula, chervil, purple basil, salad burnet; an armful of blazing zinnias or feathery cosmos; a chunky, crusty loaf of bread and a special jam to spread it with. A free hand may be waving a half-eaten ginger cookie or egg roll at a neighbor or a straying child, a dog tangling its leash around a cardtable leg in its attempts to touch noses with a farmer's black lab.

The West Tisbury Farmers' Market originated in 1934 during post-Depression years as a way for local farmers and cooks to earn a little extra income. It quickly grew very popular, but in 1941 it became a casualty of gas and sugar rationing. In 1974 it sprang up again. Eleven vendors showed up on that first Saturday, including the two authors of this cookbook, one offering home-smoked bluefish, bluefish pâté, and other delicacies from her kitchen; the other, potted plants and flowers. Over the years the Market has expanded to the point where assigned spaces, two co-managers, four parking attendants, strict regulations, annual kitchen inspections by the town Board of Health, and other strictures have become necessary. By 1992 the forty-eight farmers and food vendors were drawing hundreds of customers each week. Now the Market is the social highlight of the weekend, where everyone meets everyone, the place to be seen. Sellers speak of "July people" and "August people" as if they were different species.

But it remains a market in the truest, freshest sense. Some of the bakers stay up all Friday night making their pies, cakes, and breads; and all the farmers are in their fields by dawn stripping off the corn ears, picking the beans, so everything will be as fresh as possible. It is a happy, bustling, profitable undertaking that has become a fixture in the Vineyard's summer scene and holds fond memories for the "summer people" when they've gone back home.

Bluefish Lady's Pâté

The lady who provided this recipe does have a name, but when her Farmers' Market customers meet her elsewhere on the Island, they tend to greet her with, "It's the Bluefish Lady!" Since her husband owns a fishing boat, there were often surplus fish around, especially during bluefish season, and giving it away became a problem ("People used to close their doors when they saw us coming with fish"). So she started smoking the extras and making this savory pâté to sell at the Market, to the delight of countless summer visitors.

8 ounces cream cheese, softened
8 ounces smoked bluefish, skinless
1 medium onion, coarsely chopped
Approximately 1 tablespoon fresh lemon juice

Place all ingredients in a food processor, pulse five times, then blend continuously until mixed and smooth. Additional lemon juice may be added if desired to obtain preferred consistency. Serve, if you like, on good melba toast or thinly sliced rye or pumpernickel bread.

Makes 1 to 1½ cups.

Orange and Red-Berry Jam
[Charlotte's Garden]

This enterprising young woman, who named her garden-oriented business after her young daughter, began her association with the summer market in 1986 by selling mainly lilies, organically grown vegetables, and an assortment of unusual jams and jellies. She later expanded into such specialty items as dried-flower wreaths and potpourri, started a mail-order line of heirloom flower seeds, and developed other projects that now keep her busy year-round.

3 cups mashed fresh strawberries
1 cup fresh orange juice
7 cups sugar

1 tablespoon fresh lemon juice
2 tablespoons margarine
1 pouch liquid pectin

Combine all ingredients except pectin in a large pot (never use aluminum in making jam). Stir well. Bring to a rapid boil and boil hard for 2 minutes (use timer).

Stir well. Add pectin and stir well again. Boil 3 more minutes, then test jam by removing stirring spoon from pan and turning it sideways. If two drops run together and form sheet, then drop off, jam is ready. Otherwise, repeat test frequently until sheeting occurs. Remove jam from heat, ladle or pour into hot, sterilized jars, seal, and process 5 minutes in a hot-water bath.

Makes six to seven 8-ounce jars.

Four-Basil Pesto

[Charlotte's Garden]

4 large garlic cloves

1 cup walnut meats

3/4 cup virgin olive oil

Salt and freshly ground black pepper

1/2 cup lemon basil

1/2 cup cinnamon basil

1/2 cup lettuce leaf basil

1/2 cup sweet basil

1 cup grated Parmesan cheese

1/4 cup grated Romano cheese

Pulse garlic and walnuts in food processor until medium fine. Do not puree. Add olive oil, salt, and pepper as desired. Add all the basil and pulse again until medium fine. Add both cheeses and pulse just enough to mix. Pack pesto in small containers and cover with thin layer of oil to prevent basil from darkening. Store in refrigerator. Pesto may also be frozen, in which case some cooks prefer to add proportionate amounts of the nuts and cheeses just before use.

Note: These specialty basils are available at the summer Farmers' Market on Martha's Vineyard but can often be found at gourmet markets elsewhere. The pesto can be made using only sweet basil but will lack the unique taste of the four basils.

Makes 1½ cups.

Spicy Peanut Sauce

[The Kitchen Porch]

The young woman who developed this piquant sauce says it evolved from tasting and recipe collecting she did during two years of travel in Asia and Southeast Asia. She has been selling it at the Farmers' Market, along with several equally flavorful concoctions, since 1986. Asked why she chose to live on the Vineyard, she replied that it seemed like "a good place to settle down and raise a family." A qualified librarian, she also works in one of the town libraries during the off-season.

2 cups peanut butter
1 tablespoon chopped fresh ginger root
2 cloves garlic
4 scallions, cut up
1 tablespoon crushed chili peppers (or 1 tablespoon chili garlic sauce)
1/8 cup sesame oil
1/4 cup light soy sauce
1/2 cup rice vinegar
1/4–1 cup water (or coconut milk or chicken broth)

Put peanut butter in food processor. Add ginger, garlic, scallions, and crushed peppers or chili garlic sauce. Turn processor on and slowly add other ingredients. Add from 1/4 cup to 1 cup water for desired consistency. If preferred, coconut milk or chicken broth may be used in place of water.

Makes about 4 cups.

Rose-Petal Jelly

[New Lane Sundries]

A native Islander, this jam's creator learned many of her culinary skills from her Island relatives, particularly an aunt who was famous for her pickles. Starting by making jams and jellies as a hobby, she soon developed a line of fifteen sundries, including her aunt's pickles, and in 1988 she began offering them for sale at the Farmers' Market. This best-selling jelly not only is infused with the delicate flavor of the flowers that go into it but takes on their lovely color as well. It well deserved the blue ribbon it was awarded one year at the annual Agricultural Fair.

1 quart fresh rose petals, loosely packed
2½ cups water
3½ cups sugar
2 tablespoons fresh lemon juice
1 packet plus 2 tablespoons Certo

Rinse petals in cold water, place in a pan with the 2½ cups water, and bring to a boil. Cover pan and let petals cook slowly over low heat for 10 minutes, stirring once or twice. Remove pan from stove and let sit, covered, about 15 minutes.

Strain infusion, saving both petals and liquid. Put 1¾ cups liquid, the sugar, and the lemon juice in a preserving kettle, stir, and bring to a boil. Stir in about ¼ cup of the cooked petals. Add Certo, stir, bring to a boil again, and boil hard for 1 minute (use a timer). Remove from heat immediately. Skim foam from top, then pour or ladle jelly into hot, sterilized jars. Seal jars and process in a hot-water bath 5 minutes. While jars are cooling and setting up, invert them several times so petals appear to be floating.

Note: The donor of this recipe uses petals from the wild *rosa rugosas* for her jelly, for their strong fragrance and their color.

Makes four 8-ounce jars.

Champagne-Orange Mustard with Ginger

[New Lane Sundries]

1 cup good-quality dry mustard (Coleman's is recommended)
½ cup champagne
½ cup white vinegar
1 teaspoon grated orange peel
1 teaspoon grated fresh ginger, or 1 teaspoon powdered ginger
½ cup sugar
2 eggs, beaten (or equivalent amount of an egg substitute)

Combine mustard, champagne, vinegar, orange peel, and ginger in bowl. Whisk thoroughly, cover bowl with plastic wrap, and let mixture sit overnight.

The following day, combine sugar with eggs or egg substitute in medium-size bowl, then add mustard mix and mix thoroughly. Turn mixture into saucepan and cook over low to medium heat until mustard reaches desired consistency, about 20 minutes. Stir mixture continuously during cooking period, or it will scorch on the bottom. If scorching begins, lower heat immediately. When done, pour into hot, sterilized jars, seal, and process in hot-water bath 5 minutes. Mustard can be stored indefinitely in the refrigerator without processing step, if desired. Bottle, seal, and let cool before storing.

Makes about 2 cups.

Two Vinegars

[Vinegar Cottage Herbs]

This husband-and-wife team has been involved in various agricultural ventures since their marriage more than thirty years ago, and they have been full-time farmers on the Vineyard since their arrival here five years ago, doing everything from raising Thanksgiving turkeys to producing wool from their own flock of sheep. At the Farmers' Market, he displays his impeccable vegetables, she sells her colorful vinegars and other herbal products.

FIVE-HERB AND GARLIC VINEGAR

1 quart white vinegar (preferably Heinz)
About ¼ cup each leaves or small sprigs of Italian-type parsley, sage,
 rosemary, thyme, and purple basil (this imparts a lovely shade of pink)
1 medium garlic clove, crushed

CILANTRO-CHILI-GARLIC VINEGAR

1 quart white vinegar (preferably Heinz)
About ½ cup loosely packed fresh cilantro sprigs
1 medium garlic clove, crushed
2 teaspoons crushed dried chili peppers

Directions are the same for both vinegars. Pour vinegar into a clean, wide-mouth, 1-quart glass jar. Rinse five-herb mix or cilantro sprigs gently in cold water, shake, and pat dry with a paper towel. Crush herbs lightly with a wooden mallet or by hand to release flavors and add them to the vinegar. Add the crushed garlic clove. To the Cilantro-Chili-Garlic Vinegar, add the crushed chili peppers. In time these will turn this vinegar a warm amber shade. Place a double thickness of plastic wrap over the mouth of the glass jar, then cap.

Steep the vinegar in sunlight for two days, then place the jar in a dark, cool location for at least two weeks. If made in late summer or early fall, the vinegars may be put directly into the dark and left to steep all winter.

When vinegar has steeped, strain it through cheesecloth, discarding the used herbs. Use only a stainless-steel or plastic strainer. Pour vinegar into plastic-topped bottles for storage. Do not use a metal funnel unless it is stainless steel. Cut sprigs of the appropriate herbs (those in flower are most decorative) and insert a few into the vinegar. A stainless-steel fondue fork is useful for this procedure. Also add a lightly crushed fresh garlic clove. A small dried chili pepper may be added to the Cilantro-Chili-Garlic Vinegar as ornament, but it may make the vinegar somewhat hotter.

Each recipe makes about a quart.

Rainbow Pasta Salad

[Pilot Hill Farm]

½ cup Five-Herb and Garlic Vinegar (see page 299)
⅔ cup olive oil
1 clove garlic, minced
2 tablespoons fresh opal basil (or 3 teaspoons dried basil)
1 teaspoon salt
¼ teaspoon crushed red pepper
1 pound colored pasta twists, cooked al dente and drained
Raw vegetables (use as desired): thin-sliced baby yellow summer squash
* and baby zucchini; thin-sliced orange and red bell peppers; slivered red*
* cabbage; chopped scallions and Royal Burgundy (purple) beans;*
* curly parsley sprigs*

In a large bowl mix herbal vinegar, oil, garlic, basil, salt, and red pepper. Add warm pasta. Toss to coat well. Allow to cool, then mix in whatever vegetables you choose (others may be added to the above list) in whatever quantity you like. Mix well and serve, decorated with parsley sprigs.

Makes 4 to 6 portions.

Ginger Cookies

[Hidden Hill Bakery]

All kinds of delicious things emerge from the convection ovens of this Market baker. Though she says she is known as the Muffin Lady, her ginger cookies are also enormously popular. A true professional, she markets her baked goodies at various outlets on the Island throughout the year. And it looks as though she may soon also be known as the Dogbone Lady for the bone-shaped dog treats she has recently added to her repertoire.

1 cup light vegetable oil
2 cups sugar
½ cup dark molasses
2 eggs, lightly beaten
1 teaspoon salt

2 teaspoons cinnamon
2 tablespoons ginger
1 teaspoon cloves
3½ teaspoons baking soda
4 cups flour

Preheat oven to 375°F.

In large mixing bowl, beat together oil and sugar, then beat in molasses and eggs. Beat in salt, spices, and soda, then add flour, beating in 1 cup at a time. Mix thoroughly. Spoon about 2 tablespoons per cookie onto baking sheets, 2 inches apart. Form into ball shapes, then flatten with glass bottom dipped in sugar (moisten bottom of glass so sugar will adhere). Bake about 10 minutes, until edges are dry and tops are slightly crinkled. Remove from oven, let cool about 5 minutes, then lift with spatula onto rack to cool.

Note: If desired, baking sheets can be lightly oiled. If allowed to cool in ungreased pans, cookies will stick to pans.

Makes about thirty 3-inch cookies.

Sour Cream Coffee Cake

[Hidden Hill Bakery]

½ pound butter or margarine
2 cups sugar
1 pint sour cream (or no-fat
sour cream)

1 teaspoon baking soda
1 tablespoon baking powder
4 eggs, beaten
4 cups all-purpose flour

Ingredients should be at room temperature.
Preheat oven to 350°F.
In a large bowl, combine all ingredients well. Beat until smooth. Spread half of the batter in an oiled 9-inch tube pan.

FILLING/TOPPING

½ cup dark brown sugar
2 tablespoons cinnamon
1 cup walnuts, chopped

Combine all ingredients in a mixing bowl. Sprinkle half the filling/topping over the batter, making sure to spread evenly. Add remaining batter and cover evenly with the remainder of the filling/topping.

Bake on middle rack of oven for 65 minutes. Cake is done when its edges have begun to shrink away from the pan.

Makes 11 to 15 portions.

Suzanne's Piecrust

Suzanne is an accomplished pastry chef who also gardens, skis, runs marathons, and fishes. She and her husband spend part of each year in Alaska, where for ten years he worked as a bush pilot and they operated a salmon fishery that they still own. Now they are Vineyard residents, and summer finds them at their Farmers' Market stand selling all sorts of pies and fresh-squeezed lemonade. Only Crisco, Suzanne claims, will produce this tender, flaky piecrust.

2 cups unbleached, all-purpose flour
1 teaspoon salt
⅔ cup Crisco (measure generously)
¼ cup ice water

Place flour and salt in a food processor. Pulse once or twice only. Empty ⅓ cup of this mixture into a small bowl. Add the ice water and stir briskly until a smooth paste is achieved. Set aside. Add Crisco to mixture in food processor. Process just enough to form an uneven, crumbly mass. Transfer to a large bowl. Add the paste mixture. Using a wooden spoon, mix quickly until the mixture is well incorporated. Then use your hands, still working quickly, to form dough into a ball. Cover with plastic wrap and let rest 10 minutes.

When ready to fill the pie, roll pastry as follows: Tear off a 16-inch length of wax paper and sprinkle it with several tablespoons of flour. Set the pastry ball in the center of the paper and cut ball in half. Set one half aside and cover. Center the other half on the paper, cut side down. Flatten once with the palm of the hand, then roll pastry into a circle sufficient to fit a 9-inch pie pan. The dough should extend 1 to 1½ inches beyond pan's rim. Trim edges evenly.

Center pie pan upside down on the dough. Slide one hand under the wax paper, invert crust onto pan, and peel off paper. Save it to use for top crust. Turn under the rim pastry, making a fluted edge. Fill bottom pie crust with any desired filling. Repeat process for top crust, cut three vents in center, and flute edges over bottom crust.

Makes two 9-inch crusts.

Suzanne's Apple Pie

This apple pie is a best-seller. A minimum of sugar is put with the apples, and, according to Suzanne, lemon juice is imperative to enhance their flavor.

5 Granny Smith apples
Suzanne's Piecrust (see page 304)
⅓ cup sugar (or more, as preferred)
1 tablespoon fresh lemon juice
1 tablespoon cinnamon, or to taste
2 generous teaspoons butter

Preheat oven to 425°F.

Peel and quarter the apples and remove cores. Cut in generous slices to prevent loss of shape in baking. Heap apples into prepared piecrust. Taste apples to determine sweetness, then sprinkle with ⅓ cup sugar or more, as desired. Sprinkle on the lemon juice and cinnamon to taste. Dot fruit with bits of the butter. Add top crust as described in preceding recipe, including fluting and cutting three vents in top of crust. Set pie on baking sheet and place on oven's lowest shelf. After 10 minutes, reduce heat to 375°F. Bake an additional 45 minutes, or until apples feel tender when pricked with a fork. Set pie on a rack to cool. Gently press top crust down to level of apples.

Makes one 9-inch, two-crust pie.

CHAPTER 14

Vineyard Inns
and
Restaurants

T here are at least five and maybe ten times as many eating places on the Vineyard now as there were when this book was first published in 1971. Back then, it was difficult, if not impossible, to go out for a spur-of-the-moment dinner on some lowering winter night. Today there are at least half a dozen warm, welcoming year-round restaurants to choose from.

New eateries appear at the beginning of each tourist season, springing up like mushrooms after a summer rain, and a good many of them are just about as short-lived. There were seventy-six restaurants listed in the 1998 telephone directory; some will be defunct by the time a new phone book is issued.

But the good places survive. Many have existed for decades. We have assembled a sampling of recipes from some of the best-known and best-liked ones, including one in Edgartown that opened as the Island's first licensed tavern in the 1600s and has served food ever since, and a small, sprightly eatery on Vineyard Haven's Main Street that only opened in January of 1998 but quickly became known for its good food and appealing ambience.

Unfortunately, several places as we hoped to include, particularly ones in Edgartown, were closed for the winter when this revision was compiled. But we were still left with an abundance of choices and wish we had sufficient space to include more recipes. Perhaps another time.

Garlic-Crusted Codfish

THE BLACK DOG TAVERN, VINEYARD HAVEN

A real dog inspired the now famous Black Dog logo that you are as likely to encounter on a sweatshirt in a Dublin pub as on a T-shirt at a Vineyard beach. She was an amiable Labrador retriever who greeted diners with a friendly wag and often tried to sneak in with them to solicit treats in the kitchen.

The Black Dog Tavern, opened in January 1971, hasn't changed much since then. Housed in a rustic wooden building only yards from Vineyard Haven Harbor, it is still an informal, relaxed dining spot where habitués gather to eat large portions of tasty, interesting food, talk, and linger, and where parents often take their children for a special Sunday lunch.

The menu varies from day to day, but this cod dish has been a favorite for a long time.

2 cups dry bread crumbs
3 tablespoons olive oil
2 tablespoons chopped garlic
2 teaspoons dried oregano
Salt

Freshly ground black pepper
1 cup all-purpose flour
3 eggs, whipped
3 pounds codfish fillets

Preheat oven to 425°F.

Mix together bread crumbs, olive oil, garlic, oregano, salt, and pepper. Coat fish fillets in flour and shake off excess. Dip fish fillets in egg wash, then coat with bread-crumb mixture. Bake 15 minutes on a greased baking pan.

Makes 8 portions.

Vegetable Lasagna

LOUIS'S TAKEOUT CAFÉ AND RESTAURANT, VINEYARD HAVEN

One of the Vineyard's busiest and most successful year-round restaurants is located in an unpretentious former dwelling on the outskirts of Vineyard Haven. Opened by its owner as a takeout place in 1981, the enterprise was so successful that in 1985 a simply furnished but attractive restaurant was added behind the takeout section, and soon people were lining up to get in for dinner.

The following recipe, a special favorite of the customers, is interesting because the lasagna noodles are not precooked. Putting the dish together will take less time if all the ingredients are assembled beforehand.

Two 10-ounce boxes frozen
    chopped spinach
1 tablespoon olive oil
1 medium onion, diced
    (about 1 cup)
1 medium green pepper, diced
    (about 1 cup)
1 teaspoon dried oregano
1 teaspoon dried basil
1/2 teaspoon salt
1/2 teaspoon freshly ground
    black pepper

2 cups yellow squash, sliced into
    very thin rounds
2 pounds ricotta cheese
2 cups grated mozzarella cheese
1 cup grated Parmesan cheese
2½–3 quarts your favorite tomato
    sauce (or use the Marinara
    Sauce on page 314)
1 plus pounds dry lasagna
    noodles

Thaw the chopped spinach is a microwave or overnight in the refrigerator. Squeeze dry and set aside. Heat oil and sauté onions, peppers, and seasonings until vegetables are limp. Remove from heat, add to the spinach, and toss to mix. Divide into two portions.

Divide squash and cheeses into two portions, one for each layer of the lasagna. Using a 15- by 9-by 2½-inch lasagna pan sprayed with nonstick pan coating, cover the bottom with 1 cup of sauce. Arrange a layer of dry noodles on it so they just touch. Start the layering with one portion each of ricotta, yellow squash, spinach mixture, 2 cups of sauce, mozzarella cheese, and Parmesan cheese.

Then arrange a second layer of pasta at a 90-degree angle to the first one. Break pieces to make them fit, if necessary. Cover with other ingredients as before. For the top layer of pasta, the noodles must be coated on both sides with the sauce. Then arrange them in the same direction as the bottom layer. This criss-crossing of the pasta offers stability to the finished product.

Cover with plastic wrap (not foil), and refrigerate overnight to allow noodles to "cook" in the liquid of the sauce and vegetables. Bake, covered with tented foil, for 2 hours in a 350°F oven. Let rest 15 minutes. Heat remaining sauce and pass when serving lasagna.

Makes 8 to 10 portions.

Hoisin-Glazed Calamari Salad

CAFÉ MOXIE, VINEYARD HAVEN

One of the Island's newest culinary successes, this eighteen-seat, bistro-style restaurant opened in early 1998, and its high-quality food soon attracted regular customers. The much older building that once occupied this corner site on Main Street was burned to the ground in the disastrous fire of 1883 that destroyed twenty-eight businesses, thirty-one dwellings, and the Baptist church. Café Moxie, owned and operated by the daughter of a founder of the Black Dog Tavern, provides an atmosphere brightened by leaded windows, a tin ceiling, and art exhibits that are changed bimonthly.

1 cup of yellow cornmeal
¾ cup cornstarch
2 pounds calamari, cleaned and sliced into rings
2 bunches watercress
½ bunch cilantro, chopped
½ cup sour cream
½ cup buttermilk
1 tablespoon lemon juice
Salt

Freshly ground black pepper to taste
1 teaspoon minced ginger root
2 teaspoons sesame oil
½ cup hoisin sauce
½ cup water
2 teaspoons soy sauce
2 cups canola oil
½ cup chopped cashews

Combine cornmeal and cornstarch in a medium-size bowl and dredge calamari rings in mixture. Set aside. Clean and dry the watercress. Prepare cilantro dressing by combining in blender the cilantro, sour cream, buttermilk, lemon juice, salt, and pepper. Blend briefly, then pour sauce over watercress and toss lightly till mixed. Divide greens between six chilled salad plates.

Prepare hoisin glaze by briefly sautéing ginger in sesame oil, then whisk in the hoisin sauce, water, and soy sauce. Keep sauce warm.

Heat the canola oil, gently add calamari slices, and fry them lightly for about two minutes. Remove and drain on paper towels.

To assemble salad, add calamari to warm hoisin sauce and toss lightly. Place a portion of calamari on top of each plate of watercress. Toast the chopped cashews and sprinkle some on each portion of salad.

Makes 6 portions.

Jambalaya

LOLA'S, OAK BLUFFS

In the clubhouse of a former golf course on the outskirts of Oak Bluffs, an enterprising chef has established a very popular restaurant that is a favorite of both summer visitors and Islanders, especially the many professional African-Americans who have homes on the Vineyard—among them, lawyers, doctors, politicians, and writers. Though the owner grew up relishing Southern food in Detroit, her real training as a chef took place in New Orleans, a fact reflected in the many Creole and Cajun-style dishes she prepares in her restaurant kitchen.

Jambalaya is one such speciality. It takes lots of preparation and is expensive to make. But it is worth the effort.

Jambalaya

½ cup cubed fresh tuna
½ cup cubed fresh swordfish
½ cup cubed fresh salmon
½ cup cubed chicken breast
¼ cup olive oil
2 tablespoons Cajun seasoning
½ teaspoon salt
1 tablespoon cracked black
   pepper
¼ cup hot sauce

2 cups Marinara Sauce (see
   below)
1 cup shelled bay scallops
½ cup chopped linguica or
   andouille sausage
24 jumbo shrimp, peeled and
   deveined
24 mussels, scrubbed and
   debearded
2 cups chicken or lobster broth
3 cups cooked rice

In two skillets (unless you have a super large one), briefly sauté over high heat the tuna, swordfish, salmon, and chicken in ¼ cup olive oil. Add seasonings and hot sauce. Add Marinara Sauce, scallops, sausage, shrimp, mussels, and chicken or lobster broth. Simmer 3 to 5 minutes, until mussels open. Add cooked rice and simmer until heated through.

Makes 6 to 8 portions.

Marinara Sauce

½ cup chopped red pepper
½ cup chopped green pepper
½ cup chopped onions
3 cloves of garlic, chopped
3 tablespoons olive oil

8 or 9 chopped plum tomatoes
   (or 2 cups canned chopped
   tomatoes)
1 teaspoon each dried basil and
   oregano

Sauté the peppers, onions, and garlic in the olive oil. Add the tomatoes and herbs. Simmer for 20 minutes. Remove from heat.

Grapenut Bread

THE DAGGET HOUSE, EDGARTOWN

The Dagget House opened in 1660 as the first licensed tavern on Martha's Vineyard, and it has been serving food ever since. In 1750 the building was expanded to its present size, with the additional space serving variously as, among other things, a sailors' boarding house and a counting house until 1948, when it was purchased by its present owners and opened as a restaurant and inn. The building has two features of historic interest; a beehive fireplace in the restaurant and a secret staircase room behind the restaurant's bookcase.

The popularity of this grapenut bread prompted the owners to make the recipe available at the inn's front desk. Try it toasted for breakfast.

⅔ cup Grapenuts cereal
⅓ cup wheat germ
3 tablespoons butter
⅓ cup dark brown sugar
¼ teaspoon salt
1⅓ cup boiling water

1 tablespoon yeast
1 teaspoon sugar
⅔ cup warm water
4 cups flour (more may be needed)

Mix together the Grapenuts, wheat germ, butter, sugar, and salt. Add the boiling water, stir, and let cool.

Meanwhile, combine the yeast and the sugar and stir into the warm water. Let stand until bubbly. Add yeast mixture to Grapenuts mixture and stir. Add flour and mix well. Turn dough out on floured surface and knead until soft and smooth. Add more flour if needed. Return to bowl, cover, and let rise in warm place until double in size (about 1 hour). Punch down with fist and return to floured surface. Divide into two loaves, knead a few minutes, shape, and put into greased bread pans. Let rise until doubled (about ½ hour). Bake at 350°F for 50 minutes.

Note: Butter should be at room temperature for easier combining. Also, the recipe contains very little salt. You may want to double the amount given.

Makes two loaves.

Red Pepper and Scallop Bisque

SAVOIR FAIRE, EDGARTOWN

Open from April through October, Savoir Faire is tucked behind the Dukes County Courthouse, away from the hordes of tourists swarming along the sidewalks. A fifty-five-seat, cottage-style restaurant, it offers a charming setting for a leisurely lunch or a quiet dinner since it opened in 1985—bright and sunny in the daytime, cozy at night.

Typical of the imaginative dishes on their menu is this interesting soup that features those big, beautiful red peppers from Holland.

1 cup chopped shallots
1 cup chopped red onion
1 cup chopped carrots
1 cup chopped celery
2 cups shrimp shells
¼ cup olive oil
8 large tomatoes, peeled, seeded, and chopped
2 cups clam juice
2 cups water

¼ cup dark rum
2 cups dry sherry
2 tablespoons chopped fresh tarragon
6 large red Holland peppers
6 cups heavy cream
1 teaspoon lemon juice
Salt
Freshly ground black pepper
Ground cayenne pepper

| 2 pounds shrimp, peeled and deveined | 1½ pounds large sea scallops |

Toss shallots, onions, carrots, celery, and shrimp shells in olive oil. Roast in 375°F oven for 15 minutes or until well browned. Place vegetables and shells in a heavy soup pot with tomatoes, clam juice, water, rum, sherry, and tarragon. Bring to a boil, lower heat, and simmer 1½ hours or until reduced by half.

Meanwhile, roast peppers over open flame. Peel and seed them, then puree in a food processor. Remove mixture in soup pot from heat and cool. Puree this mixture in a food processor. Combine with red pepper puree and press through a fine sieve into a soup pot. Add cream and season to taste with salt, and black and cayenne peppers. Bring to a boil, then simmer 1 hour, or until reduced by one quarter. Add lemon juice and adjust seasoning.

Grill shrimp and scallops over open flame or in a cast-iron skillet for 2 minutes on each side. Dice shrimp and scallops and divide between warmed bowls. Ladle bisque over shrimp and scallops, and serve immediately.

Makes 8 portions.

Oven-Poached Atlantic Salmon

LAMBERT'S COVE COUNTRY INN AND RESTAURANT, WEST TISBURY

Situated a mile off Lambert's Cove Road, this charming fifteen-room inn opened in 1969 in a renovated 200-year-old farmhouse still surrounded by remnants of farmland, now discreetly landscaped. As the only Up-Island eating place that is open year-round, the inn always provides its guests and diners with a homey and welcoming atmosphere, whether serving a delicious dinner in the dining room before a glowing fire or hosting a flower-decked summer wedding.

Salmon often shows up on menus these days, usually prepared in simple but innovative ways. We like this version, developed by one of the inn's former chefs.

SALMON STEAKS

Two 8-ounce salmon steaks
3 tablespoons horseradish,
    squeezed dry
3 tablespoons sour cream
3 tablespoons mayonnaise

¾ cup Japanese bread crumbs
1½ tablespoons vegetable oil
Salt, white pepper, and paprika
    to taste

Preheat oven to 425°F.

Place salmon steaks in a pie pan. Blend together horseradish, sour cream, and mayonnaise, and spread over fish. Lightly sauté bread crumbs in oil, and combine with salt, white pepper, and paprika. Spread crumbs over salmon. Add water until fish is three quarters covered. Place in oven and poach 10 minutes or until salmon flakes when pierced with a fork.

While fish cooks, prepare Remoulade Sauce (see following recipe). Serve sauce with fish.

Makes 2 portions.

REMOULADE SAUCE

1 finely chopped hard-boiled egg
1 tablespoon minced cornichons
  or sour gherkins
1 tablespoon drained capers
1 tablespoon chopped fresh
  parsley
1½ teaspoons chopped fresh
  tarragon

1 small garlic clove, minced
½ teaspoon Dijon mustard
1 cup mayonnaise
Salt and freshly ground pepper
  to taste

Stir chopped egg, cornichons or gerkins, capers, parsley, tarragon, garlic, and mustard into the mayonaisse. Season to taste with salt and pepper.

Goat Cheese Balls with Tomato Ragout and Crostinis

The Beach Plum Inn and Restaurant, Menemsha

Situated on a bluff whose banks are still thick with beach plum bushes, this aptly named inn commands an impressive view of Vineyard Sound and Menemsha Harbor and often offers spectacular sunsets. The eleven-room inn was established in 1953 by Cordon-Bleu-trained cook and author Theresa Morse. Its current owners offer an elegant four-course prix fixe or an a la carte menu to their guests and diners. A sampling from their kitchen is this much-praised hors d'oeuvre.

GOAT CHEESE BALLS

18 ounces goat cheese

6 ounces cream cheese

Salt to taste

Freshly ground black pepper to taste

1½ cups Japanese or French bread crumbs

1½ cups fresh herbs (basil, thyme, parsley, and oregano)

Flour to coat

4 whole eggs, beaten

3 tablespoons vegetable oil

ROASTED GARLIC TOMATO RAGOUT

12 garlic cloves

6 ounces extra virgin olive oil

12 large or 16 medium-size plum tomatoes

½ cup chopped parsley

4 springs of thyme, chopped

1 cup chopped fresh basil

6 ounces tomato juice or water

Salt to taste

Freshly ground black pepper to taste

SOURDOUGH CROSTINIS

6 slices sourdough bread, sliced   *Olive oil for brushing on bread*
½ inch thick

Bring cheeses to room temperature. Mix well and add salt and pepper to taste. Shape into twelve 2-ounce balls. Chill 30 minutes. Pulse bread crumbs and herbs in blender until coarsely chopped (save 2 tablespoons of herbs to sprinkle on finished dish). Dredge chilled cheese in flour, then dip in egg. Coat with herbed bread crumbs. Chill 20 minutes, or up to one day.

Sauté cheese balls, six at a time, in hot oil about 1 minute. Remove carefully and drain on paper towels. Keep warm.

Prepare Roasted Garlic Tomato Ragout as follows: In a 350°F oven roast garlic in olive oil for 12 to 15 minutes, until cloves are golden brown and soft to touch. Strain garlic, reserving oil. Mince garlic and combine with 3 ounces of the strained oil. Seed and coarsely chop the tomatoes, then sauté them in remaining strained oil for 2 minutes, stirring occasionally. Add minced garlic, herbs, and tomato juice or water. Cook about 3 minutes more. Season with salt and pepper and keep warm.

Prepare Sourdough Crostinis by brushing each slice of sourdough bread with olive oil and baking in a 350°F oven for 4 minutes. Cut each slice into four strips.

Assemble dish by placing equal amounts of warm ragout sauce on six salad plates and topping each portion with two warm cheese balls. Garnish plates with crostinis and sprinkles of reserved fresh herbs. Serve immediately.

Makes 6 portions.

Key Lime Pie

HOME PORT RESTAURANT, MENEMSHA

A window table in this big, multiwindowed Up-Island restaurant is the perfect place to demolish a baked stuffed lobster or a seafood platter as you watch the tides surge through Menemsha Bight and the late-day sun sink below the flats of Lobsterville, across the channel. Opened in 1931 as a soup-and-sandwich place, Home Port was purchased by its present owner in the late 1970s and is now probably the most popular place for seafood (eat in and takeout) on the Island.

But try to save room for dessert, so you can savor this justly famous concoction.

3 egg yolks

4 ounces lime juice

Lime zest from 1 lime

2 drops green food coloring

28 ounces condensed milk

1 10-inch graham-cracker
    piecrust (see page 188)

Whipped cream topping

Combine the egg yolks, lime juice, lime zest, and food coloring in an electric mixer. Beat on medium speed for 30 seconds. Add condensed milk. Beat on low speed for 2 minutes.

Pour into graham-cracker piecrust. Chill for 2 hours before serving. Top with whipped cream.

Note: The egg yolks in this pie are not cooked, but nowadays contaminated eggs are very rare. Just be sure the ones you use are very fresh and free from even the slightest crack.

Makes one 10-inch pie.

Pear Upside-Down Gingerbread Cake

OUTERMOST INN, GAY HEAD

This is about as "away from it all" as you can get on Martha's Vineyard—a seven-room inn perched right on the Gay Head cliffs. It opened in 1989 and was constructed entirely by its owners, husband and wife, who incorporated many special touches into its design. Each bedroom, for instance, is named for the wood used for its floor—oak, cherry, pine, and so on. And every room has a dramatic view of the Atlantic Ocean. The inn is open from mid-April to mid-October.

The menu at Outermost Inn often features special seafood dishes, but we were taken by this unusual, delectable dessert.

7 tablespoons softened butter
½ cup granulated white sugar
3 large, ripe pears
½ cup plus 1 tablespoon dark
   brown sugar
2 tablespoons grated fresh peeled
   ginger
1 tablespoon fresh lemon juice
1 egg
½ cup buttermilk

½ cup molasses
1 cup flour
1 teaspoon baking soda
½ teaspoon ground cinnamon
¼ teaspoon ground cloves
¼ teaspoon ground nutmeg
¼ teaspoon ground mustard
¼ teaspoon salt
2 cups sour cream

Preheat oven to 350°F.

Coat the bottom and sides of a 10-inch black iron skillet with 3 tablespoons of butter. Sprinkle granulated white sugar evenly over bottom of pan. Peel and core pears. Slice them into thin crescents and place in bowl. Add 1 tablespoon of brown sugar, 1 tablespoon of ginger, and lemon juice. Toss gently. Arrange the slices in pinwheel pattern on bottom of skillet.

Combine remaining 4 tablespoons of butter with remaining ½ cup of brown sugar in medium bowl. Mix until well blended. Beat in egg, then buttermilk, ¼ cup molasses, and remaining tablespoon of grated ginger. Whisk together flour, baking soda, spices, mustard, and salt. Add to buttermilk mixture and stir until combined. Pour batter over pears, and gently smooth top. Bake 40 to 45 minutes, or until gingerbread springs back when lightly pressed. Remove from oven and let cool in pan for at least 20 minutes. Invert cake on decorative platter. Garnish with remaining ¼ cup molasses beaten into sour cream when served.

Makes 8 to 10 portions.

Epilogue

Summer is over. Colorful fall leaves, most of them brilliant yellow, now brighten the ground instead of the trees, but soon they will fade, dry, and crumble. The signs on the shops have been taken down and the No Trespassing signs nailed up. Shutters are closed on the summer houses; chains hang across roadways; gates are shut. Out at Squibnocket, the rocks roll in on the rising tides and begin covering the summer sand; and the only sounds heard there besides the wash of the water and the crying of the gulls is the occasional plop of a few handfuls of sand as little by little the precious, coveted sea cliffs of Martha's Vineyard erode in the wet wind and the slashing fall rains, drop to the beach, and wash away forever into the sea. The Island is disappearing; through the millennia to come, it will be washed away.

But for the moment—and one hopes for the rest of our time—the Vineyard is safe, at least from a geological standpoint. Radical change, if it occurs, will be brought about by those who live or want to live on it. Only twenty years ago, a sandy, narrow road through the woods would often open out to a broad, tranquil meadow, then a salt marsh, a pond, dunes, and the broad sea. Now the road is likely to be posted, broadened, hard-topped. The meadow is crisscrossed with roads and marred by condominiums, and the beach is inaccessible to all but a select few. Yet rum cherries, wild grapes, beach plums, rose hips, and late blackberries still hang richly ripe on the moors and in the thickets. Schools of tinker mackerel and pollock swarm in and out of the Great Ponds with the tides. The fat black-faced Canada geese settle in Donnie Mill's stripped cornfield beside the tattered scarecrows and glean the last hard kernels of grain; restless, they take off again and circle aimlessly over West Tisbury in a loose V, then head for Chilmark and the Keith pond, debating noisily en route whether to migrate or count on being fed all winter on the Island.

The opulence of fall pervades the Vineyard, as all the people and creatures who live on it and plants and trees that grow on it prepare for the short, cold days of winter. For Martha's Vineyard is not only a summer place but a place to be born and grow up, a place to live and work and thrive year-round, nourished by the bounty that its soil and shore offer to all who are provident enough to seek and use it.

Index

About the Authors

LOUISE TATE KING cooked professionally for more than thirty years. She was one of the cofounders of Blueberry Hill Farm in Chilmark, Martha's Vineyard, and for several years owned and operated a highly successful French-provincial–style restaurant in Edgartown during the summer–into-early-fall season. She studied at the Cordon Bleu in Paris, spent considerable time visiting the great vineyards in France and Italy, and supervised various restaurants in the West Indies during the winter months. Now she lives quietly with her marmalade cat in her gingerbread cottage on the Oaks Bluff campground.

JEAN STEWART WEXLER grew up in North Carolina and Kentucky. After living and working briefly in Italy and Switzerland, she moved to Washington, D.C., and then to New York City, where she worked for various book publishers. She now spends all year on Martha's Vineyard with her husband and her poodle, tending to several large flower gardens, fishing, studying jazz piano, writing gardening pieces for the *Vineyard Gazette* and other publications, and—of course—cooking.